Greg Perry

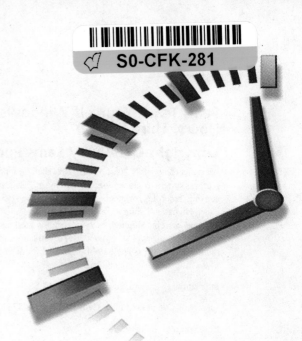

SAMS
Teach Yourself

Windows 95

in 24 Hours

THIRD EDITION

SAMS

A Division of Macmillan Computer Publishing
201 West 103rd St., Indianapolis, Indiana, 46290 USA

Sams Teach Yourself Windows 95 in 24 Hours, Third Edition

Copyright © 1998 by Sams Publishing

International Standard Book Number: 0-672-31482-7

Library of Congress Catalog Card Number: 98-87470

First Printing: *August 1995*

Second Printing: *March 1997*

00   99   4   3   2

Printed in the United States of America

Trademarks

All terms mentioned in this book that are known to be trademarks or service marks have been appropriately capitalized. *Sams* cannot attest to the accuracy of this information. Use of a term in this book should not be regarded as affecting the validity of any trademark or service mark.

Warning and Disclaimer

Every effort has been made to make this book as complete and as accurate as possible, but no warranty or fitness is implied. The information provided is on an "as is" basis. The authors and the publisher shall have neither liability or responsibility to any person or entity with respect to any loss or damages arising from the information contained in this book

EXECUTIVE EDITOR:
Grace Buechlein

ACQUISITIONS EDITOR
Grace Buechlein

DEVELOPMENT EDITOR
Laura Bulcher

MANAGING EDITOR
Brice Gosnell

PROJECT EDITOR
Sara Bosin

COPY EDITOR
Kelli Brooks

PROOFREADER
Benjamin Berg

TECHNICAL EDITOR
Ron Ellenbecker

LAYOUT TECHNICIANS
Ayanna Lacey
Heather Hiatt Miller
Amy Parker

Contents at a Glance

Contents

Dedication

A guy couldn't ask for a more intriguing and eclectic brother-in-law than Steve Wiseman! Steve, this one's for you!

Acknowledgments

My sincere thanks go to the editors and staff at Sams Publishing who strive to produce computer books that teach all levels of computer users from beginners to experts. The people at Sams Publishing take their jobs seriously because they want readers to have only the best books possible.

The crème of the crop is Grace Buechlein, a friend more than an Editor. Grace, you are the best. Helping Grace make sense of my writing is Laura Bulcher who started development on the most challenging author to work with at Sams, *me*.

As I've said before, Sam's Dean Miller deserves praises and raises. Dean has his hand somewhere in most of my successful books and my books are better because of Dean. Behind every successful man is a great wife and a greater mother-in-law. I don't know about the in-laws, but I know that Dean and his family are super and they help make my experience with Sams remarkably enjoyable.

Other editors and staff at Sams who produced this book, namely Sara Bosin, Kelli Brooks, Erika Millen, and Benjamin Berg, are also responsible for this book's excellence, and I alone am responsible for any problems if there are any.

My lovely and gracious bride, Jayne, keeps supporting my ups and downs. Thank you, my Dearest Jayne. Thanks also to my Dad and Mom, Glen and Bettye Perry, who are my biggest fans. I love you all.

Greg Perry

About the Authors

GREG PERRY is a speaker and writer on both the programming and the applications sides of computing. He is known for his skills at bringing advanced computer topics down to the novice's level. Perry has been a programmer and trainer since the early 1980s. He received his first degree in computer science and then a master's degree in corporate finance. Perry is the author of nearly 1.5 million computer books sold, including *Teach Yourself Windows 98 in 24 Hours*, *Teach Yourself Office 97 in 24 Hours*, *Teach Yourself Programming in 24 Hours*, *Teach Yourself Visual Basic in 21 Days*, and the *Absolute Beginner's Guide to C*. He also writes about rental-property management and loves to travel.

Tell Us What You Think!

As the reader of this book, *you* are our most important critic and commentator. We value your opinion and want to know what we're doing right, what we could do better, what areas you'd like to see us publish in, and any other words of wisdom you're willing to pass our way.

As an Executive Editor for the Operating Systems team at Macmillan Computer Publishing, I welcome your comments. You can fax, email, or write to me directly to let me know what you did or didn't like about this book—as well as what we can do to make our books stronger.

Please note that I cannot help you with technical problems related to the topic of this book, and that due to the high volume of mail I receive, I might not be able to reply to every message.

When you write, please be sure to include this book's title and author, as well as your name, email address (if appropriate), and phone or fax number. I will carefully review your comments and share them with the author and editors who worked on the book.

Fax: 317-581-4663

Email: opsys@mcp.com

Mail: Grace Buechlein
Operating Systems
Macmillan Computer Publishing
201 West 103rd Street
Indianapolis, IN 46290 USA

Introduction

You probably are anxious to get started with your 24-hour Windows 95 tutorial. It won't be long now before you begin your first lesson. Take a few preliminary moments to acquaint yourself with the design of this book described in the next few sections.

Who Should Read This Book

This book is for *both* beginning and advanced users of Windows. Readers rarely believe that lofty claim for good reason, but the design of this book and the nature of Windows 95 make it possible for this book to address such a wide audience. Here's why: Windows 95 is a major improvement over previous Windows operating environments.

Readers unfamiliar with windowed environments will find plenty of introductory help to bring them up to speed quickly. This book teaches you how to start Windows 95, how to exit Windows 95, and how to manage almost every aspect of Windows 95. This book talks to beginners but does not talk *down* to beginners. Once you get the fundamentals, the final lesson shows you tips and traps, before only well-known by the Windows 95 experts.

Windows 95 operates using a completely new style from previous versions of Windows such as Windows 3.1. Although Windows 95 is similar to the earlier versions, almost every Windows 95 action differs slightly from the Windows 3.1 equivalents. There are more than enough new features to keep Windows 3.1 users interested and happy for a long time. In addition, your skills won't be lost if you ever move up to Windows 98 because most of Windows 98's features can be found in Windows 95, and many of those are taught here when they overlap Windows 95 features.

If you are extremely new to computers, you may want to read Appendix A, "Understanding Your Computer." This appendix gives PC newcomers a step-up by quickly covering all the basics of computer hardware and software.

What This Book Will Do for You

Although this is not a reference book, you'll learn almost every aspect of Windows 95 from the user's point of view. There are many advanced technical details that most users will never need, and this book does not waste your time with those. This book knows that you want to get up to speed with Windows 95 in 24 hours, and fulfills its goal.

This book presents both the background and the theory that a new Windows 95 user needs. In addition to the background discussions, this book is practical and provides more than 75 useful, step-by-step tasks that you can work through to gain hands-on experience. The tasks guide you through all the common Windows 95 actions you'll need to make Windows 95 work for you, instead of your working to use Windows 95.

Can This Book Really Teach Windows 95 in 24 Hours?

Yes. You can master each chapter in one hour or less (by the way, chapters are referred to as "hours" in the rest of the book). Although some chapters are longer than others, the material is balanced. The longer chapters contain several tasks, and the shorter chapters contain background material. The balance provided by the tasks, background, and insightful explanations and tips make learning Windows 95 using this book fresh at every page.

What You Need

This book assumes that you have a Windows 95-compatible computer with Windows 95 installed.

Conventions Used in This Book

Each chapter contains a glossary to explain the important new terms in the chapter. There is a question and answer section at the end of each chapter to reinforce ideas. This book also uses several common conventions to help teach the Windows 95 topics. Here is a summary of the typographical conventions:

- The first time a new term appears, the term is *italicized*. The glossary will contain that term in the first hour the term is mentioned.
- Commands and computer output appear in a special monospaced computer font.
- Words you type appear in a boldfaced computer font.
- If a task requires you to select from a menu, the book separates menu commands with a vertical bar. Therefore, this book uses File | Save As to select the Save As command from the File menu.

In addition to typographical conventions, the following special elements are included to set off different types of information to make them easily recognizable:

Special notes augment the material you are reading in each hour. They clarify concepts and procedures.

You'll find numerous tips that offer shortcuts and solutions to common problems.

The caution sections warn you about pitfalls. Reading them will save you time and trouble.

PART I
Wake Up Windows 95!

Hour

HOUR 1

What's Windows 95 All About?

Who says that a productive computer user cannot have fun being productive? Microsoft Windows 95 is fun, friendly, and powerful. This hour introduces you to Windows 95. You will learn how Windows 95 improves upon previous versions of Windows.

The highlights of this hour include:

- How Microsoft designed Windows 95 to be as easy and intuitive as possible
- What makes Windows 95 powerful
- How to start Windows 95
- How to log on to Windows 95 if you use a network
- How to access and manipulate common Windows 95 controls such as command buttons and check boxes
- How to perform a shut down of Windows 95

Getting a Feel for Windows 95

Most users like the look and feel of Windows 95, and they appreciate the fact that Windows 95 is also enjoyable to use. Although Windows 95 is both fun and easy to master, it is also a computer interface system that offers tremendous power for anyone who uses PCs. With Windows 95, you will be able to access your computer's hardware and data files easily even if you have not used a computer much before. As a matter of fact, Microsoft spent many hours and many dollars streamlining the way that Windows 95 helps people work. If you are new to computers, you might want to turn to Appendix A, "Understanding Your Computer," and review it now to get an overview of the basic parts of a computer.

Windows 95 contains a computer interface that attempts to please all groups of people including novice computer users, previous Windows 3.1 and *MS-DOS* users, and advanced computer programmers. MS-DOS was a pre-Windows *operating system*, a system program that controls the flow of information through PCs. To achieve the lofty goal of pleasing a broad spectrum of users, Microsoft designed an interface that is intuitive without being intrusive.

Figure 1.1 shows a Windows 95 screen that Windows 95 users see much of the time. The Windows 95 screen is often called a *desktop*, and you'll learn to manage items on the Windows 95 desktop just as you do with your own desktop where you sit. Other than some pictures and text here and there, the Windows 95 desktop screen is very clean and clear of the clutter that previous Windows users so often saw.

FIGURE 1.1

The Windows 95 screen, like a clean desktop, is free of clutter

The pictures that appear on the Windows 95 desktop are called *icons*. Figure 1.1 contains icons along the left side of the screen. Icons can also appear elsewhere such as on the ribbon across the bottom of Figure 1.1's desktop.

Your Windows 95 screen might contain more or fewer icons than Figure 1.1's screen depending on the way your version of Windows 95 is configured. For example, if your PC is not connected to a computer network, you may or may not see the icon labeled Network Neighborhood. In addition, you might see artwork on your Windows 95 desktop. Many figures in this 24-hour tutorial use a version of Windows 95 that supports an *active desktop*. The active desktop offers several Internet-based features as well as a slightly different interface from the one in Figure 1.1. If your icons are underlined, the chances are good that your desktop is set up to be active.

The artwork that forms the background for a Windows 95 screen is called *wallpaper*. The wallpaper comes from a graphics file called a *bitmap* file. In Hour 7, "Manage Your Desktop," you'll see how you can change or remove the wallpaper if you don't like the artwork used on your system. Figure 1.2 shows the same Windows 95 desktop as before only the desktop contains a graphical wallpaper file to make things more interesting. In addition, you'll see active desktop items, such as underlined icons and an Internet channel bar, that you'll learn about as you progress through these 24 lessons.

FIGURE 1.2

Wallpaper can make your desktop less boring

Internet channel bar

Underlined icon titles

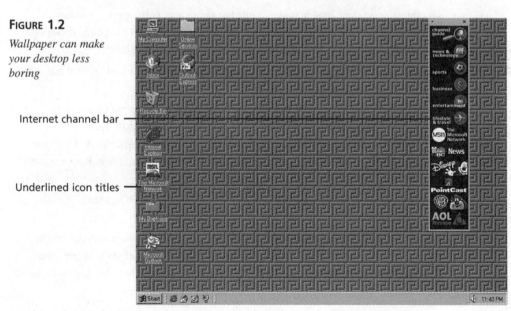

The Windows 95 screen acts like a desktop from which you work on your computer. If you want to write letters using a word processor, you start the word processor program from the Windows 95 environment. Windows 95 always remains in the computer's memory to help you interact with your programs and the computer hardware.

Computers controlled by graphical user interfaces (*GUIs*), such as Windows 95, no longer require the tedium of typed commands that computers used to require. Windows 95 is a graphical environment. Instead of typing a command that directs the computer to start a program, you use the mouse or keyboard to point to an icon on the screen to activate the icon's matching program.

Microsoft developers proudly promote the effort they put into the Windows 95 interface. In designing Windows 95, Microsoft took people who had never before used a computer and placed them in front of other operating environments, such as previous versions of Windows, and requested that the new users perform certain tasks such as starting game programs. As a result, Microsoft learned a lot about the way people approach a visual environment. Windows 95 is the result of countless hours of this kind of usability testing.

If you are fairly new to computers, you might not understand why you would want to use Windows 95. Perhaps you've used a word processor or a spreadsheet but never taken the time to learn about MS-DOS or find out what this Windows stuff is all about. Other newcomers to Windows 95 might have migrated to the PC world from a Macintosh or mainframe computer. In a nutshell, Windows 95 is all of the following:

- An operating system that manages your hardware and software interactions. Windows 95 provides uniform access to your system so that programs can more accurately use your system's resources (such as disks and printers).

- A graphical user interface (GUI) that lets you start programs and control hardware graphically using a mouse and keyboard.

- A *32-bit environment,* which is a fancy computer technical term meaning that Windows 95 utilizes your computer's internal architecture to its fullest, unlike Windows 3.1 and MS-DOS, which were only 16-bit environments. A 32-bit environment does not necessarily guarantee double-speed performance, but programs often run much faster than in 16-bit environments.

- An improved replacement for MS-DOS–based computers. DOS stands for *disk operating system.*

- A networked interface that helps seamlessly integrate a network and the Internet into your work environment. If you do not currently use a network or the Internet, Windows 95 will help you transition to either of those new technologies when you are ready.

If one were to state the single greatest reason to use Windows 95, that reason would be this: Microsoft designed Windows 95 so that you can concentrate on using your software and hardware—*not* so you have to concentrate on using Windows 95. As you'll see throughout this book, use of the keyboard and mouse complement each other to give you easy control over every aspect of Windows 95.

Perhaps you know that Windows 98 is now available. If you have Windows 95 and take advantage of the active desktop that you'll learn about in Hour 3, "Take Windows 95 to Task," you'll have mastered the primary features of Windows 98 as well as Windows 95. Although internally different, Windows 98 differs only slightly from Windows 95 when the Windows 95 user accesses the active desktop.

How to Operate the Mouse

The odds are good that you've used a mouse if you've used a computer before. Using the mouse involves following the *mouse cursor* (sometimes called the *mouse pointer*) around the screen. The mouse cursor is the pointing arrow that moves as you move your mouse.

Here's a quick summary of the possible mouse actions you can perform:

- When you move the mouse, you physically move the mouse across your desk. Some mice are actually trackballs; trackballs remain stationary and you spin the trackball's sphere to move the mouse. Other kinds of mice are touchpads that you move your finger on to move the mouse cursor. Both trackballs and touchpads have mouse buttons that work just like a regular mouse. The screen's mouse cursor follows your mouse movements. To point to an object on the screen, you move the mouse to that object.

- When you click the mouse, you press and immediately release either the left or right mouse button. To select graphical screen objects, you often click the left button. You use your right mouse button to display special pop-up menus. Hour 4, "Understanding the My Computer Window," explains how to swap the left and right mouse button actions if you are left-handed.

- When you double-click, you press and immediately release the left or right mouse button twice in succession.

- When you drag screen objects with the mouse, you move the mouse cursor over an object that you want to drag and press and hold the left mouse button (keeping the button pressed). The item under the mouse cursor is now temporarily welded to the mouse cursor. As you move the mouse (while still holding the mouse button), the screen object moves with the cursor. When you eventually release the mouse button, Windows 95 anchors the object in the mouse cursor's new position.

You can almost always use the keyboard instead of the mouse to perform just about any Windows 95 operation, but the mouse is a lot easier than the keyboard for most Windows 95 operations. If you are uncomfortable with using a mouse, don't fret, because the mouse actions soon become second nature. One of the fastest ways to master the mouse is to play a game such as Solitaire that comes with Windows 95. Hour 3, "Take Windows 95 to Task," explains how to start Solitaire.

First Things First

Windows 95 contains a complete operating system (called the *kernel* because the operating system is the heart of everything you do on the computer and controls all the actions that take place in the PC), in addition to a graphical user interface. Except in rare cases where someone configures his computer to run Windows 95 along with another version of Windows, Windows 95 starts automatically when you turn on your PC. Therefore, you don't have to learn how to start Windows 95; Windows 95 automatically loads itself when you turn on your computer or *reboot* it (which means to reset the computer using the strange Ctrl+Alt+Del keystroke sequence or press a reboot button, if your PC has one).

The keystroke Ctrl+Alt+Del might be confusing to you. To issue that key combination, you press and hold down the keys sequentially: Press and hold down the Ctrl key, then press and hold down the Alt key, and then press the Del key (you actually hold down all three keys). Let up on all three keys at once to begin the reboot process.

Logging On

If you are not connected to a network, little in this section applies to you now, but it's a good idea to read through it anyway. If you ever share your PC with others, even without a network connection, you will need to know how to log on to Windows using a user name and password as described here.

If your PC is connected to a network or set up for multiple users (using *profiles* you'll learn about in Hour 7, "Manage your Desktop"), you have to *log on* to the PC. When you log on, you type a user name and password that you or a *System Administrator* in your company has set up. Figure 1.3 shows the logon screen that you might see if you are running in a networked computer environment.

FIGURE 1.3

Network users have to log on to Windows 95

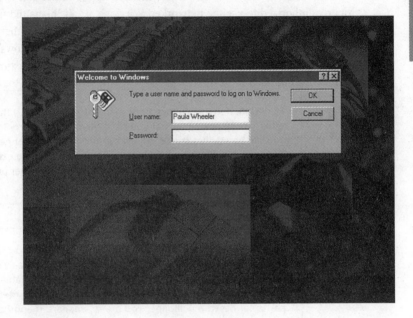

Task 1.1: Logging On to Windows 95

Step 1: Description

You have to ask the person responsible for installing the networked Windows 95 for your logon information. After you get the user name and initial password, you can log on to the computer and access Windows 95.

Step 2: Action

1. When you see the logon screen, type your user name exactly as the System Administrator set it up. Often, your user name is your full name or your first initial and last name.

2. Press the Tab key.

3. Type your password exactly as the System Administrator set it up. Asterisks appear in place of the actual password you type so that no one looking over your shoulder can read your password.

4. Press Enter to start Windows 95.

▼ Step 3: Review

If you get an error message, check with the System Administrator to make sure you are properly authorized to use the networked Windows 95. If this is the first time you or anyone else has logged on with your user name, the initial password that you enter is the ▲ permanent password, unless you change the password later. Windows 95 requests that first password twice to be sure that you type the initial password exactly as it should be.

By design, networks allow more than one user access to the same files. In other words, assuming that you have the proper electronic authorization, you can access files stored on any person's PC that is connected to your PC. The extra benefits that a network provides also require extra security precautions so that unauthorized users do not bother other people's files.

Your Network Administrator can set up different *user profiles* for each network user. A user profile defines your interface preferences and the file access you have. The Windows 95 interface is customizable as you'll see throughout this book. When you log on, your custom interface, such as a particular desktop wallpaper you prefer, appears. If another user uses your computer, that user's profile will determine that user's interface design.

You can change your password by double-clicking the Windows 95 Control Panel's Password icon and entering your current and new password. If you need further help with the Control Panel, you'll learn how to use the Control Panel for managing your system in Hour 4, "Understanding the My Computer Window."

Welcome to Windows 95

Windows 95 is helpful. In fact, Windows 95 is *extremely* helpful! Each time you turn on your PC and start Windows 95, Windows 95 displays the *Welcome Screen* with a different tip (such as the one shown in Figure 1.4). (If you don't see the Welcome screen, this feature has been turned off on your system. If you want to reactivate the Welcome screen now, see Hour 6, "A Call for Help," to learn how to display the Welcome screen.)

FIGURE 1.4

Learn something new every time you start Windows 95

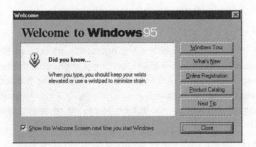

The Welcome screen is an example of a *window*. In Windows 95, windows appear all over the place, often overlapping and hiding other windows. Keep in mind that Windows 95 works as if it were a 3D set of images on your screen. If one window covers up a screen object (such as text, an icon, or another window), the objects the new window covers are still underneath the new window. When you move the window or make the window disappear (called *closing* the window), you'll see the hidden objects again.

The Welcome screen is helpful when starting Windows 95. In addition to a different tip, you can access any of the following services from the Welcome screen:

- Browse a brief onscreen tour of Windows 95
- Find out how Windows 95 differs from its predecessors such as Windows 3.1
- Use your modem (if one is connected to your PC) to register your copy of Windows 95 so Microsoft can inform you of its latest products
- Learn what other Microsoft products are available
- Read additional tips

Much of the time, you'll read the Welcome screen tip and close the window with the button labeled Close so you can begin working with Windows 95. After a while, the tips will begin to repeat themselves, and you won't need the services of the Welcome screen any longer. Uncheck the caption next to the check box at the bottom of the screen when you want to stop seeing the Welcome screen.

Command Controls

As you work with Windows 95, you'll see all kinds of windows appear and disappear. Windows such as the Welcome screen are called *dialog boxes*. Dialog boxes contain all kinds of various *controls* with which you can manage Windows 95.

There are six *command button* controls down the right side of the Welcome screen. Command buttons (often just called *buttons*) give you pushbutton access to various options. These onscreen graphical buttons look and act as if they are physical pushbuttons. There are three ways to select an onscreen command button:

- Click the button with the mouse.
- Press Tab to highlight the buttons in succession. Shift+Tab moves backwards. You'll know that a button is highlighted when a dotted outline appears around the button's caption. Moving the highlight between onscreen controls is called *changing the focus*. After the focus (the dotted highlight) appears on the button you want to select, press Enter to activate that button.
- Press Alt plus the underlined letter on the button's caption. This combined keystroke is called a *hot key*. For example, you can select the Welcome screen's Next Tip command button by pressing Alt+T.

There is another kind of control at the bottom of the Welcome screen called a *check box*. Certain windows need check boxes to indicate a yes or no possibility. If the Welcome screen's check box is checked (a check mark appears in the white box when checked), Windows 95 shows the Welcome screen (with a different tip) the next time you start Windows 95. If you uncheck the check box, Windows 95 does not show the Welcome screen again.

There are three ways to check (or uncheck) a check box:

- Click either the check box or the message next to the check box with the mouse.
- Move the focus to the check box text (by pressing Tab or Shift+Tab) and press Enter.
- Press Alt plus the hot key of the check box's message.

Perhaps you just started Windows 95, but the Welcome screen did not appear. The last person to use your PC might have unchecked the Welcome screen's check box control. If you'd like to see a Welcome screen tip when you start Windows 95, you'll learn how to add the Welcome screen to the startup sequence in Hour 6, "A Call for Help." Although activating the Welcome screen is not difficult to do, you need some additional Windows 95 skills before you should try this task.

Close the Welcome screen window if it still appears on your monitor. When you close a window, the window goes completely away. You can close the window by clicking the command button labeled with an X (the *Close* button). In Hour 2, "Tour Windows 95 Now," you'll learn how to leave a window without completely closing the window; the window is out of your way but you can return to that window whenever you want.

Keep Before You Quit

1

You are probably anxious to get started, but before you learn more about using Windows 95, you must learn how to quit Windows 95 properly. Due to the integration of Windows 95 and your computer's hardware and software, you must take a few extra steps when quitting your Windows 95 session and turning off your computer.

> If you do not properly shut down Windows 95, you could very easily lose work that you just completed. At the worst, you could damage a Windows 95 configuration file that will mess up Windows 95 the next time you start your PC.

Surely you've noticed the button in the lower-left corner of the Windows 95 screen labeled Start. This area of the screen is part of a bar known as the *taskbar,* and this button is called the *Start button.* The taskbar is perhaps the most important element in Windows 95 because you'll use the taskbar to launch and switch between several programs as well as access the Internet. Windows 95 lets you run more than one program at the same time. In other words, you can download a file from another computer, print a spreadsheet, listen to an opera on an audio CD, and type with a word processor—all at the same time. The taskbar grows to list each program currently running. Figure 1.5 shows a taskbar that lists four programs running in memory at the same time. Depending on your Windows 95 configuration, your taskbar might differ slightly from the one in Figure 1.5.

FIGURE 1.5

The taskbar lists every program running

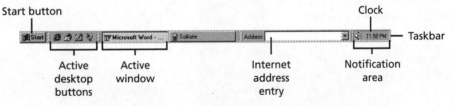

Start button — Clock — Taskbar

Active desktop buttons — Active window — Internet address entry — Notification area

> Think of the taskbar as acting like a television channel changer. When you run more than one Windows 95 program, you can switch among the programs by clicking the program names in the taskbar just as you press channel buttons on your TV.

The taskbar does more than list and manage running programs. The taskbar is the starting point for just about everything you will do in Windows 95. If you want to rearrange files, start programs, change screen colors, modify the mouse, or view the contents of files, the taskbar contains the power to do all those things and more.

The taskbar also contains the commands you need to shut down Windows 95 and your computer. In Hour 3, "Take Windows 95 to Task," you'll delve much more deeply into the operations of the taskbar. At this point though, you'll learn just enough to master the Windows 95 shut down process, because without the proper shutdown you face risky consequences of data loss.

> Place the mouse cursor over the Start button but do not click the mouse button. After a brief pause, Windows 95 displays a small caption box next to the mouse cursor that reads, "Click here to begin." If you are unsure as to what a Windows 95 button does, rest your mouse cursor over the button to see this pop-up help called a *ToolTip*.

When you click the Start button on the taskbar, the *Start menu* pops up as shown in Figure 1.6. The Start menu gives you access to every part of your computer. Table 1.1 describes what each option of the Start menu does. From the Start menu, you can start programs, check disk space, manage files, and properly shut down the computer. The latter, shutting down the computer, is the concern of this section.

FIGURE 1.6

The Start menu is the command center for the rest of Windows 95

TABLE 1.1 THE START MENU COMMANDS

Command	Description
Programs	Displays lists of program names. You can start the associated programs from this menu.
Documents	Displays a list of documents, or data files, that you've recently opened and might want to return to again. (Windows 95 works from a data-driven viewpoint that makes your data the system's focus instead of your programs.)
Settings	Lets you change the configuration of Windows 95.
Find	Lets you search your computer's files for specific data.
Help	Gives you online help for the various tasks you can perform in Windows 95.
Run	Gives you the ability to execute programs or open program group folders by typing an appropriate MS-DOS command that you could not otherwise select from Windows 95.
Shut Down	Lets you safely shut down your computer without losing data. (Depending on your system, you might see related options such as Standby or Suspend.)

The most important command on the Start menu is the Shut Down command. Before you do too much, even before you really master the ins and outs of the Start menu, you should read the rest of this section to learn how to shut down your computer safely. You don't want to write the first chapter of a best-selling novel only to find that Windows 95 sent the chapter into oblivion because you did not shut down the computer properly before turning off the power.

Activating Menu Commands

When confronted with a menu, such as the Start menu, there are several ways you can select any item you want. If you use your mouse, you can point to an item on the menu. As you move the mouse cursor over the menu items, you'll see that a highlight follows the mouse cursor through the menu, clearly showing you which menu item the mouse cursor is over. If your hands are on the keyboard when you display a menu, you can press the up and down arrow keys to move the highlight through the menu's commands.

Some menu commands, such as the Shut Down command, contain ellipses (. . .) to the right of the command name. The ellipses indicate that if you choose this command, a dialog box will appear requiring additional information.

Some menu commands, such as the Start menu's Programs and Documents commands, display arrows to the right of the command names. The arrows indicate that other command menus appear if you select from those commands. Sometimes, Windows 95 menu commands *cascade* (trigger additional menus) several levels deep, such as the one shown in Figure 1.7. You can decrease the cascade, removing one or more of the extra cascaded menu levels, by moving the mouse to the left one menu or by pressing the Esc key. In some cases, if a menu is taller than your screen, you can click the arrow at either end of the menu to scroll the menu up or down to see additional choices.

Some menu commands, such as Help, do not contain anything to the right of the command name. These commands perform an immediate service, such as displaying a Help screen, displaying a menu, or starting a program from your disk drive.

If a menu command contains an underlined letter, such as Help, you can select that menu command by pressing Alt plus the letter. Alt+H activates the Help menu command.

FIGURE 1.7

Some menus trigger other menus, producing a cascaded menu look

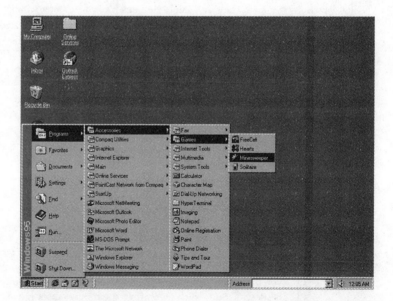

If you just explored a bit and displayed a cascaded menu or selected another command from the Start menu, press Esc until the Start menu disappears and the Start button returns to normal. As mentioned earlier, this is an important time to learn about the Shut Down command. Click the Start button again and select the Shut Down command. The ellipsis after the words Shut Down indicates that a dialog box window will appear.

Figure 1.8 shows the resulting Shut Down window. (Your window may vary depending on your PC's configuration.) There is more than one way to shut down your computer depending on what your current need is.

FIGURE 1.8

You must make a decision as to how you want to shut down the computer

Shut Down Options

The Shut Down window demonstrates a new kind of control in Windows 95. The lines inside the Shut Down window represent captioned *option buttons*. A dot inside one of the option buttons indicates that option is the selected option. When you first display the Shut Down window, the first option, Shut Down, is the selected option. If you were to select another option, Windows 95 would *deselect* the first option, thereby ensuring that only one is active at any one time.

Here are three ways to select an option from a list of option button choices:

- Point to one of the options with the mouse and click the mouse button.
- Use the keyboard's up and down arrow keys to move the focus (the focus's dotted line surrounds the selected option button) among the selections.
- Press Alt plus the underlined letter of the option you want to select. Alt+R chooses the Restart option.

Simply selecting an option does not trigger any action. After you select the desired option, you then have to click the OK command button (sometimes labeled Yes) to execute that option's command. If you choose Cancel, Windows 95 removes the Shut Down window and returns you to the Windows 95 environment. If you click the Help command button, Windows 95 displays online help that describes the options in more detail. (Hour 7, "A Call for Help!" explains the Windows 95 online help system in detail.)

If you want to restart Windows 95 without rebooting your PC, hold down a Shift key when you select the Restart option. Continue holding Shift until you see the message, `Restarting Windows 95`. Windows 95 restarts but your computer doesn't go through the time-consuming reboot and memory test.

Table 1.2 describes the shut down options. Most of the time, you'll select the first one because you are turning off the computer. When you select the first option, Windows 95 pauses briefly, and then displays a message telling you that you can turn off the computer's power. Go ahead and select the first option now. Select the first option button and click the OK button to initiate the shutdown.

TABLE 1.2   THE SHUT DOWN COMMANDS AND THEIR DESCRIPTIONS

Command	Description
Shut Down	Closes all open files and programs as well as writes any remaining unwritten data to the disk.
Restart	Performs a shut down, but then reboots the computer for you. Sometimes, you are instructed to restart Windows 95 after installing a new program or after changing a Windows 95 option.
Restart in MS-DOS Mode	Performs a shut down, but then restarts the computer in MS-DOS mode without putting you directly into Windows 95. Only those users who understand MS-DOS commands would want to use this command. From the MS-DOS mode, you can type the word exit to leave MS-DOS and enter Windows 95.

You need to develop the habit of shutting down Windows 95 properly before turning off the PC. Perhaps you can stick a note to the computer's on/off switch until you get used to running the Shut Down command. Again, the Shut Down command is cheap insurance against data loss, and using it is a good habit to develop.

TEN HIGHLIGHTS OF WINDOWS 95

Still not convinced that you want to change from the familiar Windows 3.1 to Windows 95? Here are ten good reasons to make the switch:

1. Windows 95 is faster than Windows 3.1. Windows 95 requires fewer keystrokes and mouse clicks to get work done. Most applications run faster as well.

2. Windows 95 provides a technical feature known as *preemptive multitasking* that offers much smoother operation of several programs at the same time. Windows 95 offers better multitasking and lets you download files in the background while you do something else. Although not all programs you run are written to take advantage of preemptive multitasking, many are and you benefit from Windows 95 when you run them.

1

3. The Windows 95 screen, although much cleaner than the Windows 3.1 screen, makes all your PC's programs available to you when you need them, but does not needlessly clutter the screen.

4. Windows 95 contains integrated networking and Internet capabilities if you work in a networked environment. As a matter of fact, for those on a budget, Windows 95 offers a direct-connect pseudo-networking feature that lets you connect two PCs together with just a cable.

5. Windows 95 contains a much-improved MS-DOS with true cut-and-paste capabilities and the power to run MS-DOS–based programs (such as your favorite games!) as quickly as you can run those programs in a native MS-DOS environment.

6. You do not have to match switch settings or worry about those pesky things called DMAs and IRQs when installing new hardware. With the new *Plug-and-Play* feature, Windows 95 detects when you add or change hardware and adjusts all the computer's settings automatically. (Most of today's hardware supports Plug-and-Play compatibility.)

7. Windows 95 has the capability to detect when you insert a CD-ROM in the drive and start (or install) the software stored on the CD-ROM. This *AutoPlay* feature eliminates the need for users to issue start-up instructions when they want to run a program from a CD-ROM. In addition, other areas of multimedia are more integrated into Windows 95 than before. For example, you can place a volume control at the bottom of the screen to control the speaker volume for audio playback of CDs.

8. Windows 95 utilizes that right-hand button on your mouse. Clicking the right button pops up a context-sensitive menu that gives you instant access to common tasks you might want to perform (see Hour 2 for details).

9. Windows 95 supports filenames longer than 8 characters with a three-character extension! If you want to give a file a 250-character name that even includes spaces, go ahead! (The limit is 256 characters.)

10. Perhaps the most important day-to-day improvement you'll find is Windows 95's replacement for Windows 3.1's Program and File Manager called *Explorer* (covered in detail in Hour 5, "Explore the Windows 95 System"). Explorer makes managing hardware and files actually easy for a change.

Summary

You are off to a great start! It's time to push your own Start button, gear up your mind's memory chips, and begin exploring Windows 95 to see how to use Windows 95 and what it can do for you. Over the next 23 hours of study and tutorial, you'll be mastering the Windows 95 environment and learning all kinds of shortcuts along the way.

Keep in mind that Windows 95 is not an end in itself. The application programs that you want to run are the most important parts of your computer usage. It is Windows 95's job to help you work with your applications as painlessly as possible.

Workshop

Term Review

AutoPlay   The Windows 95 feature that starts the loading and execution of CD-ROMs as soon as you place the CD-ROM in your computer's CD-ROM drive.

bitmap   The technical name for a graphics file. Windows 95 often uses bitmaps for the Windows 95 wallpaper.

Check box   A Windows 95 control that appears next to each item in a list. You use the check boxes to select one or more items from the list.

click   The process of pressing and immediately releasing one of the mouse buttons.

command button   A Windows 95 control that appears and acts like a pushbutton on the screen.

cursor   A pointing device, such as the arrow that represents the mouse pointer location and the insert bar that represents the Windows 95 text location. The cursor moves across the screen as you type or move the mouse.

desktop   The Windows 95 screen and background.

dialog box   A window containing text and one or more screen controls that you use to issue instructions to Windows 95.

disk operating system   The program inside memory that controls all the hardware and software interactions.

dragging   The process of moving an image or selected text from one screen location to another using the mouse. To drag the mouse, you move the mouse while holding the mouse button. When you've dragged the item to the final position, release the mouse to anchor the item in that position.

focus   The highlighted command button or control in a dialog box that Windows 95 automatically selects when you press Enter.

GUI   A graphical user interface, such as Windows 95, that lets the user interact with the computer primarily through graphic images as opposed to a more traditional text-based interface that requires typed commands.

hot key   The combination of an Alt keypress combined with another key that selects command buttons. The key you press with Alt is displayed with an underlined letter in the command button you want to select.

1

icons   Small pictures that represent commands and programs in Windows 95.

kernel   The internal native operating system that controls the hardware and software interaction.

log on   The process that lets you gain access to a networked computer.

multitasking   The process of running more than one program at the same time.

Option button   A Windows 95 control that appears next to each item in a list. You use the option buttons to select one and only one item from the list.

Plug-and-Play   The feature inside Windows 95 that detects and automatically configures the operating system to match new hardware that you install in your computer system.

point   The action made by the screen's mouse cursor when you move the mouse.

reboot   The process of restarting your computer through the keyboard (by pressing Alt+Ctrl+Del) without shutting off the computer's power.

Start button   The button at the left of the taskbar that displays the Windows 95 cascading menu of choices. When you click the Start button, the Windows 95 Start menu appears.

Start menu   A Windows 95 system and program menu that appears when you click the taskbar's Start button.

System Administrator   The person in charge of assigning user names and setting up new users on networked environments.

Taskbar   The bar at the bottom of a Windows 95 screen where running program icons appear along with the system clock.

User profile   The customized interface and file-access rules setup for each networked user.

wallpaper   The background graphics that appear on the Windows 95 desktop.

Q&A

Q For whom did Microsoft write Windows 95?

A Microsoft wrote Windows 95 for everybody including beginners, intermediate users, advanced users, and programmers. The primary Windows 95 goal is to be easy enough for newcomers and yet powerful enough for those who need that power.

Q **Why do asterisks appear when I enter my network password?**

A Asterisks appear in place of the actual characters that you type so that someone looking over your shoulder can't steal your password.

Q **What happens if I do not use the Shut Down procedures for my computer?**

A If you do not shut down your computer before turning off the power, you could lose data files or even system configuration files. Most of the time, you'd probably be okay if you did not shut down the computer, but your data is worth too much not to get into the habit of properly shutting down the system and safely storing all data.

HOUR 2

Tour Windows 95 Now

For the next hour, you are going to learn a lot about Windows 95's interface so that you'll know how to interact with the Windows 95 system. You will become comfortable with managing windows and icons.

By the time you finish this hour, you'll be as familiar with the basics as many veteran Windows users. This hour's techniques will follow you and help you manage almost every other aspect of Windows 95 that you work with in the future. After you master the basics of the window and screen management tools, you'll use those abilities in all your Windows 95 applications work.

The highlights of this hour include:

- Why windows management is important
- What the parts of a window are called
- How to resize and move windows
- How to use the Control menu
- How to manage window toolbars

Windows appear all over the place when you work with Windows—that's why it's called *Windows*! Therefore, taking a moment now to learn proper windows management will reap big savings and reduce confusion in the future.

I *Do* Do Windows!

The first window that you will work with is called the *My Computer window*. In this hour, you will look at that window to learn how to work with windows in general. Hour 4, "Understanding the My Computer Window," explains how to use the contents of the My Computer window, but this hour uses My Computer so you can familiarize yourself with common windows operations.

Locate the My Computer icon on your Windows 95 desktop. It's usually the icon in the upper-left corner. Double-click the icon to open the My Computer window. Most icons on the desktop open to windows when you double-click them, as you'll see throughout this book. If the icon's title is underlined, click only once to open My Computer. Your desktop is in the active desktop mode that requires only single clicks to open windows. Hour 3, "Take Windows 95 to Task," describes the active desktop.

Figure 2.1 shows the My Computer window with all its control buttons and window components labeled. This same window structure exists in almost every window that you open. Although you saw a couple of simpler windows in this book's previous hour, the window in Figure 2.1 is more typical of the windows you'll work with.

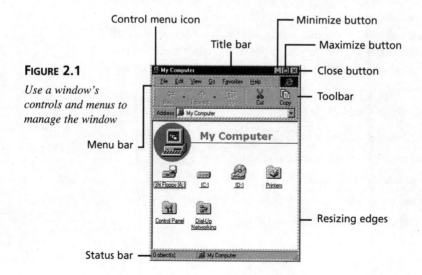

FIGURE 2.1

Use a window's controls and menus to manage the window

Your My Computer window might differ slightly in the way the icons and text appear. Depending on how your windows are set to display, the contents might appear in a list. In addition, the graphic image and toolbar might not appear in the window. You'll learn how to adjust your display's settings in Hour 4, "Understanding the My Computer Window."

2

Familiarize yourself now with the window buttons because almost every window contains these window controls or a subset of them. Here are some of the more general things you can do with such a window:

- You can shrink the window down to an icon on the taskbar, eliminating the window from the screen but keeping the window active. This process is called *minimizing a window.*

- You can enlarge a minimized window to partial or full-screen size. When you size a window to take up the entire screen, the window is *maximized.*

- You can move a window from one location to another on the screen.

- You can bring a window to the top of a stack of windows so you can work within that window. (Due to Windows 95's multitasking capability, hidden windows can still perform data processing, such as calculating and printing.)

- You can close a window completely, removing its icon from the taskbar and stopping the application that is running inside the window.

You can have one or more windows on your screen, some overlapping other windows, some completely covering others; and you will sometimes see windows side by side or above other windows. In a typical Windows 95 user's day, the user might have two or more applications running at the same time. Each of those applications might display one or more windows of its own.

Having multiple windows open at one time doesn't necessarily cause confusion. On a typical desk, even the desks of the most organized people (the author not being one of them!), you'll find all sorts of paper stacks, and those stacks don't imply disorganization. The desk's user simply has to know how to organize the stacks and bring the most important stacks to the forefront when she wants to work on them.

When you start a program, the taskbar gets a new taskbar button with the name of that application appearing on the taskbar button.

Some applications display single windows. Other applications might display multiple windows. For example, there are word processors that can display two documents side by side in two different windows.

Minimizing Windows

If you temporarily finish working with a window, you can minimize that window by clicking the window's Minimize button. Minimizing a window keeps the program in the window loaded and active but puts the program out of the way until you are ready to return to that program again. Even if you minimize a window, the window's icon and description remain on the taskbar at the bottom of the screen. The taskbar continues to hold the application's button until you completely close the application.

Task 2.1: Minimizing a Window

Step 1: Description

The Minimize button clears the window from your desktop. The program that you have running inside the window is still loaded and active, but the program no longer takes up screen space. The taskbar continues to list the program because the program is still active.

Step 2: Action

1. Find the Minimize button on your My Computer window.
2. Click the button with your mouse pointer. Look closely at the screen as you minimize the window. You'll see that Windows 95 graphically and quickly shrinks the outer edges of the window down into the taskbar button labeled My Computer.

Step 3: Review

When you minimize a window, whatever window or icon is behind that window then appears. Remember that the way you know a window is still active is that its icon and description still appear on the taskbar, as shown in Figure 2.2.

FIGURE 2.2

The window's taskbar button still appears after you minimize a window

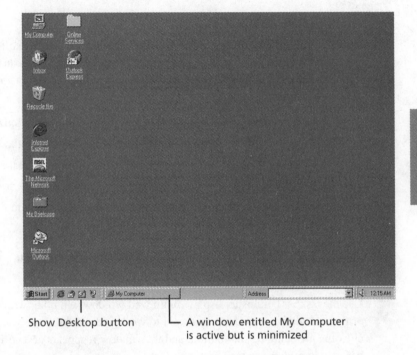

2

Show Desktop button ⌐ A window entitled My Computer
is active but is minimized

The taskbar button in Figure 2.2 contains the caption My Computer. The caption says My Computer because the minimized window's title bar contained the title My Computer. The taskbar button always contains the same title that is listed in the window's title bar.

Notice the set of buttons on the taskbar. (These buttons appear only if you have Internet Explorer 4 installed.) The Show Desktop button minimizes all open windows. Therefore, if you quickly want to minimize all open windows and work with your Windows 95 desktop, click Show Desktop. Programs will continue to run in the minimized windows.

Depending on the length of the title and the number of items in the taskbar, the taskbar might only show the first few letters of a window's title. You can drag the right edge of the taskbar area that holds the buttons to the right to increase the room given to the buttons.

Enlarging Windows

Windows 95 supplies several ways to enlarge a window. You can enlarge a minimized window from its taskbar status to the window's regular size. You can also maximize a window that's already showing so that it takes up the entire screen space. Here are the ways to enlarge a window:

- Click the window's taskbar button when the window is minimized
- Click the window's Maximize button to enlarge the window to full screen
- Drag one of the window's corners or edges outward to increase the size of the window or inward to shrink the size of the window manually

The next task discusses the first two methods for enlarging a window, and the next section explains how to enlarge a window manually.

Task 2.2: Enlarging a Minimized Window

Step 1: Description

Use the taskbar buttons to display minimized windows. In other words, if you have one or more minimized windows and want to work with one of those window's programs, click the matching taskbar button, and the window reappears at its original size (its size before you minimized the window).

Step 2: Action

1. Click the My Computer taskbar button. The My Computer window reappears.
2. Notice how the window quickly and visually grows from the taskbar back to its original size? Perhaps you want to see that again. Minimize the now enlarged My Computer window again to shrink the window down into the taskbar.
3. Click the My Computer taskbar button and watch the window return to its original and enlarged state.

Step 3: Review

The taskbar lists buttons that represent all running programs and active windows. Some of those programs might have their windows showing on the screen; other programs are minimized so they take no screen space but are still loaded. Clicking a taskbar button

 causes a minimized window to return to its original size.

Icons other than the open windows may appear on your taskbar. In the standard default setup of Windows, the time of day and other icons such as the speaker icon appear on the rightmost side of the taskbar.

Task 2.3: Maximizing a Window

Step 1: Description

As long as a window contains a Maximize button, you can maximize that window to the screen's full size. (Some windows are designed to be no larger than a preset size; these windows do not have Maximize buttons.) When you want to dedicate the entire screen to a window, you can usually maximize the window by clicking the window's Maximize button.

 You also can maximize a window by double-clicking the window's title bar.

Step 2: Action

1. Click the My Computer window's Maximize button. The window grows to consume the entire screen. Figure 2.3 shows what you will see. The My Computer window does not often contain a lot of items, so maximizing the My Computer window does not produce much benefit other than the practice that you're getting here. The more a window contains, the larger you'll want to make that window so that you can see the contents.

FIGURE 2.3

A maximized window fills the entire screen

A Restore button replaces the Maximize button

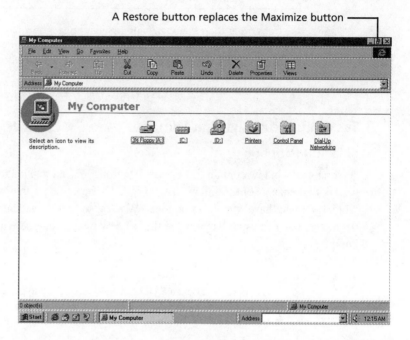

There is no need for Windows 95 to keep a Maximize button on a window that's already maximized. Therefore, Windows 95 changes the Maximize button to a Restore button as soon as you maximize any window. The Restore button, noted in Figure 2.3, always restores the window to the size it measured before you maximized it.

2. Click the My Computer window's Restore button. The window resizes (down) to its original size. As soon as you restore the window's size, you'll see that the Restore button switches back to a Maximize button again.

3. Give it another maximizing whirl, but this time, double-click the My Computer window's title bar (point the mouse anywhere over the title in the window's title bar before double-clicking). Double-clicking the title bar maximizes a window just as pressing the Maximize button does.

4. Restore the My Computer window's original size again by clicking the Restore button.

Step 3: Review

You will often maximize a window if you are working within that window's program. For example, most word processor users maximize the word processing window while typing a document so that more screen real estate goes to that document and, therefore, more of the document appears on the screen at one time. You can maximize a window by clicking the window's Maximize button or by double-clicking the title bar.

> If you load several programs and one program's window covers up another program's window, you can click the hidden program's taskbar button to bring the covered window into view.

2

Manually Changing Window Sizes

You can resize a window manually by dragging the mouse. When you point to any window's edge or corner, the mouse cursor changes from its default shape (the pointing arrow) to a bidirectional arrow. The bidirectional arrow indicates that you are at one of the edges of the window and you can drag that edge or corner inward or outward to change the size of the window.

When you drag one of the four straight edges, the window grows or shrinks left, right, up, or down. When you drag one of the four window corners, the window grows or shrinks in both height and width in the direction of the cursor's bidirectional diagonal shape.

> You will not be able to resize every window that appears on your monitor. The Welcome screen that you see when you start up Windows 95 is one such screen.

Moving Windows

The windows that appear on your Windows 95 desktop don't always appear in the location you want. That's okay. Using the mouse, you can easily drag a window to another location on the screen. The title bar acts like a handle for the window—to move the window, you drag the window's title bar.

Task 2.4: Moving a Window

Step 1: Description

Sometimes, you'll need to rearrange the windows on your screen so they form a more logical appearance as you work. To move a window, drag its title bar. As you move the window by dragging the title bar, an outline of the window follows the mouse. When you release the mouse button, the window appears in the new location.

▼ Step 2: Action

1. Move the My Computer window by dragging the title bar and moving the mouse. You'll see the outline of the window move with the mouse.

2. Release the mouse button to end the dragging session and anchor the window in its new location.

3. Move the window again. Move the window off the edge of the screen. As you can see, when you move a window over the screen's edge, Windows 95 *truncates* (chops off) a portion of the window. When you move the window back into full view, the window reappears in its entirety.

Step 3: Review

Any time you want to change the arrangement of your screen's windows, you can move
▲ one or more windows to different locations.

Closing a Window

Windows 95 is obviously full of windows, and those windows contain executing (running) programs that work with data values of all kinds. In addition, a window might contain icons to other windows and programs. This windowed concept gives you a flexible and manageable way to run and control several programs at one time. When you open a window in the real world, you are using that window to let air inside a building. *Opening* a window in Windows 95 means that you are using the program or data area located within that window. Whenever you start a windowed program or enlarge a window that's been minimized, you are opening the program's window.

When you're through with an open window, both in the real world and in Windows 95, you must *close* the window. Closing a window eliminates the window from view, and if that window contained a running program (as most do), that program ceases executing. The window's taskbar button will no longer appear on the taskbar.

Remember that *closing* a window differs from *minimizing* the window. Closing a window stops a program; minimizing a window keeps it running in the background.

If you open a window from an icon, closing the window eliminates the window from your desktop area, but the window's icon will remain on the screen in its original place. Unless you take some advanced steps to erase the icon and its contents, the icon remains on your Windows 95 desktop area whether the corresponding window is open or closed.

You can rearrange icons on your screen by dragging them with the mouse just as you rearrange windows. In addition, if you right-click over your desktop and select Arrange Icons, a pop-up menu appears that enables you to select the arrangement of your desktop icons (alphabetically, by type, size, date, or automatic arrangement).

2

Keep in mind that some windows contain running programs (such as the window you see when typing in a word processor program) while other windows contain icons and even more windows (such as the My Computer window). You can close both kinds of windows by clicking the Close button. When running a program, you can also close its primary window, and hence terminate the entire program, by double-clicking the program's icon in the upper-left corner of the window or by terminating the program (normally by selecting File | Exit from the program's menu or File | Close for open windows as described in Task 2.5). To select from a menu, point to the menu with your mouse and click on the item you want to select.

Windows 95 contains *folder* icons. These icons, when you double-click them, open up still more folders or windows of icons. When you see folder icons in file listings, the folders represent directories on your disk. Hour 5, "Explore the Windows 95 System," explains more about folders and directories.

Task 2.5: Closing a Window Using the Mouse

Step 1: Description

When you're done with a window, you can close the window by clicking the Close button (the window control button with an $\underline{X}$ that appears in the upper-right corner of the window), double-clicking the window's icon, or (if the window represents a running program) using the program's termination commands to close the program and the window.

Step 2: Action

1. Click the Close button on the My Computer window. The window will instantly disappear from view.

2. Look at the taskbar for the My Computer icon. You will see no My Computer icon! Remember that a closed window is different from a minimized window in that a minimized window is still active and loaded.

▼   3. Open the My Computer window again by double-clicking the My Computer icon
          on your desktop.

Step 3: Review

Closing a window is like taking a paper file off your desktop and storing that file away in
a file cabinet. The window is completely gone from your work area just as the paper file
would be. If you want to work in the window again, you have to reinitiate the commands
that displayed the window to begin with (usually by double-clicking an icon that repre-
▲   sents the window).

Using the System Menu

All windows contain icons in their upper-left corners. The icon is the same icon that you
see when the window is closed. For example, you clicked a large PC icon on the
Windows 95 desktop to open the My Computer window. When open, the My Computer
window contains a small icon that matches the start-up icon you double-clicked to start
the program.

Earlier (in the section "Closing a Window") you learned to double-click this icon to close
a window. The icon also represents a *System menu* (which, in earlier versions of
Windows, was known as the *Control menu*) with which you can control the window's
size and placement. Figure 2.4 shows the System menu for the My Computer window.
Almost every Windows 95 program contains this same menu.

FIGURE 2.4

You can control a win-
dow's size and place-
ment through the
System menu

What's on the Menu?

Just as a menu in a restaurant is a list of food items you can choose, a Windows *menu* is
a list of commands you can select. The System menu is a typical Windows 95 menu.
Many menus operate the same way that the System menu operates—that is, the list of
menu choices stays out of the way until you are ready to choose from it. You saw another

kind of menu in Hour 1, "What's Windows 95 All About?"—The Start menu. After you display a menu, you can move through the menu selections using the keyboard's up and down arrow keys or the mouse.

The first thing you might notice about Figure 2.4 is that the top choice, Restore, is *grayed out*. Often one or more menu items are grayed out, meaning that the choice is unavailable at this time but, depending on circumstances, might be available from this menu at a later time.

Just like the Start menu, the System menu offers a list of *shortcut keys* with which you can quickly select a menu item. For example, Alt+N selects the System menu's Minimize command as long as the Control menu is shown at the time you press Alt+N.

There's another kind of shortcut key visible on the System menu. Both Alt+C *and* Alt+F4 select the System menu's Close command. (F4 is one of the twelve *function keys* that are labeled F1 through F12 across the top of your keyboard.) The Alt+F4 key, however, is an *accelerator* key meaning that the System menu does not have to be showing when you press Alt+F4 to close the window. Accelerator keys generally involve function keys and appear to the right of their associated menu choices.

As with the Start menu, you can also select from the System menu using the mouse. You now know everything there is to know about using and choosing from Windows 95 menus!

 Want to know an alternative method for closing the Start or System menu? Press the Esc key.

Table 2.1 explains what each System menu command does.

TABLE 2.1 THE CONTROL MENU COMMANDS

Command	Description
Restore	Restores a window that you've maximized. The Restore command is available (not grayed out) only when the window is maximized.
Move	Moves a window on the screen to a different location.
Size	Resizes a window by enlarging or shrinking the window.
Minimize	Shrinks the window to the taskbar icon and description.
Maximize	Enlarges the window to full-screen size.
Close	Closes the window. If the window is a running program, the program terminates.

A Window's Menu

If you have *Internet Explorer 4* installed on your PC, many of your windows will contain menu bars. Internet Explorer is an Internet-browsing program that you'll learn to master in Hour 14, "Windows 95 and Internet Explorer 4." Even non-program windows that display information such as the My Computer window can display a menu bar. You can use the menu bar to close the window, open additional windows, copy, cut, and paste information from one window to another, get help, and even access the Internet for related information. (The Internet's never far away in Windows.)

As you progress over the next 22 lessons, you'll learn ways to use the window menu bar options to traverse windows and get to the information you need most. When you select an option from a menu bar, that option's menu pulls down to display a list of actions. For example, Figure 2.5 shows an open View menu. Throughout the rest of the lessons, when asked to select View | Details, for example, you would click the View menu bar option and select Details with your mouse or arrow keys.

FIGURE 2.5

Windows contain menus that let you control operations on and within the window

Task 2.6: Working with a Window's Menu Bar

Step 1: Description

The menu bar lets you control the way the window looks and behaves. If the window's icons are too large to hold all of a window's contents, you can select smaller icons or change the window to a list view format.

Step 2: Action

1. From the open My Computer window, select **View** | **Small** Icons. The window's icons get smaller so they display in a smaller space.

▼   2. Select **View | Details** to see the window's contents compacted even further. The list view shows extra information about the window's contents such as the size, date created, free disk space, and other statistics relative to the item in the window.

Step 3: Review

▲   Use a window's menu bar to change the window's appearance and behavior. More of the menu bar options will come in handy as you learn more about Windows.

A Window's Toolbar

A *toolbar* is a ribbon of buttons across the top of a window. Some programs have multiple toolbars. The toolbar you see atop the My Computer window is fairly common and appears throughout most windows that appear in Windows. Toolbar buttons give you pushbutton access to common actions you perform with the window. (If your toolbar does not appear at the top of the My Computer window, you need to display the active desktop as you'll learn in this hour's final section.)

As you work within a window, the toolbar changes to reflect actions that become available. For example, if you open a folder icon located in a window, not only do the clicked folder's contents replace the window's original contents, but the toolbar changes as well.

All of the window toolbars in Windows are known as *Explorer toolbars* because they mimic the actions of Internet Explorer Windows. Many toolbar buttons are standard across applications and windows, and you'll learn to recognize them quickly.

Task 2.7: Working with a Windows Toolbar

Step 1: Description

Toolbars change as you work within the window. In addition, you might want to modify a toolbar's behavior to access the toolbar's benefits more efficiently. Although toolbar management can be quite a lengthy topic, simple toolbar management is easy, as you'll see in this task.

Step 2: Action

1. Maximize the My Computer window. Notice that the Back toolbar button (the button with the left-pointing arrow) is grayed out.

▼   2. Double-click the Printers folder. The Printers folder contains an icon to let you set up a new printer that you might add to your system. It also contains icons for existing printers you've already designated. Notice that the Back toolbar button is now available. Back lets you return to the previous contents of the window.

▼   3. Click the Back button and the original My Computer contents return. (Forward would take you to the Printers folder.) No matter how many windows and subfolders you open within a window, you can always retrace your steps backward and forward again with the Back and Forward buttons.

4. Modify the way the toolbar looks. Right-click over the right end of the toolbar (an area where no buttons appear) to display the toolbar's menu. Select Text Labels. As Figure 2.6 shows, the window's toolbar buttons no longer display textual descriptions. The buttons take up less room but are not as descriptive. (The Text Labels button is a *toggle* selection. Clicking a toggle selection turns its associated condition on or off depending on its current state. In this example, Text Labels were active, so selecting Text Labels turned them off.)

FIGURE 2.6

Without the text labels, your toolbar takes up less room

Toolbar handle controls ———

5. You can repeat the menu selection to put the text labels back. The text labels make the toolbar grow to accommodate the labels. Many of the toolbar areas have toolbar handle *controls* (see Figure 2.6) that let you slide that portion of the toolbar left or right to make room for something else. Drag one of the toolbar handles left or right to see how the toolbar adjusts to the handle control. If you double-click a toolbar's handle, the tools on the toolbar handle come into view (and cover up other items) or hide to bring hidden items into focus again.

▼

▼   6. A window's contents don't dictate what you view in the window! The area of the
           toolbar labeled <u>Address</u> is not a button but describes the white box to the right of
           <u>Address</u>. The box is a *drop-down list box* that can display choices you might want
           to use. Click the list box's down arrow (at the right of the list box) to see a list of
           areas you can go to from the window. Whether your choose (by dragging the
           mouse or using the keyboard) a disk drive or the Internet, the contents you pick
           will appear inside the window and replace the window's original My Computer
           contents. As always, the Back button brings you right back where you started if
           you want to return to the My Computer window.

> The Address list box, as well as the other traversal features of the toolbar
> such as the Back and Forward buttons, proves that Windows doesn't limit
> you; just because you open a window doesn't mean that you want to stay
> with that window. The toolbar lets you move from one window's contents
> to a totally unrelated window and even to an Internet site (that will display
> in the window) if you've got a connection to the Internet.

> You can remove the Address list box if you don't want to consume the tool-
> bar space. Select **View | Toolbar** and click **Address** bar to remove the check
> mark next to the entry and hide the Address bar. (Repeat this tip to bring
> the bar back again.)

Step 3: Review

A window's toolbar appears when you traverse any part of your PC, a networked file, or
the Internet from any window. Customize the toolbars so they display the information
that helps you most. The toolbars are plentiful with pushbutton features and even contain
the standard Windows capability to copy, cut, and paste information from the window to
elsewhere in your system.

> If you delete or cut something from a window accidentally, click the tool-
> bar's Undo button to restore the deleted or cut material.

▲

One Last Note About Windows

You can completely change the way a window looks by selecting View | As Web Page from the menu. The Web view, as opposed to the Classic view that Windows 95 uses by default, makes your Windows environment look and behave somewhat like an Internet page. Hour 16, "Activating Your Desktop," explains the advantages of using the Web view. If your windows are not set up like Web pages, the window changes from an icon or list view to a view that acts like an Internet Web browser. Then, when you select an icon (select an icon by moving your mouse over the icon or by clicking once to highlight the icon), as Figure 2.7 shows, the My Computer window displays a description of the selected item.

FIGURE 2.7

You might prefer to view your windows in a Web page format

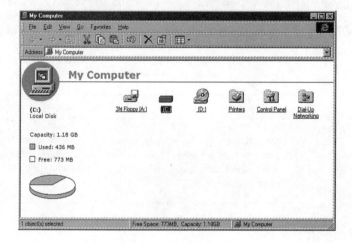

Summary

This hour taught you the ins and outs of windows management. Learning how to manage windows is a fundamental skill that Windows 95 users must understand. Windows 95 lets you open, resize, move, and close windows. The windows on your desktop contain running applications, and part of running Windows 95 programs requires being able to position those windows where you want them.

Workshop

Term Review

accelerator key   A key found on a menu, usually a function key used in conjunction with the Alt key (such as Alt+F4), that lets you initiate a menu command from the keyboard without first having to display the menu.

closing a window   The practice of eliminating a window from view and terminating any program that might be running within the window at the time.

folder   A special icon that contains other icons which are displayed when you double-click the folder icon; a grouping of related files stored under the same subdirectory.

function keys   Twelve keys labeled F1 through F12 that you press to trigger various actions.

maximized window   A window that you've expanded to the size of the entire screen.

minimized window   A window that you've shrunk down to a taskbar icon.

opening a window   The process of starting a program in a window or double-clicking an icon to display a window.

shortcut key   An underlined letter on a menu that you can combine with the Alt key to issue a menu command.

System menu   A menu available on all windows within Windows 95 that lets you move and resize windows from the keyboard; it is accessed by clicking the window's icon in the upper-left corner of the window. Also called a window's *Control menu*.

Toggle   A menu selection or toolbar button that turns on and off a condition.

Q&A

Q What's the difference between a shortcut key and an accelerator key?

A Both shortcut keys (or hot keys) and accelerator keys involve selecting commands from Windows 95 menus. The shortcut keystrokes appear as underlined letters in menu commands. When you combine the Alt key with the underlined letter (such as Alt+R to select Restore), the matching menu item executes.

Accelerator keys have the added distinction of enabling the user to select menu commands by pressing keystrokes without first having to display a menu. Accelerator keys appear at the right of their corresponding menu commands.

Q Why would I want to minimize a window?

A Often, Windows 95 users run several programs at once. Instead of having all those program windows appearing all over the screen, you can minimize the windows you aren't using currently but might need again shortly so that the windows are out of the way.

To return to the minimized window, you need only to click the window's icon on the taskbar. Therefore, the window remains active and loaded, ready to be used, but out of the way until you need the window.

Hour 3

Take Windows 95 to Task

The taskbar and the Start button are closely related. Most Windows 95 users use the Start button to display the Start menu, then select a program they want to see begin. When the program begins running (also called *executing*), the taskbar displays a button with an icon along with a description that represents that running program.

The taskbar, Start button, and the Start menu are the most important components Microsoft put in Windows 95. The taskbar is the cornerstone of Windows 95. This hour describes the taskbar and its Start menu in detail and explains how to customize the taskbar to make it perform in a manner that best suits your computing style.

The highlights of this hour include:

- Where the Start menu comes from
- How to move and change the appearance of the taskbar
- How to start programs not listed on the Start menu's Programs option
- When to use the active desktop

A Quick Taskbar and Start Button Review

In Hour 1, "What's Windows 95 All About?" you saw the Start menu and used it to shut down your computer properly. Clicking the taskbar's Start button produces the Start menu. The Start menu does all these things and more:

- It makes itself available to you no matter what else you are doing.
- It displays a list of programs using the Start menu's cascading system.
- It provides you with an easy-access list of recently-used documents that you can open.
- It enables you to return to your favorite places, whether those places are Internet sites or programs.
- It provides a search engine (a routine that scans your computer for files and folders) that navigates through all your files looking for the one you need.
- It provides online help for working within Windows 95.

The next few sections explain how you can customize the taskbar and its associated Start menu, so that when you are ready to use the Start menu, it will act and look the way you expect.

> If you do not see the Start button, your taskbar might be hidden. Press Ctrl+Esc to display the Start menu and taskbar.

Moving the Taskbar

The taskbar does not have to stay at the bottom of your screen. Depending on the program you are running, you might want to move the taskbar to either side of your monitor, or even to the top of your screen. The taskbar placement is easy to change, as you will see in this hour.

> Figure 3.1 shows that a side taskbar does not have the width necessary to display lengthy taskbar descriptions. When you place the taskbar at the bottom or top of the screen, the taskbar has more room for longer descriptions.

The newly placed taskbar

FIGURE 3.1

You can move the taskbar to any edge of your screen

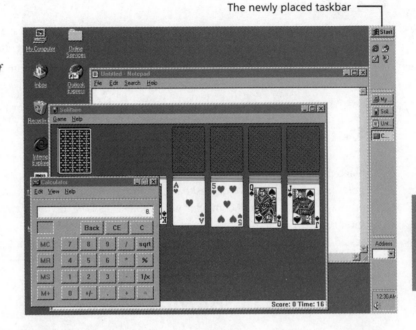

3

When you place the taskbar at the top of the screen, the Start menu falls down from the Start button; when you place the taskbar at the bottom of the screen, the Start menu pops up from the Start button.

 When working on a wide spreadsheet or document, you might want as much screen width as you can get so place the taskbar at the bottom or top of your screen. When working with graphics, you usually need more vertical screen space, so you could move the taskbar to either side of the screen when working within a graphics program.

Task 3.1: Moving Your Taskbar

Step 1: Description

The taskbar is easy to drag to any of the four edges of your screen. Simply drag the taskbar to the new location. When dragging the taskbar, you have to position the mouse pointer over a blank spot in the taskbar, such as between two buttons or to the right of the Start button if no other windows are open.

▲ To Do

▼ **Step 2: Action**

1. Find a blank spot on your taskbar and point to the spot with the mouse cursor. Be sure that you are pointing within the taskbar and not over a button on the taskbar.

2. Click and hold the mouse button while dragging the taskbar to another edge of the screen. As you drag the mouse, an outline of the taskbar moves with the mouse.

3. Release the mouse button to anchor the taskbar at its new position.

Step 3: Review

Drag the taskbar to the edge of the screen that works best for your program. You can place the taskbar at one location for one program and move the taskbar for another program later. You can move the taskbar any time, even after you've started one or more programs. If you share a computer with another user, have your Network Administrator set up a user profile for both of you. When you log on (see Hour 1), your Windows 95 session's taskbar will appear where you last left it no matter where the other user moved
▲ the taskbar before you logged on.

The Taskbar Properties Menu

A right mouse button click (or the left button click if you've set up your mouse for left-handed operation) often displays a *context-sensitive* menu of options available to you. The taskbar is one such location where the right mouse button brings up a helpful menu, called the *taskbar properties menu*. You can use it to change the appearance and performance of the taskbar and the windows controlled by the taskbar. After finding a blank spot on your taskbar, clicking the right mouse button brings up the context-sensitive taskbar properties menu shown in Figure 3.2.

> Do not click the right mouse button over one of the taskbar programs unless you want to activate that button's program or window (known as bringing the program into *focus*).

The taskbar properties menu is not necessarily a menu you'll want to display often. Most users play around with different taskbar and window settings for a while until they find preferences that suit them best. Thereafter, those users may rarely use the taskbar properties menu.

FIGURE 3.2

A click of the right mouse button on a blank space on the taskbar displays a context-sensitive menu

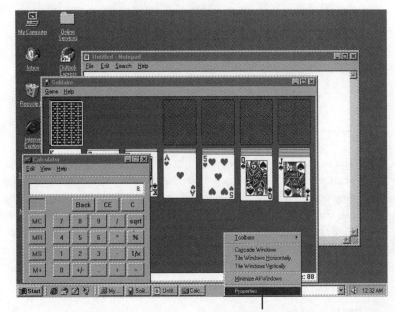

The taskbar properties menu

The menu option Toolbars enables you to customize your toolbar by selecting which items you want to see. Table 3.1 explains each kind of toolbar-based element you can place on the taskbar. Some of Table 3.1's items, such as the Quick Launch toolbar, appear only if you've installed Internet Explorer 4.

TABLE 3.1 ADD THESE TOOLBAR ELEMENTS TO YOUR WINDOWS 95 TASKBAR

Toolbar Element	Description
Address	Displays a drop-down list box on your taskbar that you can click to return to recent Web and file locations.
Links	Displays popular Web links you can quickly return to with the click of a button. You can modify the list of links.
Desktop	Puts a ribbon of icons that match those on your Windows 95 desktop. You can click on one of the icons to start that icon's program or open that icon's window instead of having to return to your desktop to locate the icon.
Quick Launch	Adds Internet access control buttons so you can quickly get on the Web. In addition, the Show Desktop icon appears in the Quick Launch section so you can minimize all open windows with a single taskbar click. Other items appear on the taskbar's right-click menu when you activate the Quick Launch taskbar icons.

continues

TABLE 3.1 CONTINUED

Toolbar Element	Description
New Toolbar	Lets you select a disk drive, folder, or Web location whose contents appear as a secondary sliding toolbar handle on the taskbar. Subsequently, the taskbar's right-click menu contains that new tool bar. To hide the toolbar again, click the toolbar name on the right-click menu.

The next three menu options are important when you want to work with more than one open window. These three menu options offer ways of arranging your open windows so they are more manageable. If you open two or more windows at once all those windows can be difficult to manage individually. You could maximize each window and display only one window at a time. There are many reasons, however, to keep more than one window open and displayed at the same time, such as when you want to copy data from one window to another. (Hour 5, "Explore the Windows 95 System," explains how to copy between windows.)

Tiling Windows

When you want to see more than one open window at a time, the taskbar properties menu gives you tools that provide quick management of those windows so you do not have to size and place each window individually. Figure 3.3 shows how too many windows open at the same time can be confusing. You'll see in the section that follows how to use the taskbar properties menu to straighten up such a mess.

Task 3.2: Organizing Multiple Windows
Step 1: Description

The taskbar properties menu provides a way to organize several open windows with the click of a mouse. There are three ways to organize the windows: cascade them, vertically tile them, or horizontally tile them.

FIGURE 3.3

Too many open win-
dows can quickly
cause disorganization

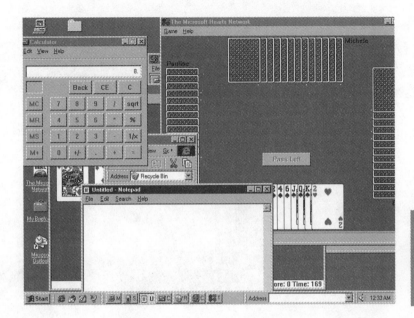

▼ Step 2: Action

1. Click the My Computer icon to open the My Computer window.

2. Click the Recycle Bin icon to open that window as well. Although you might not understand the Recycle Bin until Hour 5, the open window will show the effects of the taskbar's properties menu.

3. Display the Start menu and select the Help option. Shortly, you'll see a help window open up. Again, this window is just to put more on your desktop to work with.

4. Now that you've opened three windows, ask Windows 95 to organize those windows for you. Display the taskbar's properties menu by right-clicking the mouse button after pointing to a blank spot on the taskbar.

5. Select the first menu item labeled Cascade. Windows 95 instantly organizes your windows into the cascaded series of windows shown in Figure 3.4.

FIGURE 3.4

The windows are now more manageable

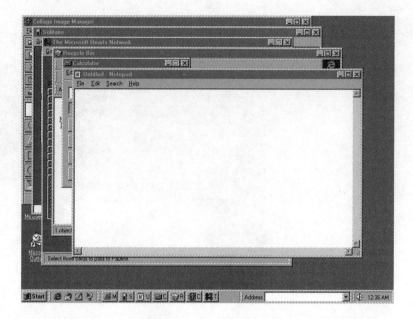

▼ Notice that the title bars of *all* open windows appear on the desktop area. When you want to bring any of the hidden windows into focus, click that window's title bar, and the window rises to the top of the stack of the screen's windows. The cascading effect always gives you the ability to switch between windows. As long as any part of a hidden window is peeking out from under another, you can bring that hidden window into focus by clicking the mouse button on that hidden window's title bar.

6. Sometimes, you need to see the contents of two or more windows at the same time. Windows 95 lets you *tile* the open windows so you can see the actual body of each open window. Windows 95 supports two kinds of tiling methods: horizontal tiling and vertical tiling. Display the taskbar's properties menu and select Tile Horizontally. Windows 95 will properly resize each of the five open windows as

▼ shown in Figure 3.5.

FIGURE 3.5

The windows are now tiled horizontally

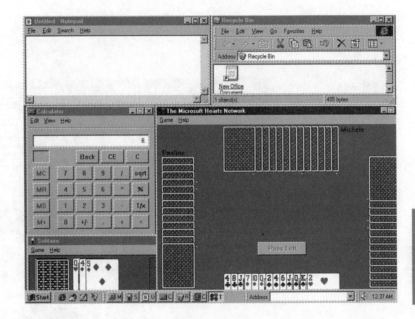

In this example, Windows 95 does not show you a *lot* of any one of the windows. Keep in mind that all the window resizing and moving tools work even after you have tiled windows. Therefore, you can move the Help window toward the top of the screen after tiling the windows, if you want to see more of that window. (Scrollbars automatically appear in tiled windows if the contents of the window consume more space than can be displayed at once.)

Figure 3.6 shows a scrollbar on the right window. Scrollbars always appear when an active window contains more information than will fit in the window. Click the scrollbar arrows, or drag the scroll box, to scroll the information up or down in the window.

7. The vertical tiling method produces side-by-side windows that are fairly thin but offer yet another kind of open window display. Select Tile Vertically and Windows 95 reformats the screen to look something like Figure 3.6. Now that you've changed the look of your open windows by using the taskbar properties menu, you can revert the windows to their previous state through the taskbar properties menu as well. You can restore the original placement of the windows by selecting Undo Tile.

Drag the scroll box
to scroll up or down

Click to scroll up

FIGURE 3.6

The windows are now
tiled vertically

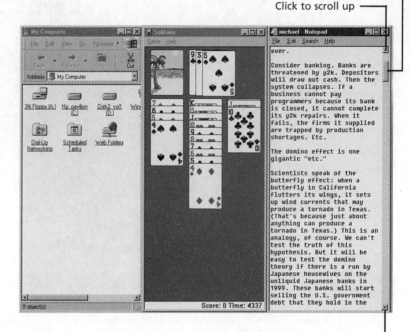

Click to scroll down

8. The Show Desktop taskbar button that appears if you activate your desktop as explained in this lesson's final section minimizes all open windows. Show Desktop is easier than using the Minimize All Windows taskbar properties menu option. Don't minimize the windows now, however, as you'll need them open for the next task.

No matter how you tile or cascade the windows, each window's Minimize, Maximize, and Restore buttons all work as usual. Therefore, you can maximize a cascaded window at any time by clicking that window's Maximize button.

▼ Step 3: Review

You can use the taskbar's properties menu to control the appearance of the open windows on your screen. The nice thing about using the taskbar to manage open windows is that you don't have to size and place each window individually. Instead, leave the hard work

▲ to Windows 95 when you want to see a tiled or cascaded series of windows at one time.

Working with Taskbar Properties

The taskbar properties menu not only controls the appearance and performance of open windows, the taskbar properties menu also controls the appearance and performance of the taskbar itself. The Properties menu option displays the Taskbar Properties tabbed dialog box shown in Figure 3.7. With the Taskbar Properties dialog box, you can change the way the taskbar appears and performs, and you also can change the contents of the Start menu.

3

FIGURE 3.7

You can change the taskbar's appearance and performance by using the Taskbar Properties dialog box

In Hour 7, "Manage Your Desktop," you'll learn how to change the contents of the Start menu.

Using Dialog Boxes

You can see an example of a tabbed dialog box in Figure 3.7. The pages in a tabbed dialog box are often called *property sheets*. When Windows 95 displays a tabbed dialog box, it is offering you more than one dialog box at one time. Instead of displaying two or more dialog boxes at once, the tabs save screen space and organize the property sheets inside the dialog box. Windows 95 might put command buttons, option buttons, check marks, text boxes, or other kinds of controls all together inside a dialog box. When you click the dialog box's OK button, Windows 95 closes the dialog box, and your dialog box settings go into effect.

In addition to the OK button, some dialog boxes have an Apply button. Generally, these dialog boxes change a Windows 95 setting such as the font size. If you click Apply, Windows 95 puts your dialog box settings into effect but does not close the dialog box. Therefore, you can see the results of your dialog box settings without getting rid of the dialog box.

Task 3.3: Using the Taskbar Properties Dialog Box

Step 1: Description

The Taskbar Properties dialog box accepts from you information that controls the way the taskbar appears on the screen. You can allow (or disallow) windows to overlap the taskbar if those windows are large enough to do so; you can eliminate the clock from the taskbar; and you can even minimize the taskbar so that it does not appear until you need it. (Normally the taskbar appears no matter what else you have displayed on the Windows 95 screen, as you've already seen.)

Step 2: Action

1. With the three windows still open on your screen from the previous task, display the taskbar properties menu again by right-clicking the mouse button on the taskbar.

2. Select the Properties command to display the tabbed Taskbar Properties dialog box shown in Figure 3.7.

   The first check box option, Always on Top, is usually checked because Windows 95 normally sets the taskbar to be displayed at all times. The taskbar is most helpful when it is on the screen, right? The only problem with the taskbar's being on the screen at all times is that one complete row of the screen is consumed by the

▼   taskbar instead of by your own windows. Uncheck the option by clicking over the check mark or anywhere on the words beside it. The graphic inside the dialog box actually changes when you remove the check mark to show a window overlapping the clock in the taskbar.

    Click the OK command button to see the results of the unchecked option. (If you clicked the Apply command button, Windows 95 would have changed the taskbar immediately while still displaying the dialog box.)

5. Display the Taskbar Properties dialog box again. Check the Auto Hide option and click the OK button. Where did the taskbar go?

6. The taskbar is now out of sight and out of the way. The taskbar hasn't gone far—point the mouse cursor to the bottom of the screen and the taskbar will reappear. You can now have your taskbar and hide it, too!

> If you display the Taskbar Properties dialog box but decide that you don't want to make any changes after all, click the Cancel command button and Windows 95 will remove the Taskbar Properties dialog box and leave the taskbar unchanged.

7. Although only a little of the taskbar is still showing, you can display the Taskbar Properties dialog box again, check the Always on Top option, and uncheck the Auto Hide option.

8. The third check mark option controls how the Start menu's icons are displayed. If you want to save some screen room when you display the Start menu, you can request small icons, and the Start menu will consume less screen space. If you uncheck the last option labeled Show Clock, the clock will go away from the taskbar after you click the OK command button on the dialog box.

> You'll learn what that speaker icon is at the right of the taskbar in Hour 22, "Multimedia is Really Here."

▼ 9. Display the Taskbar Properties tabbed dialog box again and set the check mark options to your desired values. Before clicking the OK command button, click the tab labeled Start Menu Programs (at the top of the dialog box). You'll see the second dialog box, which is shown in Figure 3.8.

FIGURE 3.8

*The second dialog box
appearing from behind
the taskbar options*

▼   The Start Menu Programs page enables you to change the appearance of the Start
         menu.

         The second half of this dialog box controls the contents of the Start menu's
         Documents command. When you select Start | Documents, Windows 95 displays a
         list of your most recent data files. All data files are known as *documents* to
         Windows. If the list gets too full, erase it by clicking the Clear button.

    10. Click the Cancel command button to close the dialog box and return to the regular
         Windows 95 desktop. Close all windows that are now open by clicking the Close
         button in each window's upper-right corner.

Step 3: Review

There are several ways to change the taskbar's properties and performances through the
taskbar properties menu. The menu appears when you click the right mouse button. The
menu contains commands to modify the appearance of all of the following:

    • The open windows on the screen

    • The taskbar

▲   • The Start menu's commands

Sizing the Taskbar

What happens if you open a number of windows by starting several programs? The sin-
gle-line taskbar fills up very quickly with buttons, icons, and descriptions that represent
those open windows. Figure 3.9 shows such a taskbar. If you're doing a lot of work, the
taskbar gets squeezed for space. However, you can solve that problem rather easily.

FIGURE 3.9

*The taskbar needs
more room*

Just as you can resize a window, you also can resize the taskbar. When you enlarge the
taskbar, it can more comfortably hold several buttons for open windows, and the descriptions on those buttons can be longer. Figure 3.10 shows the same taskbar as the one
shown in Figure 3.9. This time, the taskbar is larger, and you can better tell by the
descriptions on the taskbar buttons what each program is.

FIGURE 3.10

*The taskbar now has
more breathing room*

Task 3.4: Resizing the Taskbar

Step 1: Description

If you need to expand (or shrink) the taskbar, you can drag the top of the taskbar up the
screen until it reaches the middle of the Windows 95 desktop. The taskbar then has more
room for more open window buttons and descriptions. Of course, if you've moved the
taskbar to one of the other edges of the screen, you'll drag the inward-most edge of the
taskbar toward the middle of the screen to increase the size of the taskbar. If you want to
shrink the taskbar, you can reverse the dragging until the taskbar is as small as you want
it to be.

Step 2: Action

1. Move the mouse cursor to the top edge of the taskbar. The cursor changes to a
   bidirectional resizing arrow that looks like the window resizing cursor shape you
   learned about in Hour 2, "Tour Windows 95 Now."

2. Drag the taskbar toward the center of the screen. As you drag the taskbar, Windows
   95 expands it one taskbar row at a time until you complete the dragging operation.

3. Release the mouse button and you'll see the resulting (and larger) taskbar with
   more room for descriptions and open window buttons.

4. You can leave the taskbar at its present size or shrink the taskbar back down again
   by dragging the top edge of the taskbar toward the outer edge of the screen.

> If you drag the top of the taskbar all the way down to the bottom of your
> screen, the taskbar goes away. It is easier to shrink the taskbar with the
> mouse than by using the Taskbar Properties dialog box to hide the taskbar.
> To bring the taskbar into view, move the mouse to the bottom of the screen
> until the mouse cursor changes to a bidirectional arrow. Drag the arrow up
> the screen and the taskbar appears.

Step 3: Review

When you need more room for the taskbar, drag the taskbar's edge until the taskbar is the
size you need. You can expand or shrink the taskbar by dragging the taskbar's innermost
edge with the mouse.

Starting Programs with Start

The Start menu offers an extremely simple way for you to start the programs on your
computer. Two or three clicks start virtually any program on your disk drive. The
Programs command on the Start menu launches your programs. To start a program, just
display the menu that contains that program and then click the program's name or icon.

Task 3.5: Starting Solitaire

Step 1: Description

Microsoft gives you a Windows 95-based version of the Solitaire card game. Solitaire is
considered an *accessory* program. Accessory programs are programs Microsoft included
with Windows 95. They fall under several categories, such as multimedia programs, text
editors, and games.

Step 2: Action

1. Display the Start menu.
2. Select the Programs command. A cascaded menu appears next to the Start menu.
   Each of these items in the second menu represents either a program or a folder of
   programs. When you buy a program such as a word processor, the word processor
   usually comes with more than *just* a word processor. The word processor might
   come with several related programs that help you manage the word processor environment. The word processor folder would open to yet another window (you can
   tell by the presence of an arrow at the right of the word processor's folder) which
   would then list all the related programs in that folder.

▼ 3. Select the Accessories command to display the programs in the Accessories folder. Search down until you see the Games menu. Open the Games to see the Solitaire game (look for an opening pack of cards).

4. Click the Solitaire game to start Solitaire (see Figure 3.11).

FIGURE 3.11

Get ready to have fun!

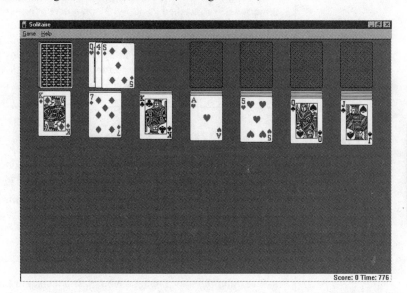

 Your Solitaire screen might differ slightly from the one in the figure because your default card deck might be set to have a different picture backing. To change the deck backing, select Game | Deck, click the backing you prefer, and click OK.

5. There's no time to play right now! This hour's closing in quickly. Therefore, terminate the Solitaire program by clicking the Close button (the button with the X, as you learned in Hour 2). Solitaire goes away and you are back to the regular Windows 95 desktop.

Step 3: Review

The Programs command launches any and all programs on your system. Depending on the way your programs are set up and because many Windows 95 programs are stored in folders, you might have to display one or more menus to access individual programs that ▲ you want to execute.

How did all those programs get on the Start menu? If you upgraded from a previous version of Windows, the Windows 95 installation program automatically updated your programs so they appear on the Start menu. If you didn't upgrade from a previous Windows version, but bought a new PC with Windows 95 or installed Windows 95 on a newly formatted hard drive, your Start menu might not have many items. Only those programs that come with Windows 95 appear. To add other programs on your system, you have to install those programs all over again. When you reinstall the program, Windows 95 adds the program to the Start menu. Hour 9, "Adding Programs to Windows 95," explains how to install new programs.

Explaining the Run Command

In addition to the Start menu's Programs command, you can use another method to start programs that aren't set up on the Programs' cascade of menus. The Run command on the Start menu provides a way for you to execute specific programs. When you select Start | Run, then enter a program or data filename at the prompt, Windows 95 starts that program or loads that data file.

Before using the Run command, you must understand the basics of disk drive names (such as C: and D:) and pathnames of files (such as C:\WORD\DEC99). You must also know the exact name of the program you want to run. Most newcomers to Windows 95 stay away from the Run command for good reason; Run requires a fairly comprehensive level of understanding of the underlying program you are trying to start. Many Windows 95 users work inside Windows 95 for years and never need the Run command.

Reaching Your Files

A *pathname* is the exact computer system location of a file. The document and folder concept in Windows 95 makes working with paths much easier than before Windows 95 came along. Most often, you will specify pathnames visually by clicking folder icons instead of typing long pathnames as you had to do before Windows 95.

The folders in Windows 95 are more technically known as *directories*, as explained in Hour 2. A directory is just a collection of files (and sometimes other directories). In file listings, Windows 95 often displays a folder icon with a name to represent a directory that holds other files. Directories also can hold subdirectories so the location of a file, the file's *path*, might be deep within several nested directories on a disk or CD-ROM drive.

A full pathname begins with a disk drive name followed by a colon (:), followed by a backslash (\). If the file resides in the disk drive's top directory (the *root directory*), you then type the filename. If, however, the file resides in a directory, you must list the directory after the backslash. If the file resides in several nested directories, you must list each directory in order, from the outermost directory to the innermost directory, and separate each directory name with a backslash. For example, both of the following are full pathnames to specific files on my computer:

```
c:\autoexec.bat
d:\Sherry\WordProc\Home\Insure\Fire and Casualty
```

The first filename is autoexec.bat located in the root directory. The second filename is Fire and Casualty located within a series of nested directories.

Windows 95's icon folder concept makes specifying long pathnames almost obsolete. Aren't you glad? Clicking folders to open them is much easier than typing the long streams of characters that often represent pathnames.

Introduction to Your Active Desktop

Windows 95's Active Desktop not only changes Windows 95's look but also the way you work with Windows 95. Your Windows 95 desktop can display icons, text, and windows, but also more active content. You can display *Internet-based documents* (written in the special *HTML language* used for Internet Web pages) on the Windows 95 background.

You can place Internet Web pages on the Windows 95 background's wallpaper. If those

If you are new to the Internet, and especially if you are new to Windows, you might not see the full purpose of the Active Desktop at this time. Before this 24-hour tutorial is over, you'll learn all you need to know to use Windows 95 and the Active Desktop efficiently and effectively.

Web pages contain the special *ActiveX controls* that some Web pages contain (ActiveX controls energize Web pages with sound, videos, and interactive features) that active content appears as well. If you've set up special "push" content, your Internet provider brings your requested Internet information directly to your Windows 95 desktop. Hour 16, "Activating Your Desktop," explains more about push content.

Even if you're not connected to the Web, you can still benefit from the
Active Desktop features such as the single-click icon selection. The Active
Desktop is not available to you unless you install Internet Explorer 4 with
your Windows 95 system.

If you've used a Web browser before, you might remember that you can select a Web
page object (an object's color highlights when you select that object) just by pointing
your mouse to the object, such as an icon, and you can open items by clicking over
them one time. In pre-Internet Explorer 4–based Windows 95 systems, you have to
click once over a Windows item to select (or highlight) it and double-click the item to
open that item. You've already learned how to open windows in Hour 2, by double-
clicking windows. By providing the same kind of select and open capabilities as the
Web provides, your PC moves one more step closer to integrating your desktop with
the online world.

The Active Desktop means that you don't have to start a Web browser and
request information, such as current stock prices, to see that data while you
work in Windows 95.

Task 3.6: Setting Up Web-Like, Single-Click Mouse Selections

Step 1: Description

Hour 16, explains how to integrate Windows 95 and Internet Explorer 4 to prepare you
for the Active Desktop. In the meantime, you might want to convert your Windows 95
desktop to the Web-like desktop that simplifies the way you select desktop items and
open windows. This task explains how to change your single- and double-mouse clicks
to the Web-browser equivalents.

Step 2: Action

1. Select Start | Settings | Folder Options. The first dialog box page, the one with the
   General tab, contains three options that determine how your desktop items respond
   to your mouse selections. The Classic style option, the Windows 95 way, requires
   that you click once to select (highlight) an icon and double-click to open an icon's
   window. Web style gives you a Web-like selection ability so that the window's contents (as well as your desktop itself) display in a Web-like browser style, complete
   with a left window pane for descriptions and a right window pane for details. The
   Custom option activates the Settings button so you can control a combination of
   Web-like and normal Windows 95 selections.

▼   2. Click the Web-style option and then click OK to close the Options dialog box. Windows 95 asks once more, with a Yes or No dialog box, if you want to convert your icon selections to single-click selections. Answer Yes and your Windows 95 desktop changes immediately; the icons there now have underlined labels. Although your desktop changes immediately, you must make one more change to activate the Web-style icons in open windows.

3. Click once on the My Computer icon to open the My Computer window.

4. Select My Computer window's View menu bar option and then select the As Web Page menu option by placing a check mark next to that option. (Maximize the window to see the full effect.) The My Computer window now changes to the Web-style view to complement your desktop. The window's left pane displays graphical information about objects that you select in the right pane.

Step 3: Review

After you change your window and desktop view to a Web-style view, you can select items by pointing to them with your mouse and open windows by clicking once instead of double-clicking over their icons. Your desktop now more fully mimics the Web. When you integrate Web pages into your Active Desktop, Windows 95 responds more uniformly.

> You can revert back to the classic view by again selecting a window's View |
> Folder Options | Classic style menu option.

▲

Summary

This hour concentrated on the taskbar. The taskbar gives you a play-by-play status of the open windows on your system. As you open and close windows, the taskbar updates with new buttons to show what's happening at all times. If you start more than one program, you can switch between those programs as easily as you switch between cable TV shows—just click a button on the taskbar. In addition, you can adjust the taskbar to look and behave the way you prefer.

The taskbar works along with the Start menu to start and control the programs running on your system. Use the Programs command on the Start menu to start programs with a total of two or three mouse clicks. Although you can use the Run command to start programs, the Programs command is easier as long as the program is set up properly in Windows 95.

Workshop

Term Review

accessory programs   Programs that Microsoft includes with Windows 95. They fall under several categories such as multimedia programs, text editors, and games such as Solitaire.

active desktop   The Windows 95 desktop, combined with Internet Explorer 4, to make Windows 95 look and behave more like Internet screens.

cascade   The effect of neatly stacking all open windows on the screen so that each window's title bar appears.

classic view   The default Windows 95 desktop that requires double-clicks to open objects and single-clicks to select objects.

context-sensitive   The ability to analyze what you're doing and respond accordingly, perhaps with a pop-up menu that provides commands you can perform.

dialog box   A special window in which you can enter information needed by Windows 95.

HTML   A special language that formats Internet Web pages.

tabbed dialog box   Two or more cascaded dialog boxes appearing on the screen at the same time.

taskbar properties menu   The menu that appears when you click the right mouse button over an empty spot on the taskbar. You can control the performance and appearance of the taskbar and Windows 95 through the taskbar properties menu.

Taskbar Properties tabbed dialog box   A tabbed dialog box that appears when you select the Properties command on the taskbar properties menu. The Taskbar Properties tabbed dialog box lets you modify the appearance and performance of the taskbar and the Start menu.

tiling   The effect of placing all open windows on the screen so that the body of each window appears next to, above, or below, the other windows.

Web-style view   When activated using Internet Explorer 4, Windows 95's active desktop takes on an appearance similar to Internet Web pages.

Q&A

Q How can I use the taskbar properties menu to change the appearance or performance of the taskbar?

A The taskbar is set by default to appear, no matter what else is on your screen. To maximize the screen space and clear away as much as possible, you can change the taskbar's performance so that onscreen windows cover the taskbar giving you an additional line for the open window. In addition to letting open windows cover the taskbar, you can choose to have Windows 95 hide the taskbar completely, showing you the taskbar only when you point to the bottom of the screen with the mouse cursor. Even if you increase the size of the taskbar you can still hide it from view. The increased size appears when you show the taskbar, but the taskbar is not in the way when hidden.

The taskbar properties menu also controls the size of the Start menu's icons so you can decrease the width of the Start menu if you prefer. You also can eliminate the clock from the taskbar so that the taskbar has room for another window's button. You can add the clock back to the taskbar at a later time, if you like.

Q Help, my taskbar has fallen and I can't get my Start menu up! What did I do and how can I fix it?

A You've changed the options in the Taskbar Properties dialog box to hide the taskbar. The taskbar is not gone for long, however. To see the taskbar again, all you need to do is point to the very bottom of the screen with the mouse, and the taskbar appears once again.

Q I've opened a lot of windows. How can I get more room on my taskbar to see more buttons?

A You can drag the innermost edge of the taskbar to expand the taskbar so that more open window buttons and icons fit within the taskbar comfortably.

3

Hour 4

Understanding the My Computer Window

The My Computer icon opens to a window that contains information relating to your computer's hardware and software. The My Computer window provides access to many different areas of your computer, as you will see as you progress through this book. Many beginning and advanced PC users ignore the My Computer window more than they should. The My Computer window, which always appears on your Windows 95 desktop, lets you access every hardware device on your system in a uniform fashion.

People often spend the first few sessions with any new operating environment getting to know the environment and modifying the appearance to suit their own preferences. This hour lets you learn about the My Computer window while you modify your work environment.

The highlights of this hour include

- What the contents of the My Computer window are
- Where to go for mouse control changes

- How to change the screen's wallpaper
- How to test your modem
- How to create a startup disk to help you recover from system problems

Searching My Computer

Your computer system is a mixture of hardware (the system unit, monitor, keyboard, CD-ROM, and so on), *firmware* (the internal memory), and software (for example, Windows 95, MS-DOS, word processors, spreadsheets, and games). There are several ways to access your computer's hardware and software through different areas of Windows 95. The My Computer window contains one of the most helpful hardware and software management resources available in Windows 95.

If your My Computer window is not open from the previous hour, open the My Computer window now by clicking the My Computer icon. Use either a single or double-click, depending on your active desktop settings.

If you do not see an open window, you might have double-clicked the My Computer icon too slowly. Double-click again until you open the icon's window. If you have trouble double-clicking the icon, you can open the icon by clicking once on it (thus highlighting the window's icon) and pressing Enter.

This lesson assumes a standard desktop setting throughout the instructions whenever a double-click is required. For example, to open the My Computer window, you need to double-click the My Computer icon. If, however, you have the active desktop set, you need to click the icon only once to open the My Computer window. The active desktop is made obvious by underlines beneath your desktop icons. If you see the underline, a single click opens the icon. Without the underlined icon, a double-click is required to open the icon because your desktop will be set up as a standard desktop.

Introducing the My Computer Window

The My Computer icon must be important or Microsoft wouldn't have put it in the upper-left corner of your screen. Its importance will show itself in many ways throughout this book and in your own work as you learn more about Windows 95.

People's needs for the My Computer window differ greatly, depending on which systems they use to run Windows 95. For example, a network user would probably display the My Computer window more often than a single user working primarily on a spreadsheet program. The network icon appears inside My Computer and makes all the drives and folders of the network available through the My Computer window.

> If you have a computer that is plug-and-play compatible (that is, Windows 95 automatically recognizes new hardware as you add hardware to your PC) and you add plug-and-play hardware to the computer such as a new internal high-speed modem, Windows 95 should be able to detect that you've installed that new modem. A modem icon automatically appears inside the My Computer window the next time you start the computer and open the My Computer window. Some devices, such as *PC card* devices that plug into most laptops and some desktop systems, automatically configure themselves when you insert the cards; they don't require that you first turn off your PC.

Before looking at a sample My Computer window work session, you should understand that there are three ways to view the My Computer window, as well as most other Windows 95 windows:

- As a Web page, as you learned in Hour 3, "Take Windows 95 to Task"
- In the icon view (with large or small icons)
- In the list view (with or without detail)

The icon view is the default view that is set when you install Windows 95. Newcomers often prefer the familiarity that an icon view provides. In Hour 5, "Explore the Windows 95 System," you will learn how to move files from one disk drive to another by dragging a file to the disk icon where you want to put the file. You can use this dragging method instead of typing a disk drive name as computer users of older operating systems have to do.

As you progress in your experience with Windows 95, you might prefer to switch to a list view of the My Computer window. A list view shows window contents in a list of items similar to a table of contents. The items show folders and filenames as well as their size and last-revised dates. The list view gives you the ability to see more items without the clutter of large icons filling the screen that occurs in other kinds of views.

When you first open the My Computer window, the difference between the icon view and the list view is not extremely important because the My Computer window shows a high-level overview of the system. Figure 4.1 shows an icon view of the My Computer window, and Figure 4.2 shows the list view of the same window. Notice that the list view

4

is more difficult to see when only a few items are present in the window. If more items appeared in the window, however, the list view would provide more information at one time; you would not have to click *scrollbars* (vertical and sometimes horizontal bars) as often to see all the items listed in the window.

FIGURE 4.1

The My Computer window shown in icon view

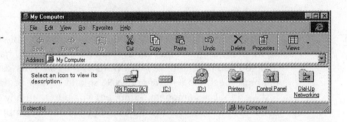

FIGURE 4.2

The My Computer window shown in list view

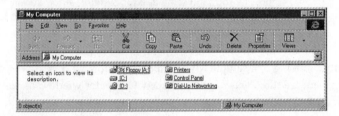

When you first explore the My Computer window, just look around for a bit. The next task walks you through a sample exploration session of the My Computer window so you'll quickly get acquainted with some of the window's more useful investigative features.

Task 4.1: Navigating the My Computer Window

Step 1: Description

The best way to begin learning about the My Computer window is to work within the window. Follow the steps in this task to see some of the things that are possible with My Computer.

Step 2: Action

1. Open the My Computer window if you don't have it open already.

2. From the menu bar, select View | List. The view instantly changes to the list view.

3. Select View | Details. The list view expands to tell you more about items in the list that appear. The list includes such items as drive names on the system, each drive's name, free space available, and the total space on each drive.

▼ 4. Go back to the View | Large Icons display. The View | Small Icons display provides extremely small icons on most systems (when that small, the icons do not improve readability over the list view).

5. Maximize the My Computer window by clicking the Maximize button or by double-clicking the title bar.

6. Double-click the C disk drive icon. You should see a window of folders and other icons appearing similar to the one shown in Figure 4.3. Each folder represents a *subdirectory* on your disk drive. A subdirectory is a list of files stored together in one group. The subdirectory name appears under each file folder. Anytime you see a folder icon, you are looking at a subdirectory icon. If you also see a hand holding the folder, the folder is known as a *shared folder*—it is available to others on the network you're working on.

FIGURE 4.3

Looking at the directories on drive C

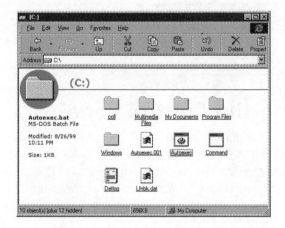

4

The icons that look like pieces of paper are document icons that represent individual files, including programs and text files, on your system's C drive. You'll also find other kinds of icons. If you see the list view when you display the C disk drive, use View | Large Icons to see the icons.

The window you're now looking at is a completely different window from the My Computer window. Minimize the window to see the My Computer window come back into view.

7. Maximize the drive C window (click the taskbar button). To look at the contents of a file folder, double-click the file folder. When you do, another window opens. You are leaving a trail of windows that describe your hard drive.

▼ 8. Close the folder's window so you can return to the drive C window. If you have lots of files on drive C, and most people do, you might have to use the scrollbars to see all of the window's contents.

9. Close the drive C window to return to the My Computer window. Leave the My Computer window open for the next section.

Step 3: Review

The My Computer window displays information about your computer and its contents. All the computer's hardware and files are located on the hard disk. As you add more hardware, you'll see more icons appearing in the My Computer window. The view that you select determines how much information you can see at one time. If you press Ctrl

▲ while opening icons, the new contents replace the current window's.

> The Printers folder contains information about any printers attached to your computer. You'll learn how to manage the Printers folder in Hour 20, "Fonts and Viewers."

Introducing the Control Panel

The Control Panel icon lets you adjust and manage the way hardware devices are attached to and respond to your computer. From the My Computer window, open the Control Panel icon. You'll see a window like the one in Figure 4.4. From the Control Panel, you can change or modify system and hardware settings.

> Be certain that you know what to change before modifying values within the Control Panel. Incorrect changes can result in you needing to do a complete re-install of Windows 95.

This section does not explain all the ins and outs of the Control Panel. You will find more information about the Control Panel and its functions in other chapters of this book. The next task demonstrates use of the Control Panel so that the Control Panel is more familiar to you.

FIGURE 4.4

Modify the system settings from within the Control Panel

Task 4.2: System Modification with the Control Panel

Step 1: Description

One of the best ways to explore the Control Panel without making a major change to your system is to modify the behavior of your mouse. This task changes the mouse cursor's default shape and lets you reverse the buttons on your mouse.

Step 2: Action

1. Open the Control Panel window within the My Computer window if you have not yet done so.

2. Open the Mouse icon. The icon indicates that the mouse settings are found here. You see the Mouse Properties dialog box appear as shown in Figure 4.5.

3. If you are left-handed but your mouse is set for a right-handed user, you can select the option button marked Left-Handed to change the mouse button functions. The buttons then change their orientation. (The change does not take effect until you close the Mouse Properties dialog box or click the Apply button.) You can change the button back to its original state by clicking on the option button.

4. Click the tab marked Pointers at the top of the Mouse Properties dialog box. From the Pointer portion of the dialog box, you can change the default appearance of the mouse. A scrolling list of mouse shapes indicates all the kinds of cursor shapes that appear when certain Windows 95 events take place.

To Do

4

FIGURE 4.5

*You can change the
behavior of the mouse*

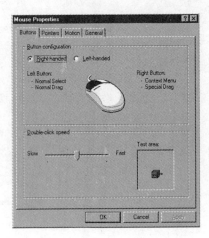

5. To change the normal mouse cursor (called the *Normal Select* shape), double-click
   the row with the Normal Select text. Windows 95 displays the screen shown in
   Figure 4.6. Different mouse cursors appear for different reasons. The Pointers dialog box lets you select diferent shapes for your mouse cursor.

FIGURE 4.6

*Select a mouse cursor
shape file*

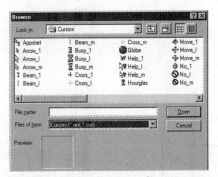

6. If you want to change the mouse cursor to a new shape, Windows 95 needs to
   know the name of the file that holds the new cursor image. (This screen is not the
   easiest screen in Windows 95 to figure out, by the way.) Just for grins, double-click
   the Hourglass row in the choices listed under Look in, and Windows 95 changes
   the pointing cursor arrow to an hourglass.

It's best to stick with the default cursor shape and *not* keep this change permanent so that others who use your computer will know what the cursor indicates. If you change the mouse cursor to other shapes, you might even forget which shape means what.

7. Before leaving the Mouse Properties window, click the Use Default button to return the standard mouse cursor to its default pointer shape. If you've already returned to the Control Panel, you have to click the Mouse icon again to set the cursor back to its default shape.

8. Click OK and close the Control Panel. You can now close the My Computer window.

Step 3: Review

Through the Control Panel located in the My Computer window, you can change various hardware settings so Windows 95 interacts with your computer's hardware differently. This task peeked into the Control Panel by showing you how to reverse the mouse buttons and change the default mouse shapes.

Windows 95 supports *animated cursors* that move when they appear. If you use Microsoft's add-on Windows 95 product called *Plus!,* or if you've installed one or more of the numerous software products that add animated cursors to your system (such as Office 97), you can select cursors that change shape during their display. Instead of looking at the standard hourglass cursor while you wait on your computer, why not display a hand patiently tapping on the desktop? The animated cursors all reside in files that have the .ANI filename extension. If your cursor name display (see Figure 4.6) does not show filename extensions, click on the cursor names and look at the Preview area of the dialog box to see whether the cursor provides animation.

The Right Mouse Button

If you use a right-handed mouse, you probably have had little use for that right mouse button. The same is true for the left mouse button for left-handed users. Beginning with Windows 95, Microsoft added a shortcut feature to the mouse button: Depending on where you are pointing the mouse, clicking the right mouse button (or left, if you changed the mouse to a left-handed mouse) brings up a menu of things you can do at that time.

The menu is context-sensitive, depending on the context, Windows 95 displays commands appropriate to that current cursor location.

Task 4.3: Using the Right Mouse Button

Step 1: Description

To Do ▲

This task shows you don't always need the My Computer window to make changes to your system. In Hour 1, "What's Windows 95 All About?" you learned that *wallpaper* is the name for the background you see on the screen when you start Windows 95 and work within its windows. You can change that wallpaper to a different picture or eliminate the wallpaper altogether with a right mouse click.

Step 2: Action

1. With all windows closed or minimized from a click of the Show Desktop button (the Show Desktop button appears on your Windows 95 taskbar), move the mouse cursor over the wallpaper in the middle of the screen. If your screen has no picture behind the icons and displays only a solid color, you *do* have wallpaper, but it's boring!

2. Click the right mouse button if you are right-handed or the left mouse button if you are left-handed. Windows 95 looks to see that your mouse is pointing to the wallpaper and displays a menu of choices that are relevant to your position.

3. Select the Properties command from the menu. Windows 95 opens the Display Properties screen shown in Figure 4.7.

FIGURE 4.7

A right click displays a wallpaper selection screen

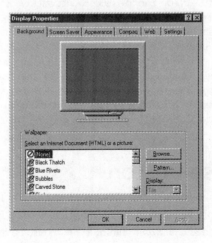

▼

▼   4. Find the lower-right section entitled Wallpaper. Scroll through the list of choices looking for an interesting name, such as Red Bricks, and click on that selection. Windows 95 models the new wallpaper style in the small screen to give you a preview of that style. You can go with that selection or choose another.

5. When you are happy with your selection, click the OK button and *presto*, you've hung new wallpaper without messy cutting or gluing!

Step 3: Review

You'll learn other uses of the right mouse button as you progress through this book. You learned here how to change the wallpaper pattern so you don't get too bored by the same
▲ old look.

Test Your Modem

Due to its technical nature, modem communications can be difficult to understand and troubleshoot. If you are having trouble communicating with another computer, the first place to look is the My Computer's Control Panel folder. Learn how to diagnose your modem problems now so you will know what to do if you experience the problems that invariably come with modem usage.

Task 4.4: Diagnosing Your Modem

Step 1: Description

This task shows you how to let Windows 95 find a potential problem. Windows 95 includes a modem diagnostic tool that tests your modem connection and lets you know if everything is fine or if a problem exists.

Step 2: Action

1. Double-click the My Computer window.

2. Double-click the Control Panel folder to open the Control Panel window.

3. Open the Modems icon to open the Modems Properties tabbed dialog box.

4. Click the Diagnostics tab.

5. Click your modem's port name (such as COM2) to highlight your modem.

6. Click the More Info button. After a brief pause, Windows 95 displays a More Info... dialog box similar to the one in Figure 4.8. If the More Info... dialog box finds an error, you will see a description of the error. (The Q&A section that
▼   appears at the end of this lesson explains how to address a modem failure.)

To Do

4

FIGURE 4.8

The modem is responding properly

7. Click the OK button to close the More Info… dialog box.

8. Close the Modem Properties dialog box and the My Computer window.

Step 3: Review

The Windows 95 modem test is another one of those nice features that even Windows 95 gurus often forget about. Although the modem test does not describe detailed problems that might exist with your modem, the modem test does tell you if Windows 95 recognizes your modem properly.

Startup in Emergencies

Now that you've familiarized yourself with Windows 95, its environment, and the Control Panel, this is a great time to ensure against a minor or major disaster. During the course of using Windows 95, you will add hardware and software. Windows 95 makes adding such components relatively easy; however, in some cases, problems can occur.

By making a *startup disk*, you can safely get your computer started and access your hard disk when you otherwise cannot start your machine. The startup disk is little more than an MS-DOS boot disk, although the disk does contain several MS-DOS and Windows 95 utility programs (such as the ScanDisk utility explained in Hour 21, "Fine-Tune with Advanced System Tools") that can help you locate disk and memory troubles that can cause boot problems.

If you use a laptop on the road, *always* carry a startup disk with you! The startup disk will help save you when you do not have Windows 95 installation disks, MS-DOS disks, or utility programs readily available.

Task 4.5: Making a Startup Disk

Step 1: Description

This task shows you how to create a startup disk. Before beginning this task, locate a high-density formatted diskette. Make sure the disk contains no data that you need, because the startup process overwrites all data on your diskette.

Step 2: Action

1. Click the Start button.
2. Select Settings | Control Panel to display the Control Panel window.
3. Double-click the Add/Remove Program icon.
4. Click the Startup Disk tab to display Figure 4.9's Startup Disk page.

FIGURE 4.9

Create a startup disk for emergencies

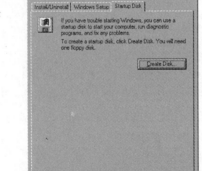

▼
5. Click the Create Disk button. The dialog box lets you know when you need to insert the disk you'll use for the startup disk.

6. After the startup disk creation process ends, close the Control Panel and put away the startup disk in a safe place.

Step 3: Review

After you create a startup disk, you'll have a disk in case of emergencies. If you find that you cannot access your hard drive or boot your computer because your system files are corrupt, you'll be able to regain hard disk access by inserting the startup disk and reboot-
▲ ing your computer.

Summary

This hour taught you how to use the My Computer window. Don't be dismayed that this hour just skimmed the surface of what's available in the My Computer window. The My Computer icon provides a launching point for many powerful hardware and software interactions that sometimes take quite a while to master. The typical Windows 95 user does not have to know all the details of the My Computer window to use Windows 95 effectively.

Workshop

Term Review

animated cursors   Cursors that display movement during the cursor's display, such as a cursor showing a picture of a running horse or a playing piano.

context-sensitive   Refers to the capability of Windows 95 to look at what actions you are currently performing (the *context*) and display help that explains how to complete those actions.

Control Panel   A folder window within the My Computer window that lets you change your computer's system settings.

desktop   The Windows 95 screen and background.

firmware   The computer's internal memory, also known as *RAM,* which stands for Random Access Memory. Firmware memory is volatile, meaning that the contents remain in memory for only as long as the PC is turned on. The disk drive is hardware, not firmware, because the disk drive retains its contents after the computer is turned off.

folder   A special icon that contains other icons that are displayed when you open the folder icon; a grouping of related files stored under the same subdirectory.

scroll bars Windows 95 controlling tools that enable you to view a window's contents more fully.

shortcut key An underlined letter on a menu that you can combine with the Alt key to issue a menu command.

startup disk A diskette you create from the Control Panel so you can start your computer when your hard disk's system files get corrupted due to a hardware or software problem.

Q&A

Q Will I use the My Computer icon a lot?

A This question's answer differs with different people. Some people use their computers primarily for one- or two-application programs. These people don't modify their computers very often and do not perform a lot of file interaction or system management, so they would rarely, if ever, need to open the My Computer window.

On the other hand, if you modify the hardware on your computer often, you might have to access the My Computer window often. As described in Hour 3, "Take Windows 95 to Task," Windows 95 is designed for use with plug-and-play hardware, which means that you don't have to configure Windows 95 every time you change hardware on your computer. Not all hardware devices are plug-and-play compatible, however. You might have to modify some Windows 95 system settings using the My Computer window when you install new computer hardware, such as a second printer.

Q I like the animated cursors but will they slow down my computer?

A If you use a slow computer, you don't want to do anything that will drain more speed from the processor. Nevertheless, the animated cursors do not seem to cause much of a drain on the processor's resources. The animated cursor icons are small and efficient. Therefore, you should feel free to use whatever cursors you want.

Q What do I do if the modem test fails?

A Unfortunately, this book cannot answer that question because the answer could come from myriad sources. The Windows 95 modem test is nice to remember because it gives you a first-step approach to tracing communications problems. If your modem tested fine but you experience communications problems, the problems are either with your software or with the computer on the other end of the telephone line. If the modem test fails, look into reinstalling the modem drivers that came with your modem. You can also try a different modem, which will solve the problem if the original modem you used is bad.

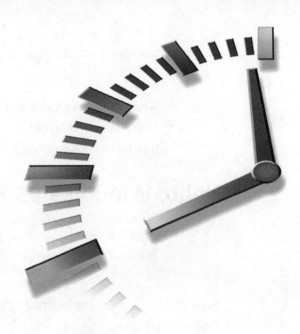

HOUR 5

Explore the Windows 95 System

The Windows 95 *Explorer* graphically displays your entire computer system in a hierarchical tree structure. With Explorer, you have access to everything inside your computer. Unlike the Internet Explorer program, which is designed to explore the Internet, Windows Explorer provides access to your PC's files and to any networked files you have access to. Even though the My Computer window also displays all the devices in your computer, Explorer can do so inside a single window. The advantage of the single window is that you have much more freedom to manage files, folders, icons, and even electronic mail using a single Explorer window.

This hour demonstrates the Windows 95 Explorer and shows you its ins and outs. After you've learned about Explorer, the hour wraps up by showing you some time- and disk-saving features of Windows 95.

The highlights of this hour include:

- How to change the various displays of the Windows 95 Explorer
- Why Explorer makes managing your computer painless

- Where to go when you want to find documents quickly
- What shortcuts are all about
- How to use the Recycle Bin

Hello, Windows 95 Explorer!

You can find the Windows Explorer program listed on the Start menu's second cascaded menu. Click the Start button's Programs | Windows Explorer. The Explorer window opens like the one shown in Figure 5.1. You can run Explorer fully maximized for more screen space or resize the Explorer screen to see other windows on your desktop.

FIGURE 5.1

Explorer's opening window

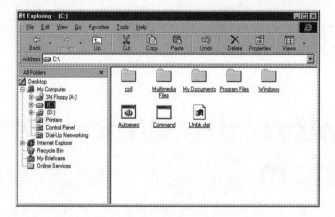

 Quickly start Explorer by right-clicking on the Start menu and selecting Explore from the pop-up menu that appears or press your keyboard's Window key (the key with the Windows logo) and the letter E at the same time to start Explorer.

The left side of the Explorer screen contains an overview of your computer system listed in a tree-like structure, often called a *hierarchical overview*. The left pane lists disk drives and folders, and you can open and close the drive and folder icons to see more or less detail. If not all of the hierarchical system tree fits inside the window at the same time, click the vertical scrollbar on the left window to see more of it.

If a folder icon appears with a plus sign to the left of it, as the Windows folder does, that folder contains additional folders. Folder icons without the plus sign contain files, but not additional folders. When you open a folder to display its contents, the plus sign changes to a minus sign, as you'll see in the first task. Thus, by clicking the plus and minus signs next to the items in the left pane, you expand and collapse the hierarchical items to see more or less detail of your computer system.

The right pane contains a pictorial overview of the contents of whichever device or folder that you select in the left window. The overview might contain large or small icons depending on the view you click. As you select different items in the left pane, the right pane changes to reflect your selection.

Task 5.1: Changing Explorer's View

Step 1: Description

This task teaches you how to adjust Explorer's display to see the Explorer screen in different ways. As you use Explorer, you can change the display to offer the best option for the information you're looking for at the time.

This task assumes that you've already started Explorer.

Step 2: Action

1. Scroll the left window pane until you see the icon for drive C in the window.

2. If you see a plus sign next to your C: icon in the left pane (you might have to scroll the window to see the C: icon), click the drive's icon next to the plus sign to display the contents of drive C. Click the plus sign to show the expanded drive contents in the left pane. The plus becomes a minus sign, and the left window opens the C: icon showing the list of folders and documents on drive C. Click the drive's minus sign again to close the left pane's detail. Click the icon and watch the right pane. As you change between these two views of drive C (detailed and overview), watch the right pane change.

The right pane always displays the contents of whatever you highlight in the left pane. Whether the C: icon is open (with a minus sign) or closed (with a plus sign), if you've selected the C: icon, the right pane displays drive C:'s contents. If you click on a folder on drive C, the right window updates to show the contents of that folder (don't click on a folder just yet).

▼ 3. Click on the highest level in the left pane labeled Desktop, and Windows 95 displays the contents of your desktop in the right pane (see Figure 5.2).

FIGURE 5.2

You can view the desktop contents in the Explorer

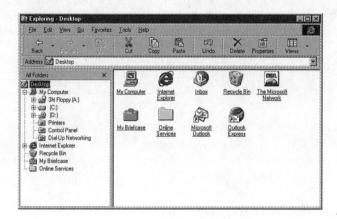

4. Click on the C: icon to display the contents of drive C. Depending on the contents and size of your drive C, the right pane might contain a few or several files.

5. Press Alt+V to open the View menu on the menu bar. Select Toolbar to display the toolbar of icons that appears right below the menu bar, if the toolbar does not yet appear there.

   The Address drop-down list box provides a third access tool for swapping between devices, folders, and files on your computer. If you ever detail too much information than will fit in the left pane, the Address list box keeps the list smaller and more manageable, always giving you more of a high-level overview of your computer system.

6. Press Alt+V to open the View menu. All of the different views are present in Windows Explorer so that you can view your disk items from a detailed or summary format. You can adjust the column widths of the three detailed columns in the right pane by dragging the column title dividers with the mouse.

   Click Name, the title of the first detailed column in the right pane. Watch the pane's contents change as you then click Type. Explorer sorts the display to appear in alphabetical order by type. Click the Modified column, and Explorer displays the items in reverse date order from most recent to the oldest. If you click any column twice in a row, Windows 95 sorts the column in reverse order.

7. If you want to see more of one of Explorer's panes, you can drag the vertical dividing line that falls between the two windows to the left or right. For example, if you
▼ want the left pane to be smaller to make room for more large icons, drag the center

▼ column to the left and release the mouse when the left pane is as small as you need it to be. (Remember that the mouse cursor changes shape when you place it at the proper position on the dividing column.)

If you make the left or right pane too small, Windows 95 adds a horizontal scrollbar to the smaller pane so you can scroll its contents back and forth to see what's highlighted or to select another item.

8. Explorer always updates itself to reflect your current actions. Therefore, the right-click menu commands change depending on whether you select a text document, folder, sound document, graphic document, executable program file, disk drive, or network drive. Click on a folder and click the right mouse button to see the menu. Now, click the right mouse button on a file, and you see a slightly different menu. The actions you might want to perform on a file are often different from the actions you might want to perform on a folder, and the menu reflects those differences. The right-click's pop-up menus are context-sensitive so they contain only the options you can use at the time. Although Windows 95 refers to most files generically as documents, many files are program files and data files used for program option settings. Windows Explorer works with files of all types.

Open a folder by double-clicking it and then return to the previous (parent) folder by clicking the toolbar's Up One Level icon. The Up One Level icon, indicated by a pop-up description when you point to it, is the button that displays a folder with a right-angled arrow pointing up. The button appears above the Address text box and to the left of the Copy button. Use the Up One Level button on the toolbar to return to the parent folder. You can also click the Back and Forward buttons to move back and forth between folders you view in Explorer.

5

9. Use Explorer to copy and move individual or multiple files at once. To select a file (called a document in Windows 95 terminology), click that document or just point to it with your mouse if you've turned on the Web-like file-selection scheme. To select more than one document at a time, hold down the Ctrl key while clicking on each document you want to select. (Press Ctrl+A to select all files.) You can even select folders as well as documents. When you select a folder, Windows 95 selects all of the document files *within* the folder. Figure 5.3 shows an Explorer screen

▼ with several document files from an open folder. After you select a file, folder, or

▼ group of files, you can drag the selection to any drive or folder in the left pane. If you first press Ctrl before dragging the selection, Windows 95 copies those files to the destination. Otherwise, Windows 95 moves or copies those files from their selected location to the destination drive and folder depending on whether you are dragging across folders or drives. To be safe, hold your right mouse button while performing the drag. When you release the item, a pop-up menu appears giving you the option of performing a copy or move of the item. The menu also enables you to create a shortcut to the item in its original location but not a copy of the item itself. To cancel a move or copy, press Esc during the operation.

FIGURE 5.3

Select multiple docu-ments and folders if you need to copy sev-eral at a time

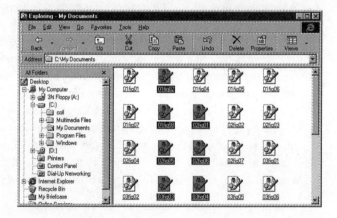

 If you want to select all but a few documents or folders, first Ctrl-click on the one or two that you *don't* want to select (to select those) and choose Edit I Invert Selection to reverse the selection. All the items that were not selected are now selected, and the one or two that you did select are no longer selected.

10. You can rename files and folders by selecting the item and pressing F2. (F2 is the shortcut key for File I Rename.) Windows 95 highlights the name so you can change it. Press Enter to save the new name.

 Do not supply an extension when you rename the file unless you've turned on the extension display. For example, if you renamed a Readme document (that is really named Readme.txt) to NewName.txt, the document would actually be named NewName.txt.txt!

▼

▼ **Step 3: Review**

Explorer gives you both high-level and detailed overviews of your computer system and the computer's files. Explorer offers two panes for two different views: A computer-level view and a folder view, if you need one. Clicking on folder icons inside either pane opens those folders and gives you a view of more documents and folders deeper within

▲ your computer system.

After you display documents and folders, you are free to copy, move, delete, and rename those items.

You cannot select parts of a document to copy or move through Explorer. After you open a document using a program, such as a spreadsheet, you see the contents of that document, and you then can copy or select parts of the document.

The Explorer Options

Explorer supports various display options for the items inside its windows. The View | Options command displays tabbed dialog boxes that let you control the items in the Explorer display.

Windows 95 uses filename extensions as a means of registering file types. Although two files of different types can have the same extension, the extension is often a clue as to the purpose of the file.

5

Task 5.2: Changing Explorer's Options

Step 1: Description

Different users require different output from the Explorer program. You simply don't need to display some document types while you work inside Explorer. The system files are good examples of files that the typical user does not need to see.

Step 2: Action

1. Select the View | Folder Options command to display the Options tabbed dialog box. (If your desktop is not set up as an active desktop, you'll select View | Options.)

▼

▼   2. Click the View tab to see the various ways you can view folders in the Folder
        Options dialog box shown in Figure 5.4.

FIGURE 5.4

*The Folder Options
dialog box determines
the appearance of
Explorer*

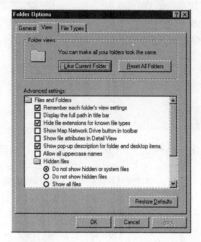

3. If you click Display the Full Path in Title Bar, Explorer displays a full pathname of
   selected documents in the title bar every time you select one of the items in the left
   window.

4. The next option is Hide File Extensions for Known File Types. Windows 95 comes
   installed with most types of files already *registered*. Registered files are files that
   Windows 95 recognizes by their filename extensions. For example, when you double-click a file with a .CDA extension, Windows 95 starts the CD Player application because CD Player is the application associated to all files that end in the
   .CDA extension.

> If you are familiar with MS-DOS and filenames, you might feel more com-
> fortable if you display the file extensions on documents appearing in the
> Explorer screen. Hiding the extensions reduces clutter in the right pane, but
> with the extension, you can determine the exact name of the file when you
> need the exact name. Fortunately, with or without the extensions, the icons
> next to the file names help remind you of the file's type.

▼

If you hide filename extensions in Explorer, Windows 95 hides those extensions in almost every other file listing. For example, if you hide Explorer's extension display, you will no longer see extensions in WordPad's Open dialog boxes. You won't even see them in applications that you purchase in addition to Windows 95, such as Microsoft Excel.

Step 3: Review

If you don't like the way Explorer displays information, you can change the display. Explorer's options let you determine how documents appear, how large their windows are, and whether or not filename extensions should appear.

Manage Documents with a Right Mouse Click

After you display the Explorer (or any other file list in Windows 95), you can point to any folder or document and click the right mouse button to perform several actions on the document. The right mouse click offers a pop-up menu in most places with Windows 95, including your applications such as your word processor. When you right-click on an item, a menu pops up from which you can manage the document and do things such as

- Select the document
- Play sound documents or open graphic documents
- Print the document
- Copy the file to a disk
- Cut or copy selected text to the Windows 95 Clipboard
- Create a shortcut access to the file so you can later open the file
- Delete the document
- Rename the document
- Change the document's system attributes

5

The *Recycle Bin* is a special location inside Windows 95 that holds the documents you delete. Recycle Bin's icon appears on your Windows 95 desktop. When you delete a document file of any type, Windows 95 sends that file to the Recycle Bin. The documents are then out of your way but not really deleted permanently until you empty the Recycle Bin. You'll learn all about the Recycle Bin in the section "Where Do the Deleted Files Go?"

Depending on your Recycle Bin's properties, obtained by right-clicking on the bin's icon and selecting Properties from the pop-up menu, not all files go to the Recycle Bin or stay there until you delete them. You can adjust the Recycle Bin's maximum size as a percentage of your free disk space. If the Recycle Bin reaches that size, the oldest files in the bin are replaced, automatically, by newer files you send there. In addition, if a file is too big to fit in the bin without violating your maximum Recycle Bin size, the file never goes to the bin but is deleted immediately. Keep in mind, also, that if you delete files from a networked drive or from an MS-DOS session, the file does not go to the Recycle Bin but is removed immediately from the system.

Task 5.3: Copy and Move Documents

Step 1: Description

A file icon's right-click menu offers advanced copying and moving of files. The *Clipboard* is the go-between for all Windows 95 copy, cut, paste, and move operations. When you want to copy a file from one place to another, you can place a copy of the file on the Windows 95 Clipboard. When you do, the file is on the Clipboard and out of your way until you go to where you want the file copied. You then paste the file to the new location, in effect copying from the Clipboard to the new location. When you copy a file to another location, the file remains in its original location and a copy is made elsewhere.

The Clipboard holds one file at a time. If you copy a document to the Clipboard, a subsequent copy overwrites the first copy.

If you want to copy a file to a disk, use the right-click menu's Send To command because Send To is easy to use when copying to a disk.

▼ When you move a file from one location to another, Windows 95 deletes the file from its original location and places the file at its new location (such as a different folder or disk drive).

> The Clipboard is like a short-term Recycle Bin. The Recycle Bin holds deleted files until you are ready to remove them permanently. The Clipboard holds deleted (or copied) documents and pieces of documents, but only until you send something else to the Clipboard or until you exit Windows 95 and turn off your computer.

Step 2: Action

1. Right-click on a text file's icon.

2. Select the Copy command. Windows 95 sends a complete copy of the document to the Clipboard. The Clipboard keeps the document until you replace the Clipboard's contents with something else or until you exit Windows 95. Therefore, you can send the Clipboard document to several subsequent locations.

3. Right-click on a folder in Explorer's right pane. The menu appears with the Paste command. Windows 95 knows that something is on the Clipboard (a copy of the text file), and you can send the file's copy to the folder by clicking Paste. Don't paste the file now, however, unless you then open the folder and remove the file because you don't need two copies on your disk.

4. Right-click again on the text file. This time, select Cut instead of Copy. Windows 95 erases the document file from the Windows folder and places the file on the Clipboard.

> Windows 95 keeps the name of the document in place until you paste the document elsewhere. The name is misleading because the name makes you think the document is still in the Windows folder. A ghost outline of an icon appears where the document's icon originally appeared. As long as the name still appears in the Windows folder, you can still open the file and do things with the file, but as soon as you paste the Clipboard contents somewhere else, the file goes away permanently from the Windows folder.

5. Right-click on a folder. If you were to select Paste, the text document would leave its original location and go to the folder. Don't paste now but press Esc twice (the first Esc keypress gets rid of the right-click menu and the second restores the cut

▼   file).

6. Windows 95 is as safe as possible. If you change your mind after a copy or cut operation, you can always reverse the operation! Right-click on the icon area and the pop-up menu contains an Undo command that reverses the most recent copy or cut.

> You cannot drag an item such as a document to just anywhere. Windows 95 changes the mouse cursor to a circle with a slash through it (the international "Do Not" symbol) when you drag the document over any area of the screen that cannot accept that document.

7. Sometimes, you might need a document for a program outside of the program you're currently working in. You can place a document on the Windows 95 desktop. Select a text file and copy the document to the Clipboard by right-clicking and selecting Copy. (You also can use drag-and-drop if you want. Hold down Ctrl and drag the document out of the Explorer window, if you've resized Explorer so you can see part of the desktop, and continue with Step 8.)

8. Move the cursor to the Windows 95 desktop to an area of the wallpaper that has no icon on it. Click the right mouse button to display a menu and select Paste. The file now has an icon on your desktop along with the other icons already there.

Placing Documents on the Desktop

The items you place on the desktop, whether by copying or by moving, stay on the desktop until you remove them from the desktop. Even after shutting down Windows 95 and turning off your computer, the desktop item will be there when you return.

Too many documents on your desktop cause clutter but you might want to work with a document in several different programs over a period of a few days. By putting the document on the desktop, it is always easily available to any application that's running. Also, you can drag Web pages to your desktop if you've activated the Active Desktop feature.

Step 3: Review

Windows 95 supports a complete set of menu-driven cut, copy, and paste commands from the right mouse click. With these commands, you can copy or move files from one place to another. If you can see the target location of the copy or move, such as another window's folder on the screen or the desktop, use the mouse to copy or move the document and save time.

Where Do the Deleted Files Go?

When you delete files using dialog boxes or Explorer, you now know that those files go to the Recycle Bin. After they are in the Recycle Bin, those files are out of your way and deleted in every respect except one: They are not really deleted! Those files are gone from their original location, but they stay in the Recycle Bin until you empty the Recycle Bin.

The Recycle Bin icon changes from an overflowing bin to an empty one when you empty the Recycle Bin so that you can tell at a glance whether or not your Recycle Bin is empty.

If you delete files from MS-DOS, using the DEL command or an MS-DOS program, the file does not go to the Recycle Bin but is immediately deleted because MS-DOS does not have access to the Windows 95 Recycle Bin.

Task 5.4: Using the Recycle Bin

Step 1: Description

The Recycle Bin appears on your Windows 95 desktop. Any time you want to view or delete items from the Recycle Bin, display your desktop and access the Recycle Bin icon.

Step 2: Action

1. Display your desktop by minimizing any open windows you have on the screen.

2. Double-click the Recycle Bin icon. The Recycle Bin window opens up as shown in Figure 5.5.

3. If you've been following along in this book so far, you should have one or two files already in the Recycle Bin. There might be many more, depending on what has taken place on your system.

4. Look at your Recycle Bin's *status bar* (the bar of information at the bottom of dialog boxes), to see how much free space you can regain by emptying your Recycle Bin.

▲ To Do

5

FIGURE 5.5

The Recycle Bin lists deleted files that you can recover

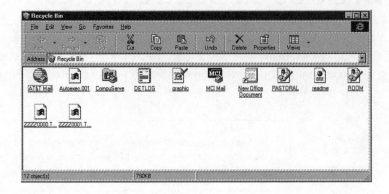

5. Open one of the Recycle Bin's items to display a Properties dialog box for that item. It tells you additional information about the deleted item, such as the date you created and deleted the item. Figure 5.6 shows a Properties dialog box. If you want to delete only that selected item, you can do so. If you selected more than one item, you can delete them also.

FIGURE 5.6

You can display the properties of any selected item

6. Perhaps the most important menu command is File | Empty Recycle Bin. This command empties the entire Recycle Bin. You can select this command now, if there is nothing in your Recycle Bin that you think you'll need later.

7. Select File | Close to close the Recycle Bin dialog box.

Select View to look at a Recycle Bin document if you want to verify the contents before deleting the document.

▼ Step 3: Review

The Recycle Bin holds deleted files until you empty the Recycle Bin. You can empty a
▲ single selected file, several selected files, or the entire Recycle Bin.

Making Windows 95 Easier

There are numerous ways to make Windows 95 easier for your day-to-day work. Three
time-saving techniques are

- Changing the Start menu
- Adding single-key access to programs
- Shortcuts

Task 5.5: Adding Time-Savers

Step 1: Description

The time-savers described in this task might not be for everyone, but they often help
users of Windows 95. You'll have to experiment with the techniques until you find the
ones that help you the most.

Step 2: Action

1. You can add programs to the Start menu by displaying the Start menu and selecting
   Settings.

2. Select Taskbar from the Settings menu.

3. The tabbed Taskbar Properties dialog box appears. Click the Start Menu Programs
   tab to display the Start Menu Programs page shown in Figure 5.7.

5

FIGURE 5.7

*Add or remove pro-
grams from the Start
menu here*

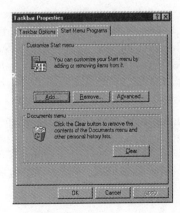

▼

▼ 4. Suppose that you want to put the Windows 95 Calculator program (normally found on the Accessories menu) on the Start menu. You would click the Add command button to display the Create Shortcut dialog box.

> Before adding programs to the Start menu, you must know the command and location of the program you are adding. If you do not know the path to the program, you can use the Browse command button to search for the program.

5. Type **c:\windows\calc.exe** at the command-line text prompt. The Windows 95 calculator program's exact filename is `calc.exe`, and the program is stored in the Windows 95 directory (folder), which is usually named `windows`.

6. Click Next to move to the next screen in the dialog box. Figure 5.8 shows the dialog box that appears.

FIGURE 5.8

You must tell Windows 95 where to store the shortcut

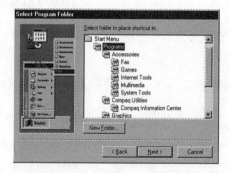

7. The Select Program Folder tells Windows 95 where to place the icon and program labeled `Calc`. If you want to place the program on the Start menu, double-click Start Menu at the top of the scrolling list box. (If you prefer to have the calculator appear in a menu that cascades off from the Start menu, select a folder and double-click over the folder.) In the Select Program Folder dialog box, each folder represents a menu.

8. After you select a location for the shortcut, Windows 95 displays one last dialog box asking for a name that will appear as that program's title on the menu. Type **Calculator** for the title if you're following along with this example. If you leave what Windows 95 suggests for a title name, you will see **Calc** as the shortcut name
▼ on your Start menu.

The label that appears under the shortcut icon acts as the shortcut name on your disk. Given that Windows 95 assigns the shortcut name, and that the name comes from the original filename which is not always meaningful, you might want to rename the shortcut to a more meaningful and descriptive name. To rename the shortcut after it has been created, right-click on the shortcut and select Rename from the pop-up menu. After you change the name and press Enter, Windows 95 uses the new name for the shortcut filename and the label under the shortcut.

9. Click the Finish command button to finish the process. When the dialog box goes away, the Taskbar Properties dialog box reappears.

10. Close the Taskbar Properties dialog box by clicking OK.

11. Display the Start menu. As shown in Figure 5.9, the Start menu contains the calculator program, which is now only two clicks away at any time.

FIGURE 5.9

You can now access the calculator quickly within Windows 95

5

Don't change the Start menu too dramatically until you are comfortable with Windows 95. If you share a computer with others, you could confuse your co-workers if you change the Start menu too much.

Shortcuts

The name *shortcut* has several meanings in Windows 95—one of the reasons that they can be confusing.

A shortcut is actually better termed an *alias file*. When you create a shortcut—whether that shortcut is a shortcut menu command, such as having the calculator now on the Start menu bar, or whether that shortcut is a shortcut you create through Explorer and other Windows 95 locations—Windows 95 does not make a copy of the calculator program in every location where you place the icon. Windows 95 actually creates a *link* to that program, called a *shortcut* in Windows 95 terminology, that points to the program on your disk wherever its location is.

If you were to right-click on a document or folder in Explorer's right window, you would see the Create Shortcut command that creates a shortcut to the document or folder you are pointing to. Windows 95 creates a new icon and title (the title begins with Shortcut To) but does not actually create a copy of the item itself. Instead, Windows 95 creates a link to that item. The link reduces disk space taken up by multiple copies of the same files. You can create a shortcut even to a networked item or Internet page that resides on a different computer altogether; the networked shortcut appears to exist on your own computer's desktop or menu, although it actually resides on the other machine.

12. Delete the Calculator program from the Start menu (you can add it later if you really want it there) by selecting Settings | Taskbar from the Start menu, selecting the Start Menu Programs tab, and clicking the Remove command button. Instead of the Create Shortcut dialog box, the Select Program Folder box appears next. Double-click the Programs folder under the Start Menu icon.

13. Select the Calc icon and click the Remove command button to remove the calculator program from the Start menu. Now you should return to the Start Menu Programs tabbed dialog box.

14. Click the Advanced command button. Windows 95 starts the Explorer program.

15. If you click the Programs folder, Explorer displays the items in the Start menu's first set of cascaded menus.

16. Open the Accessories folder to view the contents of the Accessories group. Remember that you're viewing contents of the Accessories menu that cascades from the Start menu. You see the Calculator icon appear in this folder group.

17. Right-click on the Calculator icon to display a menu.

18. Select Properties to display the Calculator program's Properties tabbed dialog box.

19. Click the Shortcut tab to display the dialog box shown in Figure 5.10.

FIGURE 5.10

You can now add a single-key shortcut that will start the calculator program

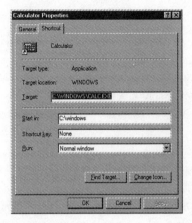

20. Press Alt+K to move the cursor to the Shortcut key text prompt. Type the letter C at the prompt. Windows 95 changes the C to Ctrl + Alt + C on the screen. Ctrl+Alt+C is now the shortcut for the Calculator program. If you run a program that uses a shortcut key you've added to Windows 95, the program's shortcut key takes precedence over the Windows 95 shortcut key.

21. Click the OK command button to close the dialog box.

22. Select File | Close to exit Explorer.

    Whenever you press Ctrl+Alt+C, Windows 95 starts the calculator program. This single-key shortcut (actually a simultaneous three-key shortcut) lets you start programs instantly, from virtually anywhere in the Windows 95 system, without having to locate the program's menu or icon.

Step 3: Review

You can now add a shortcut to the Start menu, to any of Start's cascaded menus, to the desktop, and even a single-key shortcut to the programs you use most often. Although it might not always be obvious how to create shortcuts, each presented in this section helps you get started faster with the programs that you want to run.

Hour 7, "Manage Your Desktop," explains a faster way to add programs to your Start menu if you use an active desktop. As you'll learn throughout this book, Windows 95 typically gives you many ways to do different jobs.

5

Summary

This hour showed you how to use the Explorer to search your computer system for documents and folders, as well as how to manage the computer system using a uniform interface for all your storage devices. Copying and moving among folders and documents are painless functions when you use Explorer's two-window interface. You can display the item to be moved in the right window and drag that item to any device listed in the left window.

Not only can Explorer help you manage your system, it also helps you locate information quickly. By using the Find command in Explorer (also available from the Start menu), you can search for files based on the filename, contents, size, and date last modified. There are three shortcuts that help you access your programs. You can create: a shortcut on the desktop, a shortcut on the Start menu system, and even a shortcut via the keyboard to start programs quickly.

Workshop

Term Review

Explorer   A powerful system-listing application that gives you both high-level and detailed descriptions of your computer system and the files on the system.

hierarchical overview   An expandable and collapsible view of your computer system that appears in the left pane of Windows Explorer.

registered   A file is registered when you've associated an application with that file's extension.

search string   A string of one or more characters, such as a filename, that you want to search for.

shortcut   You create a shortcut either by adding programs to the Start menu or from within Explorer by choosing the Create Shortcut option from the right-click menu. Windows 95 creates a link (the *shortcut*) to that item instead of wasting disk space with two separate files that have the same contents. A third shortcut is when you assign a key combination to launch a program.

status bar   A message area at the bottom of a window that updates to show you what is happening at any given moment. For example, when you click on a menu item, the status bar tells you what that menu item will do.

title bar   A location above many Windows 95 windows (such as the Explorer window) that describes the documents you are currently viewing.

Q&A

Q Why does it seem as if many of the Explorer functions are available elsewhere, such as in the My Computer window and in Open dialog boxes?

A You can find *many* of Explorer's capabilities elsewhere. Windows 95 is known for giving you the tools that you need where you need them. Windows 95 makes its tools available to you from a variety of locations because you'll often need to perform the same tasks while doing a wide range of activities.

Q Do files that I delete, but have yet to empty from the Recycle Bin, still consume disk space?

A Certainly. The Recycle Bin *must* keep the entire file intact or you cannot recover it from the Recycle Bin if you need the file again. Although files in the Recycle Bin consume disk space, they are retrievable at any time until you empty the Recycle Bin. Only after emptying the Recycle Bin does Windows 95 physically delete the file from your disk.

Q I'm confused; are there *three* kinds of shortcuts?

A There are three versions of shortcuts in Windows 95. They are: single-key shortcut, desktop shortcut, and Start menu shortcuts.

You can add a single-key shortcut key to any program. When you press Ctrl+Alt and that key at the same time, Windows 95 starts that program. You could be working in Explorer, at the desktop, or in virtually any other program, but when you press that shortcut keystroke, Windows 95 starts the program you've assigned to that shortcut key.

To create a desktop shortcut, you right-click on a document or folder and select the Create Shortcut command from the menu. Windows 95 creates a shortcut to the item, which is really an alias name that knows the location of the original document or folder, but that acts like a copy of the item.

When you add items to the Start menu (or any menu cascading out from the Start menu), you must create a shortcut to that item because you don't want a copy of the same program all over your disk drive. Therefore, the menu command is a shortcut to the program that, after you select that menu item, finds the program on the disk drive and starts the program.

5

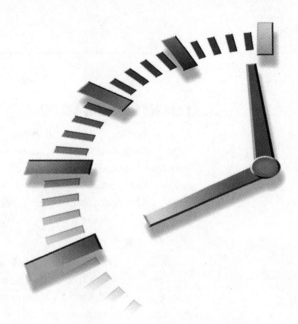

HOUR **6**

A Call for Help

This hour shows you how to find help when using Windows 95. Although this book is *really* all you'll ever need to use Windows 95 effectively (self-promotion was never one of the author's weak points!), when you get confused, Windows 95 offers a set of online tools you can access to find out how to accomplish a specific task.

If you're accustomed to a previous version of Windows, parts of the Windows 95 screens might be confusing. The Windows 95 online help system lets you point to an item on the screen and request specific help on that item.

The highlights of this hour include

- Why Windows 95 includes online help
- How to access the help system
- What Pop-up Help is all about
- How to use the help system to display the Welcome screen

Introducing Help

Even Windows 95 experts need help now and then with Windows 95. Despite its simple appearance and desktop, Windows 95 is simply too vast for users to know everything about the system. Windows 95 includes an *online* help system. Because it is online, the help system is available whenever you need it. For example, if you are working with Explorer and forget how to send a document to the disk, you can search the online help system for the words *send to* and Windows 95 gives you advice on how to locate and use the Send To command.

There are a tremendous number of ways you can request help while working in Windows 95. There are also a tremendous number of places from which you can get help. This hour focuses on the most common ways you'll use online help and also offers tips along the way. The next task explains how to access the top-level online help features.

> To use every help feature available to you in Windows 95, you'll need
> Internet access. Microsoft keeps up-to-date helpful advice on the Web. In
> addition, some help is available on all Windows 95 installations, but you'll
> need your Windows 95 CD-ROM to access the Windows 95 Tour described in
> this hour.

Task 6.1: Accessing Help from the Start Menu

Step 1: Description

The taskbar is always available to you no matter what else you are doing in Windows 95. Even if you've hidden the taskbar behind a running program, the taskbar is available as soon as you point the mouse at the bottom of the screen. You can find a Help command on the taskbar's Start menu. The Help command displays the online help's primary dialog boxes that enable you to access the help system.

Step 2: Action

1. Click the Start button to display the Start menu.
2. Select Help to request online help. After a brief pause, you see a Help tabbed dialog box similar to the one in Figure 6.1.

FIGURE 6.1

*The Help Contents dia-
log box displayed from
the Start menu*

The dialog box shown in Figure 6.1 shows the initial Help command's screen with
the first tabbed dialog box selected. Task 6.2 explains how you access this dialog
box's help information.

 Depending on the date of your Windows 95 release, you might see a slightly
different screen.

3. Actually, your help dialog box might differ from the one in Figure 6.1 because,
   depending on your system's recent usage, another tab might be selected in the dialog box.

   Figure 6.2 shows the dialog box that appears if the second tab, labeled Index, is
   selected when you see the Help screen. If you do not see this dialog box now, click
   the Index tab to display Figure 6.2's dialog box.

FIGURE 6.2

The Index dialog box

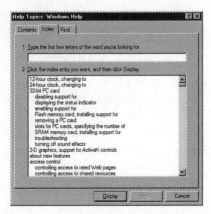

6

▼   Task 6.4 explains how to use the Index dialog box's helpful information.

    4. If you click the third tab labeled Find, you might get the help dialog box shown in Figure 6.3, or you might get a dialog box labeled Find Setup Wizard shown in Figure 6.4.

FIGURE 6.3

The Find dialog box

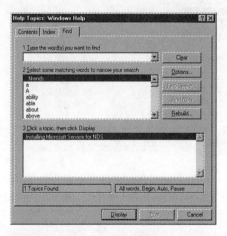

FIGURE 6.4

The Find Setup Wizard dialog box

If you see the Find Setup Wizard dialog box, you have to execute the wizard to create a table of contents for the Find dialog box. Accept the default wizard values as you follow the wizard screens to build the Find contents. After a brief pause, Windows 95 displays the Find dialog box shown in Figure 6.3. Unlike the Index tab, the Find tab enables you to locate every occurrence of a word inside the help files. Often, Find is more cumbersome than the other two pages in the dialog box. As a matter of fact, Microsoft has removed the Find page from online help written after Windows 95 (such as the help you find in Windows 98). Given the Find page's archaic and confusing nature, this text does not refer to the help system's
▼   Find page again.

5. Click the first tab labeled Contents to prepare for the next task.

> **Time Saver:** Increase your help text's font size if you have difficulty reading the help windows. Right-click over the help window and select Options from the pop-up menu. Click Tab to display the Tab dialog box and select a font size option. When you close the dialog box, your help windows will display their text in the new font size.

> **Wizards in Help**
>
> A *wizard* is a step-by-step procedure in Windows 95 that guides you through a process of some kind. The wizard that executes when you first select the Find help dialog box builds a table of contents for the Find searches. You can build a small online help database (the default recommended choice) or a large online help database that offers a more complete base of online help but consumes a tremendous amount of your disk space. Rarely will a Windows 95 user need to take up as much disk space as the maximized help database would take.
>
> If you don't see the wizard's screens, someone else might have already run the wizard and built the help database for you.

Step 3: Review

The Start menu contains a Help command that displays a tabbed dialog box of online help information. The first time you use the online help system, Windows 95 has to build a table of contents for the Find dialog box. If you are using Windows 95's help system for the first time, you'll probably have to follow the wizard's instructions to build the table of contents.

Task 6.2: Using the Contents Help Dialog Box

Step 1: Description

The Contents dialog box portion of the Start menu's Help command offers an overview of the Windows 95 environment. You might want to scan through the Contents dialog box, but if you've covered Hours 1 through 5 already, you now know enough Windows 95 that much of the information will be repetitious for you.

> Your version of the Contents dialog box might differ from the one shown in this task depending on the date of your Windows 95 system.

6

▼ Step 2: Action

1. You might find an item at the top of the Contents dialog box—Windows, the Web, and You—that starts your Internet browser and connects you to the Internet (assuming you have Internet access). From the Internet, you can read the online Windows 95 help on Microsoft's Web site. The site includes documentation not available at the time Microsoft created your Windows 95 CD-ROM. In addition, the site includes help with maximizing your use of Windows 95 and the Internet. The Web-based help entry appears only in some Windows 95 installations. If you don't find the entry, you can still access the Microsoft Windows 95 Web site from the Internet if you have Internet Web access. You can find the Microsoft Windows 95 Web site at www.microsoft.com/windows95/default.asp.

2. The second item in the Contents dialog box starts a ten-minute tour of Windows 95. Your Windows 95 distribution CD-ROM must be in the drive. When you click on the item labeled Tour: Ten Minutes to Using Windows, the tour begins, and after a brief pause, you will see the tour control screen shown in Figure 6.5.

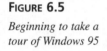

FIGURE 6.5

Beginning to take a tour of Windows 95

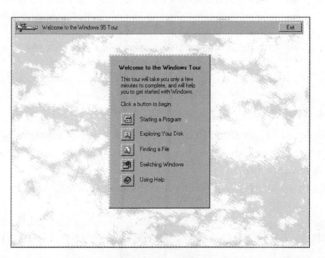

If you want to take a break and watch the Windows 95 tour, do so now. Click the Exit button to return to the Contents dialog box when you finish. If you installed the tour option when you installed Windows 95, you do not need the CD-ROM.

3. The remaining items on the Contents dialog box are items marked with book icons. If you double-click an item next to a book, the book opens up and additional topics appear (like a folder that opens to show other documents and folders). Click the topic labeled How To, and you'll see a long list (scrollable with the vertical scrollbar to the right of the window) of topics you can choose from.

If you double-click on an open book icon, that topic (and the book) closes and the subtopics disappear. The closed and open books work like the collapsed and expanded Explorer folders that display plus and minus signs to show their open and closed states. (Refer to Hour 5, "Explore the Windows 95 System," for more details.)

4. Keep clicking on the topics (opening each book icon) until you see an icon next to a topic that contains a question mark sitting on a document. When you click on one of these document icons, Windows 95 displays a help screen like the one shown in Figure 6.6.

FIGURE 6.6

A Windows 95 help topic

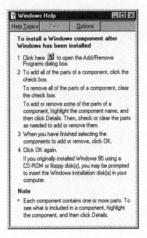

The small help topic dialog boxes stay on your screen even when you switch to other tasks. Therefore, if you want help on a topic such as moving a file, you can first display the help topic related to file moving and then start Explorer. The help topic remains on the screen while you use Explorer.

You can move and resize a help topic dialog box just as you can other kinds of windows.

When a help topic's dialog box contains green underlined text, that text is a *cross-referenced help topic*. You can click on the text to display a description of its topic. The help topic dialog box remains on the screen while you read the underlined text's cross-reference.

6

5. Most help topic dialog boxes contain buttons labeled Related Topics. When you click this button, Windows 95 displays a list of cross-referenced topics. When you click on one of them, it displays a different dialog box containing a description of the related topic.

Step 3: Review

The Contents dialog box offers an overview of tasks that you might want to perform while working in Windows 95. When using the Contents dialog box, your goal (unless you want to take the Windows 95 tour) is to find the topic you want help with and display that topic's dialog box. From the topic dialog box, you can look at cross-referenced help items and related topics.

Task 6.3: Traverse Help Topic Dialog Boxes

Step 1: Description

Rarely do you view one help topic dialog box at a time. Typically, you'll get help on a topic and then decide that you want help on another topic. You'll use the help topic dialog box command buttons to move back and forth between other help dialog boxes.

Step 2: Action

1. Figure 6.7 shows a help dialog box with three command buttons at the top of the box labeled Help Topics, Back, and Options. (Small command buttons also appear on the help page itself so you can link to other help topics.)

FIGURE 6.7

Help topic dialog boxes appear with command buttons

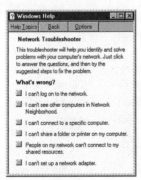

2. If you click the Help Topics command button, Windows 95 displays the Contents dialog box again.

3. If you need to select several related help topics in succession, each topic appears in its own dialog box. You can back up one topic at a time by clicking the Back command button.

▼ 4. The Options command button displays a menu of commands you can use to change the way you use the help system. If you select the Annotate command, Windows 95 displays a miniature text editor on which you can type notes that Windows 95 will attach to the help topic.

Subsequently, when you display that annotated help dialog box, you'll see a paper clip icon at the top indicating that there is an annotated reference available when you want to read it. Click the paper clip to read, change, or delete the annotation.

5. The Copy command sends the dialog box's help text to the Windows 95 Clipboard. From there, you can later paste it into another document.

6. The Print Topic command is used to print the contents of the help dialog box. When you click the print command button, a Print dialog box appears. Print dialog boxes are explained in Hour 20, "Fonts and Viewers."

7. There are three font sizes: small, normal (the default), and large. You can change the font size by selecting Option | Font from the help topic dialog box. By making a help topic dialog box's font smaller, you can display more help in a smaller dialog box.

8. The next command on the Options menu determines whether or not the help menu stays on the screen on top of all other windows when you change to a different task. As mentioned earlier in this hour, the help dialog box always stays on the screen. You can change this default behavior by modifying the value of the Keep Help on Top command on the Options menu.

9. The last command on the Options menu changes the help topic dialog box colors to the Windows 95 system colors so the information inside the help dialog boxes matches the colors of your regular Windows 95 windows. Ordinarily, the help topics display is a pale shade of yellow, simulating the yellow sticky notes you can attach to papers around the house or office.

10. If you've been following along and viewing the menu commands so far, close the help topics dialog box now. You can press Esc to close the dialog box quickly.

6

Time Saver: All of the Options menu commands are available if you right-click the mouse button on the help topic dialog box.

Step 3: Review

The command buttons at the top of the help topics contain extra power that lets you maneuver back and forth within the help system, as well as change the appearance of the

▲ help you request.

Task 6.4: Using the Index Help Dialog Box

Step 1: Description

When you want Windows 95 to find a specific topic in the online help system, click the tabbed dialog box labeled Index. Windows 95 displays the Index dialog box. Here you can ask the online help system to search for topics for you. (You had to find your own topics when using the Contents help system.)

All three of the online help system's tabbed dialog boxes eventually display their helpful advice using the same set of small dialog boxes. The help method that you decide to use depends greatly on how you want to approach that topic. If you want to find help on a specific topic, you are better off looking for that topic in the Index or Find tabbed dialog boxes rather than the Contents dialog box.

> The Index dialog box (described in this task) searches for help when you enter topics to search for. Windows 95 searches only help dialog box titles.

Step 2: Action

1. When you want Windows 95 to find help for you, display the Index dialog box and type the first few letters of the help topic you want to find. For this example, type mov. As you type mov in section 1, Windows 95 narrows the possible help topics matches in the list under section 2. Windows 95 displays all titles that begin with the letters mov, as shown in Figure 6.8.

FIGURE 6.8

Make Windows 95 look for a topic for you in the index of help titles

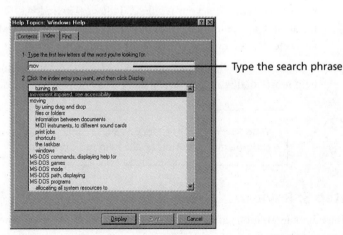

Type the search phrase

▼

▼   2. Most of the time, you do not need to finish typing the search phrase. As soon as you type two or three characters, Windows 95 narrows the list of help topics close to the one you want help with. If you want help with moving files and folders, the typed letters mov get a list in the Index dialog box's lower section that is close to the topic Moving Files or Folders.

3. If the topic you double-click on (in the lower section) appears in two or more help topic dialog boxes, Windows 95 displays yet another dialog box with every help topic title that contains that topic. Select the topic you want help on, and Windows 95 displays the matching dialog box with the helpful information at your disposal. This is a good way to see several related topics at a glance.

Step 3: Review

The Index tabbed dialog box searches through all the help topic titles, looking for the subject you want to find. Although the Contents dialog box requires that you scan through all the help topics looking for the subject you want, the Index dialog box search-es every help title for your word or phrase and displays the resulting dialog boxes when
▲   you click over the listed topics.

Pop-up Help

Sometimes you'll be in the middle of a dialog box working inside Windows 95 when you spot a command button or a control that you do not understand. Look in the upper-right corner of the window for a question mark on a command button. If you find such a com-mand button, you've found Windows 95's *Pop-Up Help* command button and cursor (sometimes called Roving Help).

Although a help search on that dialog box would produce a description of the entire dia-log box, the Pop-up Help lets you narrow the focus and request help on a specific item on the screen. Not all dialog boxes or screens inside Windows 95 contain the Pop-up Help feature so look for the question mark command button, to the left of the window minimizing and resizing buttons, in the upper-right corner of whatever window you're working on.

6

Task 6.5: Using the Pop-up Help Feature

Step 1: Description

As long as a dialog box contains the command button with a question mark on it, you can request Pop-up Help for the items on your screen.

▼ Step 2: Action

1. Display the Help screen again by selecting Help on the Start menu.

2. Click the Contents tabbed dialog box (see Figure 6.1). In the upper-right corner of the dialog box, you'll see the Pop-up Help command button and its question mark.

3. Suppose you forget what the large list box of topics in the center of the screen is for. Click the question mark command button once, and the cursor changes to a question mark that follows the mouse cursor as you move the mouse.

4. Point the question mark mouse cursor to the list of topics in the middle of the screen and click the mouse button. Windows 95 displays a pop-up description box, shown in Figure 6.9, that describes the topic list and what you are to do with it.

FIGURE 6.9

The Pop-up Help helps you when you point to a place on the screen

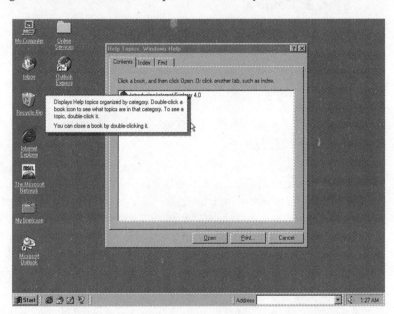

5. Press Esc to get rid of the pop-up description box and return to the regular Contents screen.

6. There's another way to produce the Pop-up Help. Point the regular mouse cursor over the item. Right-click now over the list of topics in the middle of the Contents screen. Windows 95 displays a pop-up description box that contains a one-line menu with the command What's This? in the menu.

7. Click on the What's This? command, and the same pop-up description box appears that's shown in Figure 6.9.

▼

The Pop-up Help is also known as context-sensitive help. Windows 95 looks at what you are currently doing when you request the help and displays help that matches the context of your current actions.

Step 3: Review

The Pop-up Help feature of Windows 95 comes in handy if you forget what to do when displaying a dialog box or when working in a Windows 95 application. Click on the question mark icon and then click over the control that you want help with. Windows 95 looks at the control you clicked and displays helpful advice and a description for that control.

The F1 function key is the shortcut access key for the Pop-up Help. When displaying a dialog box, you can often press F1 to get a helpful description of what you can do next.

I Want My Welcome Screen Tips!

Do you still see a Welcome screen when you start Windows 95? Hour 1, "What's Windows 95 All About?" described the Welcome screen and explained how the Welcome screen provides you with tips every time you start Windows 95. It also told you how to get rid of the Welcome screen but *not* how to get the Welcome screen back! The next task finally shows you how to get the Welcome screen back again so it appears every time you start Windows 95.

Task 6.6: Adding the Welcome Screen to Windows 95 Start-Up

Step 1: Description

The reason you're learning how to add the Welcome screen in this hour is that Windows 95 requires that you use the help system to add a Welcome screen. In this instance, the help topic not only describes helpful advice, it actually does work for you.

Step 2: Action

1. Select the Help command from the Start menu.

2. Click the Index tab to display the Index dialog box (shown in Figure 6.2).

3. In the top input prompt, type `Welcome`. When you type `Welcome`, Windows 95 highlights the Welcome screen, seen in the lower window.

6

To Do

4. Double-click the selected topic and you see the help topic dialog box shown in Figure 6.10.

FIGURE 6.10

This help topic dialog box displays the Welcome screen

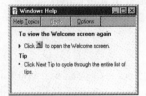

5. Read through the dialog box text. Do you see the command button with the crooked arrow inside the text? Click on that command button. After a brief pause, Windows 95 displays a Welcome screen with a helpful tip.

6. If you want to see the Welcome screen every time you start Windows 95, be sure to check (by clicking) the option at the bottom of the screen labeled Show this Welcome Screen Next Time You Start Windows.

7. You can now close the Welcome screen. Each time you restart Windows 95, the Welcome screen will appear.

8. Close the help topic dialog box.

Step 3: Review

The help system often does work for you. When you see a command button inside a help topic dialog box, you can often click that command button to accomplish a task. In this task, you learned how to add back the Welcome screen every time you start Windows 95.

 Some versions of Windows 95 provide a Tip Tour option on the Accessories menu. You can display the Welcome screen and run the Windows 95 tour from this option. If you do not see this menu option, you have to initiate the Welcome screen from the help system as described in this task.

Summary

This hour showed you how to access the powerful help features of Windows 95. When you have a question about Windows 95, you can ask Windows 95 itself for help. There are several ways to access the helpful dialog boxes about a variety of topics. The most common method of getting detailed help is to select the Help command from the Start menu.

The Help command displays a Help tabbed dialog box containing three different help search screens. The first, the Contents dialog box, displays an overview of Windows 95 in a book-like form that you read at your leisure. In addition, the Contents dialog box can start a ten-minute tour of Windows 95 if you have a CD-ROM with your Windows 95 system. (The tour requires heavy use of graphics and sound, so Windows 95 needs the storage capacity found on the CD.) You can also get online help if you have Internet access.

There are two ways to search for help using the help tabbed dialog boxes. If you select the Index dialog box, Windows 95 searches the help topic titles for the word or phrase that you need help with. If you display the Find dialog box, Windows 95 searches the help topics themselves for the word or phrase you're hunting for.

The pop-up context-sensitive help feature is nice because it lets you click over an item, such as a control in a dialog box, and Windows 95 displays help on that item. Usually, the Pop-up Help displays a description as well as advice on what you can do to make the control work for you.

Workshop

Term Review

context-sensitive help   Refers to the capability of Windows 95 to look at what actions you are currently performing (the *context*) and display help that explains how to complete those actions.

cross-referenced help topic   Green underlined text inside help dialog boxes that displays definitions when you click it.

online   Information that is available interactively as you use Windows 95.

Pop-up Help   With certain dialog boxes, Windows 95 lets you point to items on the dialog boxes and click the window's question mark command button to get help about that item. You also can display this Pop-up Help by right-clicking on an item to see a description of that item and learn the commands you can perform.

wizard   A step-by-step procedure that leads you through the execution of a Windows 95 task. Many Windows 95 programs, such as Microsoft Word for Windows, include specific wizards of their own.

6

Q&A

Q There are so many kinds of help available; which one should I use?

A The method of help that you access depends on the task you're trying to accomplish. Generally, there are several ways to get help on the same topic. If you want help on a procedure such as moving files, you probably can find related topics grouped together in the Contents dialog box. There, you can find topics, grouped by subject, which you can browse.

If you want to search the help system for *all* topics related to the one you want, such as changing icons on folders and documents, you probably want to search the Index or Find dialog boxes. The Index dialog box searches topic titles for key words that you specify. The Find dialog box searches the text itself for the topic you want to find. The Find dialog box can locate more help topics than the Index dialog box can.

When you see a Windows 95 control or menu command that you do not understand, click the question mark icon (if one is available) in the upper-right corner; then point and click on the item you want help with to get specific help (called Pop-up Help) about the screen.

Finally, if you cannot find help on a topic, especially if you want help with the Windows 95 Internet interface, check out Microsoft's Web site for help.

Q Is Pop-up Help always available?

A Sadly, the Pop-up Help system is not always available. When you want to know how to perform a task, such as copying a file, you'll probably have to issue the Help command on the Start menu and search for your topic.

Pop-up Help is a great tool to use when you want a description of a screen element. For example, when displaying a dialog box, you can display the Pop-up Help cursor to find out what commands the controls on the dialog box perform.

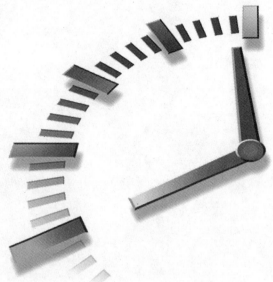

Part II

Accessories in the Afternoon

Hour

Hour 7

Manage Your Desktop

This hour is a little different from the other hours. Instead of studying a single central aspect of Windows 95, such as Explorer, this hour contains a *potpourri* of desktop management tips and procedures that improve the way you use the Windows 95 environment.

You can activate your desktop with the Windows Active Desktop feature, and you can place Web and other files directly on your desktop to customize your Windows 95 wallpaper. Windows 95 comes with several screen saver designs, and you can purchase and download additional screen savers. Screen savers not only provide something for your computer to do while it is idle, but they also offer security features.

This hour offers a collection of tips that simply help make your use of Windows 95 even easier. Start Windows 95 and walk through this hour, trying the shortcuts and advice, and decide which topics suit your needs best. Now that you've mastered the major Windows 95 tools such as Explorer and the Settings menu (covered in Hour 5, "Explore the Windows 95 System"), you are ready to streamline the way that you use Windows 95.

The highlights of this hour include

- How to place Web pages on your desktop
- Why screen savers improve the use of your computer's idle time
- How screen savers add security while you are away from your computer
- How to change your PC's date and time
- When to let Windows 95 arrange the desktop icons for you
- How to use the mouse to add programs to your Start menu
- What to do when you get tired of your Windows 95 colors
- How to create a new user profile

Activate Your Desktop

This hour introduces you to the Windows Active Desktop feature. Hour 16, "Activating Your Desktop," takes the active desktop to its next level by describing additional features such as push technology. Push technology lets you subscribe to various online services, such as news agencies, that send Web content directly to your PC at preset time intervals. You don't have to go as far as push technology to enjoy many benefits of the active desktop. You've already seen in Hour 2, "Tour Windows 95," how to specify the one-click selection of desktop icons. The active desktop is Windows 95's way of more seamlessly integrating your Windows desktop into the online Internet world.

 Remember, when asked to open an icon or folder, you are to double-click that icon or folder if you use the standard desktop, and single-click that icon or folder if you use the active desktop.

Web pages look the way they do because their underlying language, *HTML* (which stands for *HyperText Markup Language*), defines the colors, pictures, and embedded *applets* (small programs that activate Web pages using yet another language called *Java*). Why would you put a Web page on your desktop as wallpaper? Perhaps the page is a support page that you need to tweak Windows 95. Perhaps the page contains a game applet that you want to play in your spare time. Whatever the reason, you can change your wallpaper to any HTML file easily as the next task demonstrates.

Task 7.1: Making an HTML File Your Wallpaper

Step 1: Description

▲ To Do

The desktop can hold any HTML file as wallpaper. Previous Windows versions let you set up graphics files as a wallpapered desktop background, but Windows 95, in conjunction with Internet Explorer 4, lets you place HTML documents there as well. (HTML documents end with the .HTML or .HTM filename extension and display a Web page icon in Explorer views.)

Step 2: Action

1. Click the right mouse button over the Windows 95 wallpaper to display the pop-up menu.

2. Select Properties. The Display Properties dialog box, shown in Figure 7.1, appears.

FIGURE 7.1

You can set wallpaper to any HTML or graphics file

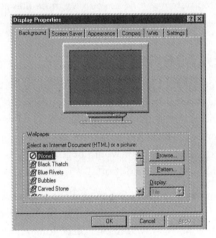

3. The Background page (the default dialog box page that shows in Figure 7.1) lets you set up a wallpaper file. You can select one of the supplied wallpaper files by scrolling and selecting from the Wallpaper list box, or you can click the Browse button to search for an HTML file.

4. When you locate the HTML file you want to use as your wallpaper, click the Open button to select the file. The file and its pathname now appear in the Wallpaper list and are available for subsequent selections.

5. When you click OK and return to your desktop, the HTML file appears as the wallpaper.

▼

7

▼ Step 3: Review

The wallpaper on your desktop can hold graphics or HTML files. You can easily select
HTML files as your desktop wallpaper background from the Background page in the
▲ Display Properties dialog box.

What if you have no HTML files on your system? That's okay because in
Windows 95 you can easily go out and find HTML files on the Web and store
them on your PC. If you browse any Web page using your Web browser, the
menu's File I Save command saves any page and its contents to the location
you specify.

Virtually *any* file can be an HTML file. If you use Word, Excel, WordPad, or
just about any other major Windows program on the market, you can often
save your data files in the HTML format. Therefore, you can place text files
on your desktop system as long as you save those files as HTML files.

SOS: Save Our Screens!

Want to know an insider's computer industry secret? Here it is: Screen savers really
don't save many screens these days. In the past, computer monitors, especially the mono-
chrome green-letters-on-black kind, would *burn in* characters when left on too long without being used. In other words, if you left the monitor on for a long time and did not
type anything, the characters on the monitor would begin to leave character trails that
stayed on the monitor even after you turned it off.

To combat character burn-in, programmers began to write *screen savers* that blanked the
screen or displayed moving characters and pictures. The blank screens had no burn-in
problems, and the moving text never stayed in one place long enough to burn into the
monitor. The screen savers would kick into effect after a predetermined length of non-
use. Therefore, if you walked away from your computer, the screen saver would begin
after a few minutes. Upon returning, you could press any key to restore the computer
screen to its original state where you left it.

Almost everybody has heard of screen savers these days. Computer software stores contain shelf after shelf of screen saver programs. There are screen savers that display pictures of your favorite television characters. There are screen savers with cartoons. There
are screen savers that continuously draw geometric and 3D designs. Microsoft designed
Windows 95 to include several screen savers. Therefore, you don't have to buy a screen
saver because if you have Windows 95, you already have an assortment of them to
choose from.

Why, then, during an age when they are not needed, are screen savers more popular than ever before? The answer is simple: Screen savers are fun! Screen savers greet you with designs and animated cartoons when you'd otherwise look at a boring screen.

If you think that you might want to try one of the store-bought screen savers, first try one from Windows 95 to see if you like screen savers. Some people decide they don't like them after they begin using screen savers.

Screen savers aren't just for fun and games so don't rule them out before you've looked at them! Even though you might not care for screen savers, the Windows 95 screen savers offer an added benefit not found in many other screen savers: The Windows 95 screen savers provide password protection. If you need to walk away from your screen for a while but you want to leave your computer running, you can select a password for the screen saver. After the screen saver begins, a user has to enter the correct password to use your computer. This ensures that payroll and other departments can safely leave their computers, without fear that somebody will see confidential information.

Task 7.2: Setting Up a Screen Saver

Step 1: Description

Windows 95 contains several screen savers from which you can choose. Through the Screen Saver dialog box, you can set up a blanking screen saver or one that moves text and graphics on the screen. You control the length of time the monitor is idle before the screen saver begins.

Step 2: Action

1. Click the right mouse button over the Windows 95 wallpaper. The display menu appears.

If you are working in Windows 95, using a word processor or other program, you might not see the wallpaper. Minimize your current window so that you can see the wallpaper and right-click over the wallpaper.

2. Select Properties, and the Display Properties dialog box appears.

7

▼   3. Click the tab labeled Screen Saver. Windows 95 displays the dialog box shown in
        Figure 7.2.

FIGURE 7.2

*The Screen Saver page
of the Display
Properties dialog box
controls the screen
saver's timing and
selection*

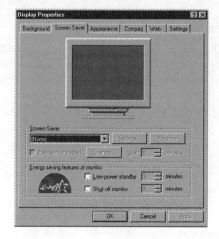

Depending on your attached hardware, the bottom portion of the Screen Saver
page may or may not be grayed out. If your monitor is designed to be *Energy Star-*
compliant, the lower dialog box settings are available to you. You can adjust these
options to save energy. The Energy Star controls work independently and override
any screen saver settings you might use.

   4. Click the down arrow directly below the Screen Saver picture to display a drop-
      down list of Windows 95 screen savers. Click the box now to see the list. When
      (None) is selected, no screen saver will be active on your system.

   5. If you select Blank Screen, Windows 95 uses a blank screen for the screen saver.
      When the screen saver activates, the screen goes blank, and any key that you press
      (or password entry, if you set up a password as described next) returns the screen
      to its original state.

> Task 7.3 explains how to use the password option with the screen saver.

The remaining screen savers are more fun than a blank screen saver. Click any one
of the remaining screen savers in the list now (such as Flying Windows), and
Windows 95 gives you a preview of it on the little monitor inside the dialog box as
▼   shown in Figure 7.3.

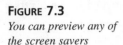

FIGURE 7.3
*You can preview any of
the screen savers*

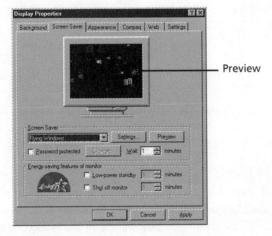

Preview

6. The animated screen savers can move fairly fast. If you want to adjust their speed,
    click the Settings button. In some cases, you also can adjust the number of animat-
    ed items that appear on the screen saver screen.

7. If you want a better preview than the one provided in the small screen inside the
    dialog box, the Preview button lets you view the screen saver full-screen. Click
    Preview to see the actual screen saver in action. Press any key or move the mouse
    to terminate the screen saver preview and return to the dialog box.

8. The Wait prompt determines how many minutes your computer must remain idle
    for the screen saver to activate itself. By pressing Alt+W (the shortcut key combi-
    nation for the Wait prompt), you can enter a new minute value or click the up and
    down arrow keys to change to a new minute value.

9. When you click the OK command button at the bottom of the dialog box, Windows
    95 activates the screen saver program. The screen saver remains active in all future
    Windows 95 sessions until you change it again using the Screen Saver dialog box.

10. The screen saver operates in the background but never shows itself, until your comput-
    er sits idle for the specified minute time value. (Unlike other programs that are active
    but hidden from view, the screen saver never shows up on the taskbar.) Don't touch
    the keyboard or mouse during the waiting time period, and you'll see the screen saver
    go into action. Press any key (or move the mouse) to return to the desktop.

Step 3: Review

Screen savers are easy to set. If you right mouse-click on your desktop and select
Properties from the resulting menu, you will activate the Display Properties tabbed dialog box where you can launch a screen saver. Not only can you control which screen

7

▼ saver is used, but you also can control the number of minutes your computer must be idle
before the screen saver is activated. You can control the speed of animated screen savers
▲ as well.

> If you don't want a screen saver, select (None) in the screen saver's dialog
> box.

Task 7.3: Securing Your Screen Saver

Step 1: Description

Using the Display Properties box, you can add a password to any of the Windows 95
screen savers, including the blank screen saver. After the screen saver executes, it
requires a password before relinquishing control to you or anyone else who wants to use
your computer.

Step 2: Action

1. Display the Screen Saver dialog box again.
2. Click the Password Protected check mark prompt.
3. Press the Change button. You must tell Windows 95 the password you want to set
   for the screen saver. The Change Password dialog box, like the one in Figure 7.4,
   opens.

FIGURE 7.4

*Tell Windows 95 the
secret screen saver
password*

4. Windows 95 requires that you type the password twice. The password appears on
   the screen as asterisks, as you type, so that no one looking over your shoulder can
   read your password. Due to the asterisk protection, Windows 95 asks that you enter
   the password twice in case you make a typing mistake the first time you type the
   new password. Type the same password at both prompts on the screen.

5. Press the OK command button. Now when Windows 95 starts the screen saver, you
▼   have to enter the password to use the computer.

The screen saver password does *not* guarantee total computer security. Someone can reboot your computer and use the computer's files. The password-protected screen saver does, however, keep people from looking at the work you were performing before you left the computer idle.

Step 3: Review

The password lets you protect your computer's screen from view by others. By setting a password, you ensure that people cannot stop the screen saver to look at what you were doing with the computer before the screen saver took effect.

Check the Time

A clock showing the current time appears at the right of your taskbar in the typical setup of Windows 95. (The clock's position might differ depending on where moved your taskbar.) In addition to the time, your computer and Windows 95 also keep track of the date. To see the date, point to the taskbar's time and the date pops up.

There are several reasons why you might want to change the computer's time and date settings. Perhaps you've moved to a different part of the world and need to change the computer's clock. Perhaps your computer contains a time and date memory that runs on a battery, and now the battery has gone bad. Perhaps the person who set up your computer simply didn't know the right time or date when she installed Windows 95. Whatever the reason for setting the time and date, you'll see here that these settings are simple to adjust.

Windows 95 uses the international settings (found by opening the Regional Settings icon in the Control Panel) to format all date and time values displayed from within Windows 95. Therefore, the selected country in the Windows 95 international settings determines the appearance of all time and date values.

Task 7.4: Changing the Time and Date with the Mouse
Step 1: Description

The taskbar gives you access to the time and date settings of your computer. Open the taskbar clock to display the time and date modification dialog box.

To Do

7

If you don't see the time on your taskbar, select the Start menu's Settings | Taskbar command and check the Show Clock option.

Step 2: Action

1. Open your taskbar's clock. Windows 95 displays the Date/Time Properties tabbed dialog box shown in Figure 7.5.

FIGURE 7.5

A double-click displays this Date/Time Properties dialog box

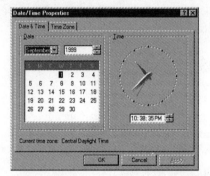

2. Click on a day inside the month to change to that date.

3. Click over the hour, minute, or second to change the time. If you highlight the hour, the minute, or the second, then click either the up or down arrow next to the time. The highlighted value increases or decreases by one unit. As you change the time value, the analog clock face changes also.

4. When you are done modifying the date or time, click the OK command button to close the dialog box, and the taskbar's time reflects your changes. You can now turn off your computer, and the computer's new settings will still be in effect (up to the second) when you turn on the computer again.

5. Windows 95 is smart and can handle time zones easily. If you display the Date/Time Properties dialog box and click the Time Zone tab, Windows 95 displays the time zone dialog box shown in Figure 7.6.

   To set a different time zone, click the drop-down list box arrow to display the world's time zones. The list box contains a list of every possible time zone in the world.

FIGURE 7.6

Change the time zone using a drop-down list box

Not all time zones adhere to daylight saving time. For example, in many parts of Indiana, residents don't have to change their clocks every six months because they don't follow daylight saving time. For those who don't want Windows 95 to adjust for daylight saving, uncheck the option at the bottom of the screen.

6. After you select the proper time zone and daylight saving time setting, click the OK command button to close the dialog box, and the settings then take effect.

Step 3: Review

Changing the date and time requires opening your taskbar's clock icon. The tabbed dialog box that appears lets you change the time, the date, and the time zone.

If your computer adjusts the clock due to daylight saving time, Windows 95 lets you know about the change with a dialog box the first time you use Windows 95 after the time change.

Rearrange Your Start Menu

Want to add programs to the Start menu quickly or rearrange them? Hour 5, "Explore the Windows 95 System," taught you how to access the powerful Settings | Taskbar dialog boxes that allow you to modify the way the taskbar behaves. The Settings | Taskbar dialog boxes include several options that let you rearrange the Start menu and add or remove programs to and from the Start menu.

7

If you don't like the location of a menu item on one of your Start menus, drag the item to another location. When you've opened one of the Start menus, such as the Programs | Accessories menu, you can click and drag any menu item to another menu.

Suppose you use Notepad a lot to edit text files and want to place the Notepad program at the top of your Start menu so you don't have to traverse all the way over to the Accessories menu. Open the Accessories menu and drag the Notepad option to your Start menu. You'll notice two things:

- The menu option's name does not drag, but the mouse cursor displays a box showing the movement.
- If you try to drop the item onto the lower section of the Start menu (the section with the Settings and Programs options), Windows 95 does not accept the change. The cursor turns into the international *Don't* symbol as you drag the Notepad over the Start menu's lower portion.

When you drag the item to the upper section of the Start menu and release your mouse button, the menu option appears on the upper section Start menu.

Deleting Menu Items

To remove a Start menu item, drag the item to the Recycle Bin. When you release the mouse over the Recycle Bin, the item goes to the Recycle Bin and leaves the menu. If you change your mind about removing the item, you can restore it from the Recycle Bin up until the time that you empty the Recycle Bin.

> Your desktop must be set up as the Windows Classic interface and not the Web view if you want to drag menu options to the Recycle Bin. You can select the Start menu's Settings | Folder Options and select the Classic style option to convert windows and the desktop to the classic view. If you want to delete items when your desktop is set up for Web view, you must do so from the item's properties dialog box described in the next Tip. To read more about Classic view versus Web view, see Hour 3, "Take Windows 95 to Task."

> If you want to rearrange more than one or two items from your Start menu, consider selecting the Start menu's Settings | Taskbar option, clicking the Start Menu Programs tab, and clicking the Advanced button to display an Explorer screen. The screen's two panes let you move and rearrange entire menu groups. The click-and-drag approach to menu management works well if you need to move or remove only a few menu items.

Menu Items Are Shortcuts

The reason you can move menu options and send them to the Recycle Bin is that the Start menu contains *shortcuts* to programs. A shortcut is just a pointer to a program, not the program file itself. Therefore, when you drag a shortcut from one location to another, the pointer moves but not the file.

You can even drag a menu item to your desktop. This process creates an icon for the item on your desktop. Then, if you want to launch that program, you can open the desktop's icon rather than traversing the Start menu to start the program.

Right-Click Menu Options

When you right-click over a Start menu option, Windows 95 displays a pop-up menu similar to the one in Figure 7.7.

FIGURE 7.7

The pop-up menus give you control over a menu option

The pop-up menu ——

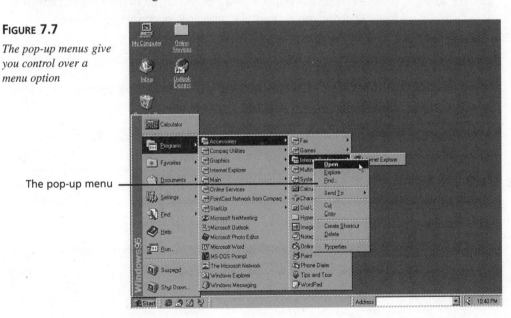

You can delete or rename menu items with the pop-up menu as well as view the item's properties. The Properties option describes the menu option and its underlying file information.

7

Paint Windows 95

Windows 95 offers several color schemes for you to select. Microsoft designed several color schemes that work well together. Depending on your taste, you can choose from conservative to very wild colors.

The color schemes that you can select have nothing to do with the colors of icons, wallpaper, or screen savers on your system. The color schemes determine the color for various system-wide items such as screen title bars, window backgrounds, and dialog box controls.

Task 7.5: Changing the Color Scheme

Step 1: Description

By selecting from various color schemes, you can determine the colors Windows 95 uses for common system-level items such as window controls. The Control Panel contains a Display icon that you use to change the color of your Windows 95 installation.

Step 2: Action

1. Select Control Panel from the Start menu's Settings menu.

2. Open the Display icon. The Display Properties tabbed dialog box appears.

> To show the Display Properties tabbed dialog box quickly, right-click over the wallpaper and select Properties.

3. Click the Appearance tab to display the Appearance dialog box shown in Figure 7.8.

FIGURE 7.8

Change system colors using the Appearance dialog box

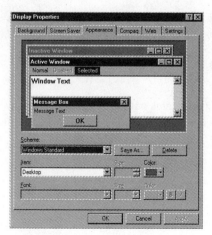

▼   4. If you want to take the time, you can change the colors of every item on the
        Windows 95 screen, including dialog boxes, window borders, and title bars.
        However, it's much easier to pick a color scheme from the list of choices that
        Microsoft supplies.

        In the Appearance page, the top half contains the selected color scheme. If you
        select a different color scheme, you'll see that scheme's color appear at the top of
        the dialog box. For example, suppose you're taking your powerful color laptop to
        Egypt while cruising down the Nile River. Open the drop-down list box labeled
        Scheme and select Desert from the list. Instantly, the top half of your dialog box
        changes colors to a Desert scheme. Now you can compute like a true Egyptian!

     5. The color scheme of your Windows 95 installation does not instantly change.
        You're still in the process of selecting colors at this point. If you don't like the
        desert color scheme, try another. As a matter of fact, try *all* of them to find one you
        really like.

There are some color schemes that include the additional benefit of large
text sizes. As Figure 7.9 illustrates, you can select a color scheme that
enlarges the character size of the Windows 95 text appearing in dialog
boxes and title bars.

FIGURE 7.9

*Not only can you
change system colors
but also common
Windows 95 character
sizes*

Large text will appear
in dialog boxes

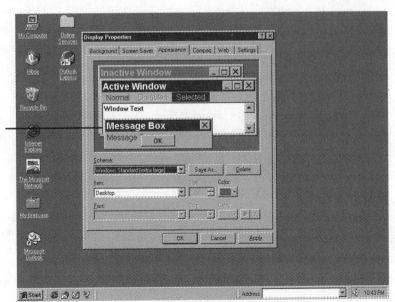

6. When you find a color scheme that you really like, click the OK command button to close the dialog box and change the color scheme to your selected colors. You can now begin working with the new color scheme; as soon as you open a window, you'll see the difference.

Step 3: Review

The Control Panel contains a display icon that lets you change the color scheme of your Windows 95 installation. After you change the colors (and, optionally, the font size), all standard Windows 95 displays, such as windows, borders, and title bars, reflect the new scheme.

> Microsoft Plus! is an add-on program you can purchase separately from Windows 95. Plus! offers several additional color schemes as well as entire desktop *themes* that let you add personality to your Windows 95 desktop.

As you change your color scheme, feel free to change the Windows 95 display font as well. By default, Windows 95 displays icons, window titles, and messages in the MS-DOS Sans Serif font. From the Appearance dialog box, you can select a different font for almost every kind of text Windows 95 displays.

Creating Profiles

If you share your PC with others, perhaps you prefer Windows settings that differ from the others. Perhaps your kids like a certain wallpaper and theme that you don't want. Perhaps you prefer one-click access to Windows icons, and your spouse is used to double-clicking icons. By creating a *profile* that defines your preferred Windows settings, you can make Windows appear the way you want it to when you use the PC, and other people, with their own profiles, will see a Windows that behaves the way they prefer.

Task 7.6: Adding a Profile

Step 1: Description

Create a profile when you want to use certain Windows 95 settings that other users might not want to use. Before you use the PC, you log on with your own user name and password so that Windows 95 can start with your preferred settings. This task explains how to create your own profile.

▼ Step 2: Action

1. Select the Start menu's Settings | Control Panel and open the Users icon. Windows
   95 begins a wizard, whose opening window appears in Figure 7.10. The wizard
   walks you through the creation of a profile.

FIGURE 7.10

*The Enable Multi-User
Settings wizard creates
a personal Windows
profile for you*

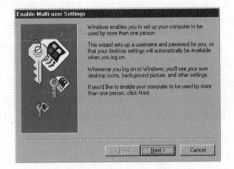

2. Click Next and type a username for yourself.

3. Click Next and enter a password. You must enter the password twice to confirm
   that you typed it accurately the first time.

4. Click Next and the wizard displays the Personalized Items Settings window from
   which you can select those specific items you want to personalize. The items you
   select, such as the Start menu, will look and behave the way you set them up and
   stay that way the next time you use the PC. If someone else uses the PC and logs
   on with her own profile, the Start menu will look and behave the way her profile
   specifies.

4. Click Next and Finish to save your profile. The next time you restart your PC, you
   are asked to supply your username before Windows 95 appears. Your username
   determines how Windows 95 looks and behaves.

> After someone finishes using your PC under his profile, you can load your
> profile without rebooting your PC by selecting the Start menu's Shut Down |
> Log Off User. Windows 95 restarts and you are requested to enter your pro-
> file.

Step 3: Review

After you set up a user profile, Windows 95 recognizes you from the username and password you enter when you begin using your PC. From your user profile, Windows 95
▲ configures itself to your preferences.

Summary

In this hour, you caught a glimpse of some tips and desktop management tools that help you work inside Windows 95 more effectively. After completing the first part of this book, you already have a good foundation regarding the tools that are available to you as a Windows 95 user. Now that you've become more comfortable with these aspects of Windows 95, you'll appreciate some of this hour's timesaving tips.

In this hour, you learned how to improve your computer's idle time by setting up a screen saver. By password-protecting the screen saver, you can add security to your system so that you can safely leave for a few minutes without exiting the program you're working in. You also learned how to change the computer's time, date, and screen colors and rearrange programs from the Start menu with just the mouse. These timesaving features help novice and advanced users use Windows 95 more fully.

Workshop

Term Review

applet   A small program, written in language such as Java, that comes to your PC through an Internet Web page.

burn-in   Characters left on older computer monitors can begin to burn into the monitor, leaving their outlines even after the monitor's power is turned off. Screen savers were originally developed to help avoid burn-in.

Energy Star   A name applied to monitors that comply with environmental guidelines that limit the use of continuous power applied to your monitor.

HTML (*HyperText Markup Language*)   The formatting commands that determine how text, colors, graphics, video, sound, and applets appear on a Web page.

screen saver   A program that waits in the background and executes only if you stop using your computer for a set amount of time. The screen saver either blanks your screen or displays moving text and graphics. Although screen savers were originally developed to help eliminate burn-in problems on monitors, newer monitors don't suffer from burn-in. Screen savers are still popular, however, because they are fun!

Q&A

Q How does a wallpaper pattern differ from a screen saver?

A The wallpaper is your desktop's background. You always see the wallpaper when you first start Windows 95 and when you minimize or close programs you are using within Windows 95. You never see the screen saver unless you quit working on your computer for a few minutes and the screen saver begins running.

Screen savers are running programs. They were originally designed to keep a screen's characters from getting burned into the screen's phosphorus. They had to be a moving pattern (or be completely blank) to accomplish that goal. The burn-in problem is not too common today, given the current design of computer monitors, so a secondary goal of a screen saver is to display an animated and often fun screen during your computer's idle times.

Q How do I adjust my computer's clock when daylight saving time occurs?

A You don't have to do anything when daylight saving time occurs, as long as you've checked the daylight saving time option in the Date/Time Properties dialog box. When you check this option, Windows 95 monitors the calendar and adjusts your computer's time appropriately. If you live in an area that does not follow daylight saving time, be sure to leave the option unchecked so your computer won't change the clock every six months.

7

HOUR 8

Desktop Accessories

Calculator, WordPad, and Paint all appear in the Accessories portion under Programs on the Start menu. As their names suggest, you can perform calculations, create text documents, and paint pictures using these three accessory programs.

The Calculator program comes in handy when you want to perform quick calculations without the need of a more powerful program such as an electronic spreadsheet. WordPad does not offer the power of Microsoft Word but you can create formatted word-processed documents quickly with WordPad, and it's a simple program to learn. Paint is a simple but effective drawing program that you can use to create colorful pictures. If you're a good artist, you might want to paste one of your creations on your Windows 95 desktop as wallpaper!

The highlights of this hour include:

- How to calculate with the Windows 95 Calculator
- How to use WordPad to create word-processed documents
- Which of Paint's advanced editing tools professionally manipulates your images

Calculate Results

Calculator, the Windows 95 calculator program, performs both simple mathematical and advanced scientific calculations. You can find Calculator in the Start menu's Programs | Accessories menu. Calculator provides you with all kinds of computing benefits. Throughout a working day, you use your computer constantly, writing letters, paying bills, and building presentations. As you work, you often need to make a quick calculation and, if you're anything like computer book authors, your calculator is probably covered up beneath papers stacked a foot high. After you start the Windows 95 calculator, it is never any farther away than the taskbar.

> Calculator actually contains *two* calculators, a *standard calculator* and a *scientific calculator*. Most people need the standard calculator for common mathematical operations required for day-to-day personal or business affairs. The scientific calculator contains additional operations, such as statistical and trigonometric operations.

Task 8.1 walks you through the use of the standard calculator.

Task 8.1: Using the Standard Calculator

Step 1: Description

The standard calculator provides full-featured calculator functions. When you use the calculator program, you can sell your own desktop calculator at your next yard sale. Windows 95 even lets you copy and paste the calculator results directly into your own applications.

Step 2: Action

1. Start the Windows 95 calculator. The calculator that you see appears in Figure 8.1. If you see a calculator window with many more buttons than the figure's, select View | Standard to work with the non-scientific calculator.

FIGURE 8.1

The Windows 95 calculator program goes beyond a pocket calculator

▼ 2. To steal from an old cliché, it doesn't take a rocket scientist to use Calculator. Calculator performs standard addition, subtraction, multiplication, and division. In addition, the standard calculator includes memory clear, recall, store, and memory add.

All of Calculator's operations produce *running totals*, meaning that you can continuously apply operations, such as addition, to the running total in Calculator's display.

Calculator has keyboard equivalent keys. Instead of clicking with your mouse to enter 2 + 2 for example, you can type **2 + 2 =** (the equal sign requests the answer). Not all keys have obvious keyboard equivalents, however. For example, the C key does not clear the total (Esc does). Therefore, you might need to combine your mouse and keyboard to use Calculator.

3. Click on the numbers 1, then 2, and then 3. As you click, the numbers appear inside the display.

4. Click the multiplication sign (the asterisk).

5. Click the 2.

6. Click the equals sign, and Calculator displays the result of 246.

7. Click C or press Esc to clear the display.

8. The percent key produces a percentage only as a result of multiplication. Therefore, you can compute a percentage of a number by multiplying it by the percent figure. Suppose that you want to know how much 35 percent of 4000 is.

   Type **4000** and then press the asterisk. Type **35** followed by the percent key (Shift+5 on the keyboard or click the % on the calculator). The value 1400 appears. The result: 1400 is 35 percent of 4000. (The word *of* in a math problem is a sure sign that you must multiply by a percentage. Calculating 35 percent of 4000 implies that you need to multiply 4000 by 35 percent.)

9. When you want to negate the number in the display, click the +/– key. Suppose that you want to subtract the display's current value, 1400, from 5000. Although you could clear the display and perform the subtraction, it's faster to negate the 1400 by clicking the +/– key, then press the plus sign and type **5000** and press the equals sign to produce 3600.

▼

> Calculator displays a letter M above the four memory keys when you store a value in the memory.

10. To store a value in memory, click MS. Whenever you want the memory value back in the display, click MR. MC clears the memory and M+ adds the display to the total in memory. If you want to store a running total, click the M+ button every time you want to add the display's value to the memory. If you want to subtract the display from the total in memory, click the +/- key before you click the M+ button. The M goes away from the memory indicator box when you clear the memory.

> When you want to switch over from your application to Calculator to perform a calculation, and then enter the result of that calculation elsewhere such as in your word processor, select Edit I Copy (Ctrl+C) to copy the value to the Clipboard. When you switch back to the other Windows 95 application, you can paste the value into that application.

11. Close Calculator.

Step 3: Review

The standard calculator performs all the operations that most Windows 95 users will need most of the time. The interface is simple and allows the use of a mouse or keyboard to enter the values. Perhaps most people will find that the keypad offers the easiest interface to the calculator as long as the Num Lock key is active.

The Scientific Calculator

The scientific version of Calculator supports many more advanced mathematical operations. Despite its added power, the scientific calculator operates almost identically to the standard calculator. The standard keys and memory are identical in both calculators. To see the scientific calculator, select View I Scientific. Windows 95 displays the scientific calculator shown in Figure 8.2. The scientific calculator offers more keys, operators, and indicators than does the standard calculator.

FIGURE 8.2

The Windows 95 scientific calculator provides advanced operations

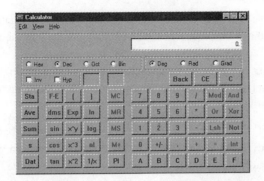

To compute a mean or standard deviation, you must work with several values at a time (a *series*). The *statistics box*, shown in Figure 8.3 and available when you click Sta, contains the series of values as you enter them because the calculator's display shows only a single line at a time. To add numbers to the series, type a value and click Dat. The first time you want to add numbers to the series, you must type the value, click Sta, and then click Dat. After you've added values to the statistics box, you can click the statistic keys such as Ave to see statistics from the series.

FIGURE 8.3

The Statistics Box keeps track of your series of values

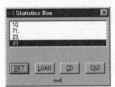

The Statistics Box contains four command buttons labeled RET, LOAD, CD, and CAD. The RET button returns you to the calculator's screen by minimizing the Statistics Box. The LOAD button sends the selected value from the series to the calculator's display. CD removes the selected value from the series. CAD removes all values from the series. If you close the Sta window by clicking X in the upper right, your values also will be cleared.

Write with Flair

Windows 95 contains a word processor called *WordPad*. WordPad appears on your Start menu's Programs | Accessories menu. Although WordPad does not contain all the features of a major word processor, such as Microsoft Word, WordPad does contain many formatting features and can accept documents created in several word processing programs. This section introduces you to WordPad.

WordPad edits, loads, and saves documents in the following formats: Word for Windows, Windows Write (the word processor available in Windows 3.1), text documents, and RTF (*Rich Text Format*) documents. As a result, when you open an RTF, Write, or Word for Windows 6 document that contains formatting, such as underlining and boldfaced characters, WordPad retains those special formatting features in the document.

WordPad contains a toolbar that you can display that helps you access common commands more easily. WordPad also supports the uses of a ruler and format bar that help you work with WordPad's advanced editing features. When you type text into WordPad, you don't have to worry about pressing Enter at the end of every line. WordPad wraps your text to the next line when you run out of room on the current line. Press Enter only when you get to the end of a paragraph or a short line such as a title that you don't want combined with the subsequent line. (Two Enter presses in a row adds a blank line to your text.)

> WordPad differs from NotePad, another text-entry program that comes with Windows 95 and also appears on your Accessories menu. NotePad does not format text for you or support the various fonts that WordPad supports. In addition, NotePad does not support the paragraph formatting that WordPad also supports. NotePad is a simple text-entry program that programmers can use to enter unformatted text into a computer program.

Task 8.2: Working with WordPad

Step 1: Description

If you have no other word processor on your system, you can use WordPad to produce most types of documents. This task leads you through the basic steps for using WordPad and its features.

Step 2: Action

1. Start the WordPad program from the Accessories menu. You see the WordPad screen shown in Figure 8.4.

2. For this task, you'll practice entering and formatting text. Type the following text:
   `A large line.`

3. Select all three words by highlighting them with the mouse or keyboard. With the mouse, select by clicking on the first character and dragging the mouse to the last character. With the keyboard, you can select by moving the text cursor to the first letter and pressing Shift+Right Arrow until you select the entire line.

Toolbar

FIGURE 8.4

WordPad offers many word processing features

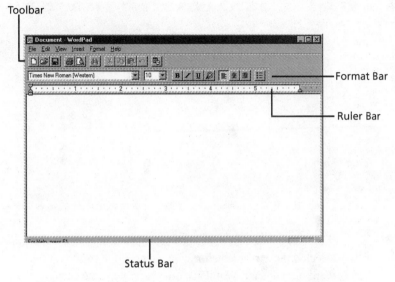

Format Bar

Ruler Bar

Status Bar

8

4. Click the Letter B on the format bar. The text stays selected but something changes; the text becomes boldfaced. Press any arrow key to get rid of the highlighting and see the boldfaced text.

5. Select the three words again. Click the letter I on the format bar. WordPad italicizes the text. Now click the letter U on the third format bar. WordPad instantly underlines the selected text. Keep the text highlighted for the next step.

   By default, WordPad selects a *font* (a typestyle) named Times New Roman. You can see the font name directly below the format bar. The font's size, in *points* (a point is 1/72 inch), appears to the right of the font name (the default font size is 10 points).

6. You can change both the font and the font size by clicking the drop-down lists in which each appears. When you select text, then select a font name, WordPad changes the font of the selected text to the new font. After selecting the text, display the font name list by clicking the drop-down list box's arrow and selecting a font name. If you have Comic Sans MS, use that font to correspond to the next figure in this book. If you do not have that font, select another font that sounds interesting.

   Open the point size drop-down list box and select 36 (you can type this number directly into the list box and press Enter if you want to). As soon as you do, you can see the results of your boldfaced, underlined, italicized, large-sized text displayed using the font name you selected. Press the left or right arrow key to remove the selection. Figure 8.5 shows what your WordPad window should look like.

FIGURE 8.5

The text is formatted to your exact specifications

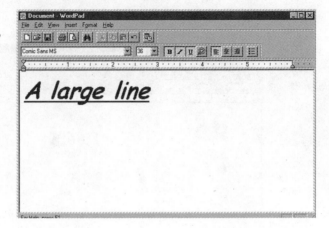

▼   WordPad applied all of the previous formatting on the three words because you selected those words before you changed the formatting. If you select only a single word or character, WordPad formats only that selected text and leaves all the other text alone.

7. Press Enter. Click the B, I, and U format bar buttons and change the font back to Times New Roman. Decrease the font size to 10. Type the following: Windows 95 is fun and press the spacebar. If you do not like the font size, click the down arrow to the right of the font size list and select a different size.

8. Suppose you want to italicize your name. If you now click the format bar for italics, all subsequent text that you type will be italicized. Click the italics format bar button now and type your first name. The name is italicized, but the other text is not italicized.

9. Click the italics format bar button again and continue typing on the same line. Type this: and I like to use WordPad.

10. As you can see, you don't have to select text to apply special formatting to it. Before you type text that you want to format, select the proper format command and then type the text. WordPad formats the text, using the format styles you've selected, as you type. When you want to revert to the previous unformatted style (such as when you no longer want italics), change the style and keep typing.

Font Controls

Ctrl+B, Ctrl+I, and Ctrl+U are the shortcut keys for clicking the B, I, and U format bar buttons. You can also change the formatting of text characters by selecting Format | Font to dis-
▼   play a Font dialog box from which you have total control over the way your text appears.

▼ 11. Select File | Print Preview to see a *thumbnail sketch* of how your document will
       look if you were to print it. By looking at a preview before you print your docu-
       ment, you can tell if the overall appearance is acceptable and if the margins and
       text styles look good. You can quit the preview and return to your editing session
       by pressing Esc.

   12. Close WordPad for now. Don't save your work when prompted to do so.

Step 3: Review

You've only seen a taste of the text-formatting capabilities available, but there's just
enough time left in this hour to discuss one final accessory program called *Paint*. Before
moving to Paint, however, browse some of the following word processing features that
WordPad supports:

- The Ruler indicates where your text will appear on the printed page when you print
  the document. Each number on the Ruler represents an inch (or a centimeter if
  your computer is set up for a metric setting in the View | Options dialog box). As
  you type, you can watch the Ruler to see where the text will appear when you print
  the document. If you select the Format | Paragraph command, WordPad displays
  the Paragraph dialog box in which you can set left and right indentations for individual paragraphs as well as tab stops.

> You can place tab stops quickly by double-clicking over the Ruler at the
> exact location of the tab stop you want.

- The toolbar's Align Left, Center, and Align Right toolbar buttons left-justify, center, and right-justify text so you can align your text in columns as a newspaper
  does. The center alignment format bar button is useful for centering titles at the top
  of documents.

- If you have a color printer, consider adding color to your text by clicking the toolbar's color-selection tool.

- The far-right format bar button adds bullets to lists you enter. Before you start the
  ▲ list, click the Bullets button to format the text as a bulleted list.

Paint a Pretty Picture

Paint provides many colorful drawing tools. Before you can use Paint effectively, you must learn how to interact with the program, and you also must know what each of Paint's tools does. The Paint screen contains five major areas. Figure 8.6 lists each of those five major areas. Table 8.1 describes each area.

FIGURE 8.6

The five major areas of the Paint screen

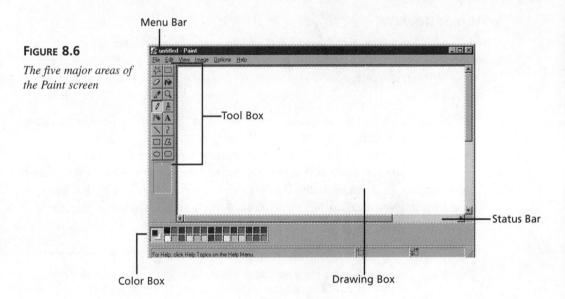

Menu Bar

Tool Box

Status Bar

Color Box

Drawing Box

TABLE 8.1   PAINT'S FIVE AREAS HELP YOU DRAW BETTER

Area	Description
Drawing area	Your drawing appears in the drawing area. When you want to create or modify a drawing, you'll work within this area.
Color box	A list of possible colors you can choose for colorizing your artwork.
Menu bar	The commands that control Paint's operation.
Status bar	Displays important messages and measurements as you use Paint.
Toolbox	The vital drawing, painting, and coloring tools with which you create and modify artwork.

There are two scrollbars on the drawing area so that you can scroll to other parts of your drawing. The drawing area is actually as large as a maximized window. If, however, Paint initially displayed the drawing area maximized, you could not access the menu bar or the toolbox or read the status bar. Therefore, Paint adds the scroll bars to its drawing area so that you can create drawings that will, when displayed, fill the entire screen.

To Do

Task 8.3: Getting to Know Paint

Step 1: Description

8

This task lets you start Paint and navigate around the screen a bit. Practice using Paint and learn Paint's features as you use the program.

Step 2: Action

1. Start Paint from the Start menu's Programs | Accessories menu.

2. Maximize the Paint program to full size. Paint is one of the few programs in which you'll almost always want to work in a maximized window. By maximizing the window, you gain the largest drawing area possible.

3. If you do not see the toolbox, the status bar, or the color box, display the View menu and check each of these three important screen areas to ensure that all five areas show as you follow along in this hour.

4. Take a look at Figure 8.7. This figure labels each of the toolbox tools. Each tool contains an icon that illustrates the tool's function. These tools help you along the way as you draw, paint, and color. When you want to add or modify a picture, you have to pick the appropriate tool. As you work with Paint in subsequent tasks, you'll want to refer to Figure 8.7 to find the tool named in the task.

FIGURE 8.7

The tools on the tool-box

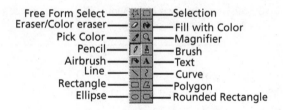

Free Form Select —— Selection
Eraser/Color eraser —— Fill with Color
Pick Color —— Magnifier
Pencil —— Brush
Airbrush —— Text
Line —— Curve
Rectangle —— Polygon
Ellipse —— Rounded Rectangle

5. Click the Pencil tool.

6. Move the mouse cursor over the drawing area, and the cursor changes to a pencil (the same icon that's on the Pencil tool).

7. Hold down the mouse button and move your mouse. Move the mouse all around the drawing area. Make all sorts of curves with the mouse. Notice that Paint keeps the pencil within the borders of the drawing area. Figure 8.8 shows what you can do when you really go crazy with the Pencil tool.

▼

FIGURE 8.8

*The Pencil tool lets
you draw freehand*

8. The default color for the pencil drawing is black. Click on a different color on the color bar, such as red or green, and draw some more. The new lines appear in the new color. Select additional colors and draw more lines to pretty the picture even more.

> You can undo up to three previous edits you've made from Paint by pressing Ctrl+Z.

9. Erase your drawing by selecting File | New. Don't save your current drawing. Paint clears the drawing area so you can start a new document image.

10. Click the Line tool. Use the Line tool to draw straight lines.

    Two coordinates define a straight line: the starting coordinate position and the ending coordinate position. In order to draw a line, you must anchor the line's starting position and extend the line to its ending position. Paint automatically draws a straight line from the starting position to the end position. You can draw lines, using the Line tool, in any direction.

11. Get used to reading *coordinate pair* numbers in the status bar. The numbers tell you the number of *pixels* (points used in your drawing) from the left and top of your window. Move the mouse around the drawing area (do not press a mouse button yet) and watch the pair of numbers at the right of the status bar change.

12. Select a different color and draw another line. Paint draws that line in the new color.

Now that you've selected the Line tool, look at the area below the toolbox. You see five lines, with each line growing thicker than the one before. By clicking on a thick line, the next line you draw with the Line tool appears on the drawing area in the new thickness. You can change the thickness, using this line size list, for any of the geometric shapes.

8

13. Click on the thickest line in the list of line sizes. Draw a couple of lines to see the thicker lines. If you change colors before drawing, the thicker lines appear in the new color.

14. The rest of the geometric shapes are as easy to draw as the lines are. Select File | New to clear the drawing area. Don't save any changes.

15. Click on the Line tool to change the line thickness size to the middle line thickness (the third thickness size). Always change the Line tool's thickness before selecting one of the geometric drawing tools. The Line tool's line size determines the line thickness for all the geometric tools.

16. Select the Rectangle tool. Rectangles, like lines, are determined by their starting *anchor position* and the rectangle's opposite corner's position. Begin drawing a rectangle at coordinates 190,75. After anchoring the rectangle with the mouse button, drag the mouse until it rests at 385,270. The status line indicator will show 200, 200, meaning that the rectangle is 200 by 200 pixels. When you release the mouse you will have drawn a perfect square.

Drawing a perfect square is not always easy because you have to pay close attention to the coordinates. Paint offers a better way to draw perfect squares. Hold down the Shift key while dragging the mouse, and the rectangle always appears as a square. Shift also draws perfect circles when you use the ellipse tool.

The three rectangles below the toolbox do not represent the line thickness of the rectangles. They determine how Paint draws rectangles. When you click the top rectangle (the default), all of the drawing area that appears beneath the next rectangle that you draw shows through. Therefore, if you draw a rectangle over other pictures, you see the other pictures coming through the inside of the new rectangle. If you click the second rectangle below the toolbox, the rectangle's center overwrites

▼   any existing art. As a result, all rectangles you draw have a blank center, no matter what art the rectangle overwrites. If you select the third rectangle, Paint does not draw a rectangular outline but does draw the interior of the rectangle in the same color you've set for the interior (the default interior color is white).

17. Now that you understand the rectangle, you also understand the other geometric tools. Click the Ellipse tool to draw ovals (remember that Shift lets you draw perfect circles). Click the Rounded Rectangle tool to draw rounded rectangles (or rounded squares if you press Shift while dragging).

     Click the top rectangle selection (to draw see-through shapes) and click the Ellipse to draw circles. Click the Rounded Rectangle tool and draw rounded rectangles. Fill your drawing area with all kinds of shapes to get the feel of the tools.

18. A blank drawing area helps you learn how to use the Polygon and Curve tools, so select File | New (don't save) to clear your drawing area.

19. Select the Polygon tool. The Polygon is a tool that draws an enclosed figure with as many sides as you want to give the figure. After you anchor the polygon with the mouse, drag the mouse left or right and click the mouse. Drag the mouse again to continue the polygon. Every time you want to change directions, click the mouse once more. When you are finished, double-click the mouse, and Paint completes the polygon for you by connecting your final line with the first point you drew.

20. Clear your drawing area again. The Curve tool is one of the neatest but strangest tools in the toolbox. Click on the Curve tool (after adjusting the line thickness and color, if you want to do so).

     Draw a straight line by dragging the mouse. After you release the line, click the mouse button somewhere just outside the line and drag the mouse around in circles. As you drag the mouse, Paint adjusts the curve to follow the mouse. When you see the curve that you want, release the mouse so that Paint can stabilize the curve.

21. The Eraser/Color Eraser tool erases whatever appears on the drawing area. The Eraser/Color Eraser tool comes in four sizes: a small eraser that erases small areas and larger erasers that erase larger areas at one time. When you select the Eraser/Color Eraser tool, you can also select an eraser thickness. (The color you choose has no bearing on the eraser's use.) Select the Eraser/Color Eraser tool now and drag it over parts of your drawing to erase lines you've drawn.

▼ 22. Clear your drawing area and exit Paint.

▼ **Step 3: Review**

The geometric tools generally require that you select a line width, a drawing style (such as rectangles that hide or don't hide their backgrounds), an exterior and interior color, and then draw the shape. You draw most of the shapes by anchoring their initial position and then dragging the mouse to extend the shape across the screen. If you make a mistake, you can use the Eraser/Color Eraser tool to correct the problem.

> Paint saves files only in the bitmap format (with the .BMP filename extension). However, it reads both bitmap and PC Paintbrush files with the .PCX extension.

> Use Paint if you want to create your own desktop wallpaper such as your company logo.

> Drawings often have titles. Graphs often have explanations. Maps often have legends. Pictures that you draw often need text in addition to the graphics that you draw. The Text tool lets you add text using any font and font size available within Windows 95. You can control how the text covers or exposes any art beneath the text. After clicking the Text tool, drag the text's outline box (text always resides inside this text box that appears). When you release your mouse, select the font and style and type your text. When you click on another tool, your text becomes part of the drawing area.

▲

The Paint Pros Modify Their Art

There are many advanced editing features available inside Paint that you'll want to study after you've mastered the basic drawing tools described in the previous tasks. You already know enough to draw virtually anything you'll ever want to draw; the Image menu, however, contains additional commands that go far beyond the fundamental drawing capabilities offered by the toolbox.

The Image | Flip/Rotate command lets you rotate the drawing area. The Flip and Rotate dialog box, shown in Figure 8.9, lets you determine whether or not you want to completely reverse the image horizontally, vertically, or by a specific number of degrees.

FIGURE 8.9

The Flip and Rotate dialog box controls the direction and amount of rotation

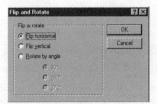

The Image | Stretch/Skew command produces a dialog box that lets you stretch the entire drawing area (or the selected area) by a certain number of degrees. By skewing or stretching an image, you can add snowy and wavy special effects to your artwork.

Artists understand better than computer book authors what color inversion is all about. All colors have complementary colors. (The red compliments the blue by telling blue how nice he looks, or something like that!) A complementary color is an offsetting color that is a color's opposite in the color spectrum; white's complement is black, for example. Artists and designers use color charts and color wheels to determine complementary colors when they need to produce offsetting colors in a painting or a room. Paint complements all colors in the drawing area or within the selected area if you select Image | Invert Colors.

The Image | Attributes menu command lets you change the size of a drawing area. Image | Attributes displays the Attributes dialog box that determines how large (you specify either in inches, centimeters, or pixels [drawing points] depending on the option you select) you want the drawing area to be. In effect, the Attributes dialog box determines the size of your drawing paper. If you want to draw in shades of black and white (as you would do if you were going to print the image on a black and white printer), you would want to create the drawing in black, white, and shades of gray. This helps you know by looking at the screen what the drawing will look like when it's printed.

Summary

This hour showed you three desktop accessory programs. Although Windows 95 is an operating system, the Windows 95 accessory programs are helpful while you perform routine tasks on your PC.

Calculator offers standard and scientific calculations. WordPad gives you introductory word processing features that let you create documents containing special formatting. Paint enables you to draw colorful pictures and save them as desktop wallpaper.

Workshop

Term Review

anchor position   The starting coordinate pair of lines and other geometric shapes.

Coordinate   A point position on the screen defined by a coordinate pair.

coordinate pair   A pair of numbers in which the first represents the number of drawing points from the left edge of the drawing area of an image, and the second represents the number of drawing from the top edge of the drawing area. In Paint, the coordinates appear on the status bar.

Font   A specific typestyle. Fonts have names that distinguish them from one another. Some fonts are fancy and others are plain.

Pixel   Stands for *picture element*. A pixel is the smallest addressable dot on your screen.

Point   A measurement of 1/72 of an inch (72 points equals one inch). Most computer onscreen and printed text measures from 9 to 12 points in size.

print preview   A full-screen representation of how your document will look when you print the document.

running total   The calculator maintains a constant display. For example, if the display contains the value 87 and you press the plus sign and then press 5, the calculator adds the 5 to the 87 and produces the sum of 92.

scientific calculator   A Windows 95 calculator that supports trigonometric, scientific, and number-conversion operations.

Series   A set of values on which you perform statistical operations.

standard calculator   A Windows 95 calculator that performs common mathematical operations.

statistics box   A box that holds your entered series of statistical values. (The calculator's display can hold only a single value at a time.)

toolbox   Paint's collection of drawing, coloring, and painting tools.

thumbnail sketch   A small representation that shows the overall layout without showing a lot of detail.

Q&A

Q Why can't I read all the text on the Print Preview?

A The Print Preview feature was not designed to let you read text necessarily. The Print Preview feature simply draws a representation of your document when you print the document on the printer. Instead of printing the document and discovering there is a margin or formatting error, you can often find the errors via the Print Preview screen, so you can correct the problem before printing the document.

Q I'm no artist, so why should I learn Paint?

A As previously stated, there are many applications that combine text and graphics. In the world of communications, which ranges from business to politics, pictures can convey the same meaning as thousands of words can. Graphics catch people's attention more quickly than text. When you combine the details that text provides with the attention-grabbing effect of graphics, you're sure to have an audience.

There are many other graphical reasons to master Paint as well. You might want to use Paint to produce these graphic publications: flyers for volunteer or professional organizations, holiday greetings, letters that include drawings by the kids, sale notices for posting on bulletin boards, and perhaps the best reason to learn to use Paint: It's fun!

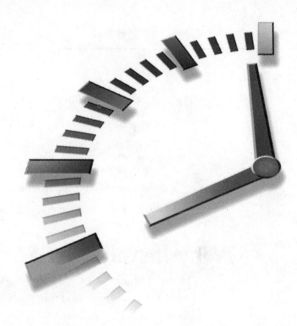

HOUR 9

Adding Programs to Windows 95

With only Windows 95, you would not be productive with your PC. You use your PC for getting work done, and that means you must add application programs, such as financial analysis, home inventory, and game programs. The best hardware is worthless without programs to drive that hardware. Over the life of your PC you'll purchase and install numerous application programs to do the work you want done. Whether you use a PC for word processing, for accounting, for home finances, for games, or for reference, you need to understand how to install the software you obtain.

This lesson teaches you how to put software you purchase onto your PC. Although *de facto* standards exist, not all software installs the same way. You might have purchased a PC loaded with Windows and application software, but you'll soon find other programs you want to use. You must install those programs before you can use them. Therefore, you should know what to expect before you face the task required of all PC owners: software installation.

The highlights of this hour include

- Why proper installation is critical
- How to use the Add/Remove Programs dialog box effectively
- Where to go when you need to add or remove a Windows option
- How to perform proper uninstallation of programs
- What to do when no adequate uninstall procedure exists

Why Install New Software?

By itself, Windows 95 does not do work for you. Your application programs do your work. You use application programs to write documents, create graphics, explore the Internet, manage database files, and play games. Somehow you have to get application programs onto your PC. Although Windows 95 comes with some applications (as described in the previous hour), you'll often add your own applications.

Today's programs come on CD-ROMs (or, rarely, on disk), and you must run those programs through an *installation routine* so that Windows properly recognizes the programs. Although every application program requires a unique, one-of-a-kind installation routine, you'll install most of today's programs the same way.

The Add/Remove Program Icon

In the MS-DOS computing environment that existed before Windows, you could add a program to your computer simply by copying a file from the diskette you purchased to your hard disk. To remove the program, you only had to delete the file. Things got messier starting with Windows, however, because Windows requires a lot from application programs. Those programs are no longer simple to add or remove, so you must familiarize yourself with the proper techniques. Fortunately, Windows 95 introduced new software-installation features that help streamline your work.

If you don't follow the proper program-installation techniques, your application probably will not run correctly. Even worse, with Windows 95's integrated set of files, a program you add to your PC incorrectly might make other programs fail.

The Windows 95 Start menu's Control Panel contains an entry you'll frequently visit to manage the programs on your PC. You can display the Control Panel by selecting Settings | Control Panel from the Start menu. The Control Panel contains several program icons you can select to modify the way Windows looks and acts. The installation icon is labeled Add/Remove Programs. When you open the icon, Figure 9.1's tabbed dialog box appears.

FIGURE 9.1

You manage your installed programs from the Add/Remove Program Properties dialog box

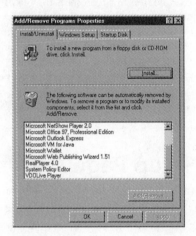

The dialog box's top half contains an Install button that you can click to install new software. Surprisingly, you'll rarely, if ever, use this button when installing Windows programs because most programs install somewhat automatically, as explained later in this hour. Nevertheless, some Windows 95 programs require that you install them using this button, and others without specific instructions often work as well.

The dialog box's lower half contains a list of application programs on your PC. The list is not exhaustive because not every program on your PC appears in the list; the list displays only those programs that you can *uninstall* (or *deinstall*) from your computer system. If you uninstall using the Add/Remove Programs Properties dialog box, you can be assured that the application will completely go away. If you created data files, the uninstall program should leave those on your disk unless otherwise noted.

ICONS AND PROGRAMS

Most icons on your Windows 95 Start menu and desktop represent programs and windows that you open. The icons are often shortcuts to your applications. You can delete the icon without actually deleting the program if the icon represents a shortcut and not the program file itself.

If you delete a program's icon from your desktop by clicking on the icon and pressing the Delete key, the icon goes away but you do not properly remove the program from Windows 95. In most cases, you remove nothing about the program except the shortcut file and icon that point to the actual program.

Sometimes an icon is not a shortcut pointer but represents the file itself, so if you delete the icon in that case, the file goes away as well. Nevertheless, Windows 95 programs most often span multiple files on your system. Some reside in the Windows folder and others in the application's folder; therefore, removing one of these files does not erase all of the application from your disk. In some cases, those extra files can cause problems, and they always consume disk space you'd probably like to recapture.

Therefore, always perform a proper uninstallation when you want to remove a Windows program. This hour's final section discusses uninstallation procedures.

The Windows 95 Setup Page

Click on the Add/Remove Programs Properties dialog box's Windows Setup tab to display Figure 9.2's dialog box page. Unlike applications, you'll never remove Windows 95 because you would be removing the operating system that controls your PC. (You wouldn't sit on the same tree branch you're sawing off, would you?) When you update to Windows 98, the new version replaces Windows 95, but you have plenty of time to worry about that later. For now, the Windows Setup page lets you change Windows 95 options.

FIGURE 9.2

Change Windows 95 settings from the Windows dialog box

Sometimes you rerun an application program's installation routine to change installation settings just as you change Windows 95 settings from the Windows Setup page. Program installations are sometimes the only place where you can modify the program's installed options. When you need to change such programs, you have to run the program's install procedure again (perhaps by clicking the Install button on the Install/Uninstall page), but it doesn't really install a second time. Instead, the program prompts you for changes you want to make to the installation.

If a program stops working properly, you might have to reinstall the program completely. Although you can run the installation again in some cases, you are probably better off uninstalling the program first (to remove all traces of the program) and then running the installation from scratch again. Be sure to back up your data files before you do that so you'll have them intact when you reinstall the program. Some uninstall programs remove all files—including data files associated with an application.

When you make a change to a Windows 95 setting, that setting might not show itself until you restart Windows 95. Most times, Windows 95 alerts you if restarting is necessary. If you make system changes and they don't appear, restarting Windows 95 is a good first step to troubleshooting.

Make sure you know what you're doing before you make a change to Windows 95! The Windows 95 setup is a fairly advanced procedure. If you read somewhere about a Windows 95 accessory program that should be on your system but is not, such as a program called *System Monitor*, you need to change your Windows 95 setup (as explained in the next section) to add that Windows 95 accessory program.

Modifying Your Windows 95 Setup

The next few steps show you how to change Windows 95 installation settings. Various Properties menu options you find throughout Windows 95 let you change settings that affect Windows 95's performance, look, and operation. The Add/Remove Program Properties section on the Windows Setup page lets you add or remove parts of Windows 95 properly.

This task requires your Windows 95 CD-ROM, so place it in your CD-ROM drive. If the Windows 95 banner automatically appears, close the window. If your system did not come with a Windows 95 CD-ROM, the Windows 95 files are probably on your hard disk, and the setup program will get its files there.

To change your Windows 95 installation settings, perform these steps:

1. Open the Control Panel's Add/Remove Programs icon.

2. Click the tab at the top of the dialog box labeled Windows Setup. The Components scrolling list box shows which groups of Windows 95 options are currently installed. An empty check mark option means that none of those options are installed to run. A grayed-out check mark means that some of the programs in the group are installed. A check mark means that the entire group is installed. If you did not install Windows 95, or if you installed it using all the default options, you might not be completely familiar with all the groups that appear.

   The checked options indicate that every program in that group is installed. For example, rarely are all of the Windows 95 Accessories group installed. You'll see a grayed-out check mark there.

3. Click the title for Accessories (if you click the check mark itself, you change the setting) and then click the Details button. You see a scrollable list of Accessories programs (these are the programs that appear when you select the Start menu's Programs | Accessories option) like the one shown in Figure 9.3.

FIGURE 9.3

In this dialog box, you can see which Accessories options are installed

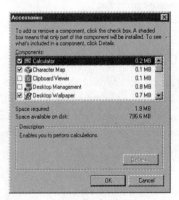

4. Scroll down to the entry titled System Monitor. Rarely do Windows users have this option checked. If you do, uncheck it to remove it from your Windows 95. (You can repeat this task later to put it back.) If your System Monitor is not installed, click to check it.

When you check or uncheck options, Windows 95 does not completely reinstall the selected option; rather, Windows 95 adds or removes the programs necessary to make the changes you request on the Windows Setup page. Whether you install or remove the System Monitor, you see the same procedure occur when you begin the update process in the next step.

5. Click OK to close the Details window.

6. At the Windows Setup page, click OK again to start the Windows setup modification. A dialog box appears, telling you the status of the update. The update can take a while if you were to add or remove several Windows 95 components.

7. Click the Close window button to close the Control Panel. The next time you restart Windows 95, you'll see System Monitor on your Start menu's Programs | Accessories | System Tools menu.

System Monitor is called a *utility program* because the program works in the background letting you analyze the performance of Windows 95 itself. If your PC ever begins to act sluggish, run the System Monitor to see which Windows 95 resources you might need. You might find that you are running too many programs at once, or that you need to add memory to your PC.

Before you install new software, you should make a backup of your system. Hour 12, "System Tools," explains how to use the Windows 95's backup program. Although rare, some software programs can confuse your system and, even if you remove the program, some traces can remain. By restoring your backup, you restore your system files to their pre-installation state.

> If you use a virus-scanning program, you might have to turn off the pro-
> gram during your new application's installation. Some virus-checking pro-
> grams interfere with program installations. Of course, as soon as you finish
> the installation, be sure to run your virus-checking program to ensure that
> the new program did not introduce a virus. (Viruses are virtually non-
> existent in software programs you obtain from reliable sources such as
> major software makers.)

Installing Applications

Almost always, when you purchase a new application program to install on your PC, you
insert its CD-ROM in the drive, close the drive door, and see an automatic message
appear, such as the one in Figure 9.4.

FIGURE 9.4

*Windows like this indi-
cate that an applica-
tion program is about
to install*

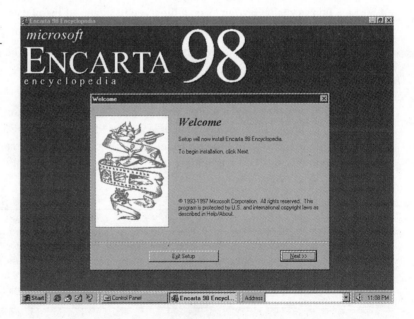

In most cases, such an application checks your PC to see if the program is already
installed. If it is not, the program gives you a prompt like the one in Figure 9.4. The software authors know that you would probably not be inserting the CD-ROM in the drive if
you did not want to install the program.

If the program is already installed, the program begins executing (without the install prompt) after you close your CD-ROM drive's door.

If you insert the CD-ROM and nothing happens, your CD-ROM's *AutoPlay* feature might be turned off so that Windows 95 does not recognize that you've inserted a new CD-ROM. See Hour 22, "Multimedia is Really Here," for AutoPlay setup instructions.

9

If the CD does not start, or if you have AutoPlay off and want to leave it off, you can open the Start menu's Run dialog box and type d:\Setup to begin the installation. (Replace the d: with your CD-ROM's drive name.) Or, if you don't know your drive's name, you can click the Browse button and locate your CD-ROM drive (its icon will have a picture of a CD-ROM) and the Setup.exe file.

For disk installations, you have to insert the first installation disk into the disk drive and type a:\Setup from the Start menu's Run command.

If you get an error message, issue the Start menu's Run command again to make sure you've entered the drive, backslash, and Setup command properly. If you have, your program might require a different command. Replace *Setup* with *Install* to see what happens. If the Run command still fails, you must check the program's owner's manual to locate the correct command.

Each application's setup is different! Therefore, unless every reader has the identical software to install, this book cannot describe every scenario that occurs past the original installation window. Nevertheless, the following list provides guidelines that almost every installation follows:

- You can often read installation notes (from a file often named *Readme.txt or Readme.doc*) by clicking the installation window's appropriate selection.
- Sometimes, multiple installation options are available. Check the printed manual (if one comes with the program) for the installation that suits you if you cannot determine which options are best from the opening window. If an option says *Typical* or *Standard*, that option works best for most situations.

- After you start the installation, a *wizard* (windows that guide you step-by-step through a process) usually guides you step-by-step through the installation.

- You can often accept all installation default answers if you're unsure whether or not to install an option during the wizard's performance. The wizard generally asks questions such as which disk drive and folder you want to install to.

- If you don't have adequate disk space, the installation program tells you. If you don't have the space for it, you have to remove other files, get a bigger disk space, reduce the installation options, or do without the program.

- At the installation's end, you probably have to restart Windows 95 for all the installation options to go into effect. If asked if you want to restart Windows 95, you can answer No, but don't run the installed program until you do restart Windows 95.

Uninstallation Procedures

Most application programs written for Windows 95 include a standard uninstallation routine that removes the application from Windows 95 and from your PC. Remember that an application program is often made up of numerous files. The program's installation routine stores those files in several different locations. Therefore, without an uninstallation routine, removing the application is a tedious task.

Before displaying the Control Panel's Add/Remove Programs window to uninstall a program you've installed, check the menu group in which the program resides. Sometimes, in a program's menu group, the installation routine sets up the uninstallation program that you can run from that group. For example, if you installed a game called Side-to-Side, you might start the game by selecting from a series of Start menus that might look like this: Programs | Side Game | Play Side-to-Side. Look on the same menu and see if there's an uninstall option that you would select, such as Programs | Side Game | Uninstall Side-to-Side. When you begin the uninstallation process, a wizard prompts you through the program's removal.

Without a menu option for the uninstall routine, you should look again to the Control Panel's Add/Remove Programs dialog box. Open the dialog box and scroll through the list of items in the window's lower part to see if the program you want to remove appears in the list. If it does, select that entry and click the Add/Remove button to begin the uninstall wizard.

If no entry appears, you are running out of options! Insert the program's CD-ROM again and see if the opening window contains an uninstall option. If it does not, look through the Readme file to see if you can get help. Also look in the program's owner's manual. Lacking any uninstall routine at all, you can try one more place if you have Internet access: the Web. See if you can find the address for the company's Web page somewhere

in the Readme or owner's manual. Lacking one, try going to the Web address
www.*companyname*.com and see if something comes up. Sometimes the company lists its
Web address in the owner's manual. (If you have no idea how to get on the Web, you'll
learn how starting in Hour 13, "Using the Online Services Window.")

A Last Resort

If your search for an uninstall procedure comes up empty, you are forced to do one of
two things:

- Leave the program on your system if you have ample disk space
- Manually remove as much of the program as you can

That last option can get messy. You need to wait until you master Windows 95 as fully as
possible before you begin to tackle such a task. To remove programs manually, you must
locate the program's files (the Start menu's Find menu option can help) and remove the
program files using Windows Explorer.

> Several software companies offer uninstallation utility programs you can
> purchase that attempt to remove all traces of unwanted programs from
> your disk. If you purchase such a program, the program should be able to
> remove most programs known about before the uninstall product was
> released. As new programs appear on the market, these software companies
> update their uninstallation utility programs, so upgrade the utility to ensure
> that you've got the latest when you need it. (You can often download pro-
> gram updates from the company's Web site.)

Summary

New software that you purchase will come on CDs (or less likely, on disk). Obviously,
you'll need to insert the CD-ROM or disk before you can install the software onto your PC.
Typically, after you insert the program's CD, the installation program automatically begins.

As you learned in this hour, software installation and uninstallation in Windows 95 can
get tricky. Much of the time there's no getting around the fact that installation is not
always simple. Newcomers have a tough time because one of the first tasks they need to
perform after they purchase a new PC is install software, yet software installation sometimes requires some advanced skills! You have to get through the installation to use the
software. Fortunately, more and more software companies are making installations as
hands-off as possible, so software installation should get easier as companies make
smarter install routines.

Workshop

Term Review

AutoPlay   The automatic loading and execution of a CD-ROM or DVD-ROM when you insert the disc in its drive.

installation routine   A procedure that guides you through the process of loading programs onto your PC that were not there before.

uninstall   Also called *deinstall*, describes the removal of programs from your PC.

utility program   A program that monitors, reports, or performs system-level operations on your computer as opposed to an application program, such as a word processor or drawing program, that you use to do work.

Q&A

Q Why don't I ever use the Add/Remove Program dialog box's Install button to install programs?

A Nobody seems to have a good answer for that! It seems as though software companies don't want to access this already-supplied installation resource. If they did, all program installations would basically require the same steps—and, one would think, users would be happier. Nevertheless, the companies seem to prefer that the installation routine begin automatically when users insert the CD-ROM.

The drawback to this approach is that many times such an installation does not work as expected. If this happens, either the AutoPlay feature is turned off or the user bought the program on disk. (No disk drive supports AutoPlay.)

Q Should I turn on AutoPlay so my CDs install automatically?

A As you learned in this hour, even those users with AutoPlay turned on don't always see a proper installation. If your AutoPlay is turned off, keep in mind that several Windows 95 users prefer to turn off AutoPlay (described in Hour 22). These users can insert a CD-ROM at any time without having to wait for a startup or installation window to appear. When they want to see the window or start the program that requires the CD-ROM, they can do so from the Start menu.

Hour **10**

MS-DOS and Windows 95

Don't believe the media…MS-DOS is not dead! As a matter of fact, Windows 95 empowers MS-DOS applications more than any version of Windows has to date.

Not all programs that you run are written for Windows 95 or even for a previous version of Windows. In the past, Windows did not always provide the support that these *MS-DOS programs* required. MS-DOS, which stands for *Microsoft Disk Operating System*, was the industry standard operating system for PCs before Windows came along. MS-DOS and its other incarnations such as PC-DOS (an IBM-only version that was compatible with MS-DOS) were text-based operating systems. It was not until PCs got powerful enough to support a graphical environment that another operating system such as Windows was possible.

Some programs are written specifically for MS-DOS and require that you open an MS-DOS window before you can run the program. Before Windows 95, you sometimes needed to exit Windows completely to run an MS-DOS program. (If you are new to computers, you might want to turn to Appendix A, "Understanding Your Computer," now and review it to get an overview of the basic parts of a computer. See also Chapter 1, "What's Windows 95 All About?")

Virtually every MS-DOS program runs under Windows 95, including many games that were previously off limits to Windows. In addition to handling memory problems that previously plagued MS-DOS programs running inside the Windows environment, Windows 95 provides modern MS-DOS features that will make you think you're running a new version of MS-DOS.

The highlights of this hour include

- When to open more than one MS-DOS session
- How to interpret and use the MS-DOS toolbar
- How to copy and paste between Windows 95 and MS-DOS programs
- Which MS-DOS Command Properties dialog box controls are important
- When to start Windows 95 programs from MS-DOS
- How to run MS-DOS programs from within Windows 95
- How to get started writing MS-DOS programs with QBasic

MS-DOS and Windows 95

If you want to run an MS-DOS program inside Windows 95, you don't have to start MS-DOS first. You can run the program from the Run command on the Start menu (as long as you know the program's path and filename), or you can add the program to one of the Start menu's cascaded menus and click on the program description or program icon.

If you want to load the MS-DOS environment, Windows 95 provides an MS-DOS icon on the Start menu's Programs group. If you click on the MS-DOS icon, the MS-DOS environment runs in a maximized or smaller window (depending on the settings in the Settings | Taskbar properties dialog box).

You can start one or more MS-DOS windows! As a result, you can run several MS-DOS programs at one time, and each multitasks inside its own window, running simultaneously.

Environment Control

In the Windows 95 Shut Down command's dialog box, there is no command to leave Windows 95 and move to an MS-DOS-only environment. In previous versions of Windows, MS-DOS was the controlling environment for Windows; Windows 95 is the controlling environment for MS-DOS so you cannot leave Windows 95 and enter an MS-DOS–only session.

The Shut Down dialog box does provide an option that lets you shut down Windows 95 and start a windowless MS-DOS environment. You would want to enter the MS-DOS environment after shutting down Windows 95 only when you find one of those rare MS-DOS programs that refuses to run under Windows 95.

10

The MS-DOS window is sometimes called a windowed MS-DOS *VM*, which stands for *Virtual Machine*. Each MS-DOS window acts as if that window contains a separate PC that does not interfere with other MS-DOS VM windows.

Task 10.1: Starting an MS-DOS Window

Step 1: Description

To Do

This task shows you how to enter the MS-DOS environment from Windows 95. MS-DOS is simply another application to Windows 95, so starting MS-DOS requires no special skills. The MS-DOS environment is known as the *MS-DOS prompt* in Windows 95 because the MS-DOS prompt collects keystrokes as you type them in an MS-DOS window.

Step 2: Action

1. Open the Start menu.
2. Select Programs.
3. Click on the MS-DOS Prompt icon. The MS-DOS window opens as shown in Figure 10.1. Notice that the MS-DOS window contains a toolbar of icon buttons at the top of the window. Previous versions of Windows did not provide a toolbar for MS-DOS windows.

▼

FIGURE 10.1

The MS-DOS window acts like any other window in Windows 95

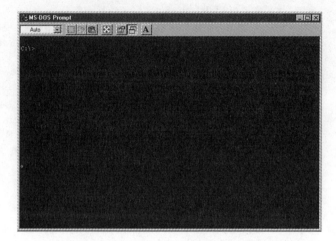

Your MS-DOS window might appear fully maximized or resized differently from the figure's MS-DOS window.

4. You can maximize MS-DOS windows. Click the maximize button (or double-click the title bar) to produce the maximized MS-DOS window.

You can also increase the MS-DOS window to full-screen size by pressing Alt+Enter.

When you increase the MS-DOS window size to full-screen by double-clicking the title bar (or by pressing the Alt+Enter shortcut key), the MS-DOS window toolbar disappears.

5. Press Alt+Enter to resize the MS-DOS window again.

6. Start yet another MS-DOS window by clicking the MS-DOS prompt's icon on the Programs menu.

7. Start one more MS-DOS window. Previous versions of Windows produced several problems when you opened multiple windows, and you could not properly multi-task the MS-DOS windows. Figure 10.2 shows three MS-DOS windows open at one time.

FIGURE 10.2

Multiple DOS windows can be open at one time

10

8. To close an MS-DOS window, you can click the close button in the upper-right corner (unless the MS-DOS window is maximized, in which case you will see no sizing buttons). You also can type EXIT at the MS-DOS command prompt. You can type the EXIT command using either uppercase or lowercase letters. Close two of the open MS-DOS windows now.

Step 3: Review

The MS-DOS command prompt icon on the Programs menu opens the windowed MS-DOS environment. From the MS-DOS command prompt, you can start MS-DOS programs or issue MS-DOS commands. This task left your Windows 95 environment with one open MS-DOS window. The next task lets you practice using the MS-DOS toolbar at the top of that window.

Task 10.2. The MS-DOS Toolbar

Step 1: Description

To Do

This task describes how to use the toolbar that appears on MS-DOS windows. Figure 10.3 shows the toolbar. Previous versions of Windows contained no toolbar. Remember that the toolbar appears only on non-maximized MS-DOS windows. The toolbar is optional, so you can remove the toolbar if you do not want to see it at the top of MS-DOS windows.

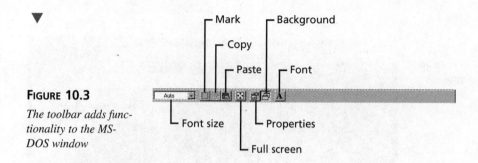

FIGURE 10.3

*The toolbar adds func-
tionality to the MS-
DOS window*

Step 2: Action

1. Click the Font size drop-down list box button (at the far left of the toolbar) to display a scrollable list of font sizes. The values determine the size, in points, of the
text characters on the MS-DOS window. The Auto setting lets Windows 95 determine the best size of the characters and MS-DOS window. If you select a different
font size, the characters inside the window, as well as the window itself, resize to
display the new character point size. If the text inside the MS-DOS window is too
small to read, you might want to select a larger point size. When you change the
font size, Windows 95 resizes the MS-DOS window to show that font more accurately. You can resize MS-DOS windows, but Windows 95 limits the MS-DOS
window size to one, two, or three sizes, depending on the font size you select.

> The double letter *T* next to a font size indicates that the font is a *True Type*
> font. True Type fonts are generally more readable than non-True Type fonts
> and appear the same on both the screen and printer.

2. The Mark tool on the toolbar lets you mark a section of the MS-DOS window to
copy to the Windows 95 Clipboard.

> You can copy MS-DOS data to the Clipboard or paste from the Clipboard.
> You cannot *cut* data from the MS-DOS window.

Issue the DIR command, (for *directory*) at the MS-DOS command prompt to display a directory listing. After you see the directory listing, click the Mark toolbar
button. With your mouse, drag from a point on the MS-DOS window down to a
second point creating a highlighted rectangle, such as one shown in Figure 10.4.

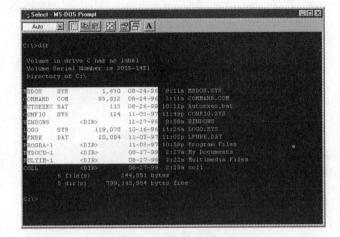

FIGURE 10.4

The highlighted portion of the MS-DOS window is marked for copying

3. Click the Copy toolbar button to send the highlighted MS-DOS data to the Windows 95 Clipboard. As soon as Windows 95 copies the data to the Clipboard, the highlight goes away.

4. To confirm that you copied the data to the Clipboard, start WordPad and select Edit | Paste. The text you highlighted inside the MS-DOS window now appears inside the WordPad window. Terminate WordPad without saving the file.

The font used inside the default MS-DOS window is a *non-proportional font*. Therefore, all character columns in the MS-DOS window consume the same width and all align properly into columns of data. It is possible that your WordPad's default font is set up as a *proportional font* so the data, when pasted into WordPad, does not align in perfect columns as the data does when shown in the MS-DOS window. If you paste MS-DOS data into a word processor and the data does not align correctly, change the font of the pasted data to a non-proportional font such as *Courier*.

5. Although you pasted the marked text into WordPad and closed the WordPad application, the data still resides on the Windows 95 Clipboard. To see that, click the Paste toolbar button. Windows 95 pastes the text into the MS-DOS window at the cursor's location.

The MS-DOS command prompt requires specific commands, and the data you are pasting probably does not fit within the normal MS-DOS command requirements. Therefore, MS-DOS might issue error messages as the data gets pasted back into the window, but you can safely ignore these messages.

▼ 6. Click on the Full Screen toolbar button to maximize the MS-DOS window to full
screen. Issue the DIR command again. A maximized MS-DOS window produces
readable text, although the toolbar and Windows 95 taskbar go away until you
resize the MS-DOS window again.

Press Alt+Enter to resize the MS-DOS window to a non-maximized size.

7. Click the Properties toolbar button to display the MS-DOS Prompt Properties
tabbed dialog box shown in Figure 10.5.

FIGURE 10.5

*The MS-DOS Prompt
Properties dialog box
controls the way MS-
DOS starts and per-
forms*

The MS-DOS Prompt Properties tabbed dialog box contains several settings that
control the way your MS-DOS windows appear and perform. For example, if you
press a shortcut key, such as *D*, at the Shortcut key prompt, you can start the MS-
DOS window by pressing Ctrl+Alt+D from almost anywhere within the Windows
95 environment.

The Run prompt determines how the MS-DOS window appears when you run programs within the window. The drop-down list box contains these three window
size prompts: Normal Window, Minimized, and Maximized.

If you want the MS-DOS window to close when an MS-DOS application finishes,
make sure that the Close on exit option is checked. Most of the time, you'll want
to leave this option checked.

Actually, most of the time you'll want to leave *most* of the MS-DOS Prompt
Properties tabbed dialog box settings alone. The default settings almost
always make MS-DOS windows perform the way you want them to.

▼

▼ 8. Clicking the Change Icon command button produces the interesting horizontally
        scrolling dialog box shown in Figure 10.6. If you want a different icon to appear
        next to the MS-DOS taskbar when running MS-DOS programs, select a different
        icon from the scrolling list of icons and click OK.

FIGURE 10.6

*You can change the
icon that appears on
the taskbar for an MS-
DOS window*

9. The remaining tabbed dialog box options are fairly advanced and are usually set to
    appropriate values. There are a couple you should know about now, however.

    Click the Screen tab to display a dialog box that controls the way the MS-DOS
    screen appears to the user. Figure 10.7 shows this dialog box.

FIGURE 10.7

*The screen options
determine how
Windows 95 displays
the MS-DOS window*

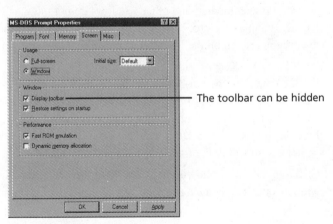

The toolbar can be hidden

If you uncheck the Display toolbar option, Windows 95 does not display the toolbar in the MS-DOS window. If you want the MS-DOS window to appear maximized when Windows 95 first displays the window (you can still resize the maximized window by pressing Alt+Enter), select the Full-screen option.

10

> Although you lose some MS-DOS functionality when you remove the tool-bar, you gain extra MS-DOS window space that otherwise is taken up by the toolbar.

10. Click the Misc tab to see another dialog box that controls several miscellaneous MS-DOS window options. You can control whether or not the Windows 95 screen saver is active during the MS-DOS session. (Some MS-DOS programs make the Windows 95 screen saver program think that no keyboard action has taken place and will trigger the Windows 95 screen saver, even when you are actively working inside the MS-DOS mode.)

    You can also see where to determine which Windows 95 shortcut keys are active inside MS-DOS. By default, all Windows 95 shortcut keys are active inside the MS-DOS window, and you should not change these settings without good reason.

    Close the tabbed dialog box now that you've reviewed the highlights of the MS-DOS properties.

11. The Background toolbar button, when clicked, makes your MS-DOS program run in the background, and when clicked again, makes your MS-DOS program run in the foreground. When in the foreground, the MS-DOS program maintains complete control of the computer, and other windows do not multitask at the same time MS-DOS is running. You would only run your MS-DOS program in the foreground if the program relied on the PC's internal clock for accurate timing, as some games require.

    Click on the Font toolbar button to display the Font dialog box from the MS-DOS Command Prompt. Figure 10.8 shows the dialog box that appears when you click the Font button. The Font dialog box lets you control the size and format of the font used inside the MS-DOS window. (The Font size drop-down list box discussed earlier controls only the font size, but not the format.)

    Click the OK command button to get rid of the dialog box. Leave the MS-DOS window open for the next section.

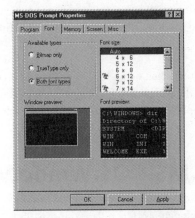

FIGURE 10.8

The Font dialog box lets you control the way characters appear inside the MS-DOS window

Although you rarely find such programs, some older MS-DOS programs and very advanced MS-DOS–based games will refuse to run if the program detects Windows 95 running. You can fool these programs into running anyway by right-clicking over their Explorer icon, selecting Properties from the pop-up menu, clicking the Program tab, and clicking the option labeled Suggest MS-DOS mode as necessary. Although some programs *might* still refuse to run because of a memory conflict, most programs will execute after using this trick even though Windows 95 is also running.

MS-DOS Commands Operate Well

The Windows 95 version of MS-DOS commands are updated to reflect the Windows 95 environment. The DIR command works in Windows 95 just as it did in previous versions of Windows and MS-DOS, except you'll see a new column to the right of the listing that contains long filenames for the files in the listing. In a directory listing, for example, you can see a file with the long name such as Exit to dos.PIF and a regular MS-DOS name of EXITTO~1.PIF. MS-DOS displays both the long and short names together in the listing.

Windows 95 uses the same internal file structure as previous versions of Windows; when you create a long filename, Windows 95 automatically converts that filename to a unique name that fits within the older (pre-Windows 95) naming convention of eight characters with a three-character extension. The DIR command lets you see both the real internal filename and the long filename that you see in Windows 95 dialog boxes.

Another MS-DOS command that you might want to use with long filenames is the COPY command. Although the following COPY command would never have worked with previous versions of Windows due to the long filenames, it works just fine in Windows 95:

```
COPY "My August sales report" "Old report"
```

(The quotation marks are required when using long filenames that contain embedded spaces.) This command copies the file named My August sales report to a file named Old report so that, at the completion of the copy, two identical files exist on your computer.

Wrapping Up the MS-DOS Window

Over time, you'll run across several items in the MS-DOS window that you'll find interesting. Here's something fun you can try: Open the Windows 95 Explorer program and resize the window so you can see both the Explorer window and the MS-DOS window. Find a filename in Explorer's right window and drag that filename to the MS-DOS prompt. As soon as you release the mouse button, the filename, including its complete drive and pathname, appears at the MS-DOS prompt!

When managing files in the MS-DOS environment, you can drag filenames from Explorer and other Windows 95 Open dialog boxes instead of typing the complete disk, path, and filename. When working inside MS-DOS windows, you can drag the file from the Windows 95 environment, and Windows 95 substitutes the filename at the cursor. For example, if you are in the middle of a COPY command, you could drag filenames from Explorer to complete the COPY command instead of typing the names.

In addition, Windows 95 has changed the CD command (*Change Directory*). As you might know, the following command moves you up one parent directory level:

```
cd ..
```

If you are buried deep within several levels of directories while in an MS-DOS session, you can add extra periods to the CD command for each directory you want to return back to. The following command returns you to the directory three levels above the current directory:

```
CD ....
```

As always, the following command takes you to the root directory no matter how many directory levels deep you are in:

```
cd \
```

Starting Programs in MS-DOS

The MS-DOS window is so fully integrated into Windows 95 that you can execute Windows 95 programs *from the MS-DOS prompt*. Therefore, if you know the filename of a Windows 95 program and you're working inside an MS-DOS window, you do not have to return to Windows 95 to execute a Windows 95 program.

Although Notepad makes an MS-DOS editor redundant and unnecessary, MS-DOS has supplied a text editor since version 1.0 of MS-DOS. There are many MS-DOS die-hards who still want to edit text files from within the MS-DOS environment.

When the Microsoft programmers wrote Windows 95, they decided to update an old stand-by program, the MS-DOS text editor, to implement the long filenames and modernize the performance of the program. If you have used an MS-DOS text editor, such as EDIT, you'll feel right at home with the updated version of EDIT included with Windows 95 (its screen is shown in Figure 10.9).

10

FIGURE 10.9

The Windows 95 text editor, EDIT, is included with Windows 95

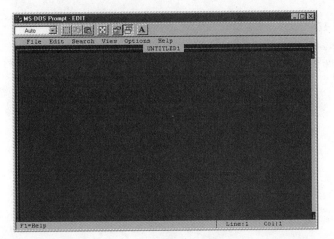

This hour does not explain EDIT because the Windows 95 Notepad program replaces EDIT. Notepad, which is a Windows-based text editor, is a Windows 95 program that makes the MS-DOS editor obsolete, except to those who prefer the older editor.

If you want to start MS-DOS in a specific directory, display the MS-DOS Properties dialog box (by clicking the Properties MS-DOS toolbar button); then type the directory's pathname at the option labeled Working.

If you use DOSKEY (the program that lets you more easily edit previously-issued MS-DOS commands), you can make Windows 95 automatically run the DOSKEY program by entering DOSKEY at the Program dialog box's Batch File prompt. (The Program dialog box is located inside the Properties dialog box).

In some cases, an MS-DOS program will refuse to run if you are running a Windows 95 screen saver. Follow these steps to allow the screen saver to work along with such a program:

1. Open Explorer.

2. Locate the MS-DOS program's icon.

3. Right-click over the icon.

4. Select Properties from the icon's menu.

5. Click the Misc tab to display the Misc dialog box shown in Figure 10.10.

FIGURE 10.10

Letting a screen saver work with an MS-DOS program

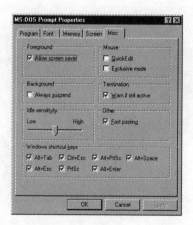

6. Click the option labeled Allow screen saver. Windows then devotes additional screen resources to the MS-DOS program.

7. Close the dialog box. The program should now let the screen saver work in conjunction with the MS-DOS program.

QBasic is Hidden but Still There!

If you have ever wondered what writing a program is like, you can give it a try with Windows 95. Windows 95 includes a programming language called *QBasic*. Many programmers got their start writing simple QBasic programs. QBasic is a programming language designed for text environments. You cannot write Windows 95 programs with QBasic but you can run QBasic programs inside an MS-DOS window and learn the fundamentals of programming.

Learning programming takes some time and effort. If you begin with a simple programming language, such as QBasic, you can avoid wading through a complicated windowed environment, and you can concentrate just on the programming language. If you want to try QBasic, you need to insert your Windows 95 CD-ROM, start Explorer, and copy the two files that begin with "Qbasic" from the CD-ROM's \Other\oldmsdos folder to your \Windows\Command folder.

To start QBasic, select the Start menu's Run menu, type **QBASIC**, and press Enter. QBasic begins with a Parameter dialog box. You can click OK to close it, and QBasic actually begins as shown in Figure 10.11.

10

FIGURE 10.11

QBasic appears on the Windows 95 CD-ROM

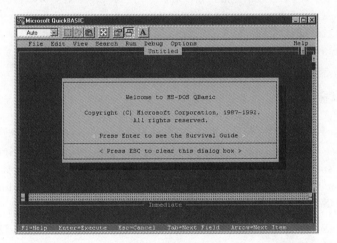

 If you want to learn how to write programs in QBasic, check out *Qbasic by Example*, Que Publishing, ISBN 1-565-29439-4.

Press Esc to remove the opening instruction screen and begin programming. When you finish, you can select File | Exit to return to Windows 95.

Summary

This hour focused on the MS-DOS environment inside Windows 95. Although Windows 95 users often work far from the MS-DOS text-based environment of olden days, the MS-DOS environment is still alive and well due to the many programs still in use today that are written for MS-DOS.

Windows 95 supports MS-DOS programs better than any previous versions of Windows. Windows 95 provides more memory for programs and allows you to open several multi-tasking MS-DOS programs at one time. In addition, Windows 95 adds a toolbar to MS-DOS windows that makes the management of your MS-DOS windows and programs much easier.

There are people who will work many hours a day with Windows 95 and never need to start the MS-DOS environment. Others still use older MS-DOS programs and current-day games that run only under MS-DOS. Because of the extra memory and runtime support provided by Windows 95, these MS-DOS programs should work comfortably inside Windows 95.

Workshop

Term Review

MS-DOS command prompt   When you work in an MS-DOS window, you must issue commands to the MS-DOS environment. The command prompt, usually shown on the screen as C:\> (indicating the current default drive and directory), accepts your MS-DOS commands as you type the commands.

MS-DOS program   A program written specifically for the MS-DOS environment. MS-DOS programs (unlike Windows 95 programs) do not provide a graphical interface.

non-proportional font   A font that contains characters where each character consumes the same width on the screen or printer.

proportional font   A font that generally makes for a more natural appearance of text. The letters within the text do not all consume the same screen width. For example, the lowercase letter *i* consumes less space than the uppercase *M*.

True Type font   A font that is generally more readable than a non-True Type font, and appears the same on both the screen and printer.

VM   Stands for *Virtual Machine*. Each MS-DOS window acts as if that window contains a separate PC that does not interfere with other MS-DOS VM windows.

Q&A

Q Why would I want to shut Windows 95 down to the MS-DOS environment?

A There are still a handful of programs written for the MS-DOS environment that will not run under Windows 95. Microsoft wrote Windows 95 to run most MS-DOS programs, even the ones that previous versions of Windows could not handle. Although the majority of MS-DOS programs work well under Windows 95, the few that do not will run as long as you shut down Windows 95 and restart (via the Shut Down menu command) your computer in the MS-DOS mode.

Q When would I want to start more than one MS-DOS window?

A If you want to run two or more MS-DOS programs at once, such as two games (whether or not you are also running Windows 95 programs), the multiple MS-DOS windows let both of the MS-DOS programs work in a multitasking mode. Each window works independently of the other(s).

Q Why would I execute a Windows 95 program from the MS-DOS prompt?

A Users of previous Windows versions found that they often wanted to execute a Windows program from the MS-DOS prompt but, until Windows 95, they were unable to do that. Perhaps you like to use an MS-DOS bookkeeping system and you suddenly want to use a calculator. If you know the Windows 95 calculator's filename, CALC (with the extension .EXE), you can type that filename (precede the filename with the file's disk drive name and pathname), such as typing `c:\windows\calc`, and the program starts immediately (your MS-DOS window still remains open as well). You don't have to type the .EXE filename extension.

Q If I like the Windows 95 Notepad program, is there any need to learn the MS-DOS editor?

A Not really. The MS-DOS editor might be good to use if you're already familiar with previous versions of the MS-DOS editor such as MS-DOS 5 and MS-DOS 6's EDIT programs. You'll find that Microsoft implemented needed changes to EDIT without changing the fundamental purpose of the MS-DOS text editor.

10

Hour 11

Aid via the Accessibility Options

This hour describes all the Windows 95 tools that provide help for users with special needs. Previous operating environments did not support these kinds of user options. Windows 95's *accessibility options* change the behavior of the keyboard, screen, and speakers so that they operate differently from their default behaviors.

Microsoft designed Windows 95 so that everybody can take advantage of the new operating environment. In addition to helping those people who need extra assistance, the accessibility options can also help users who do not normally need special help with their hardware and software. For example, if you have temporarily disconnected your speakers from your computer, you might want to turn on the visual feedback options so that sounds that normally activate the speaker appear on the screen as flashing icons instead.

The highlights of this chapter include:

- Which accessibility options might benefit you
- How to change the keyboard's response so that combination keystrokes are easier to type
- How visual clues can replace audible signals and alarms
- How to set the screen's display so that you read enlarged letters, icons, title bars, and high-contrasting screen colors
- How to make the keyboard respond as if you were moving and clicking the mouse

The Accessibility Options

The Accessibility Options tabbed dialog box contains settings for the accessibility options that you might want to set up for your Windows 95 environment. All of the accessibility options are available from this dialog box. You can set any or all of the accessibility options from the Accessibility Options tabbed dialog box.

When you double-click the Accessibility Options icon from the Control Panel, you see the Accessibility Properties tabbed dialog box shown in Figure 11.1.

FIGURE 11.1

Set one or more accessibility options from this tabbed dialog box

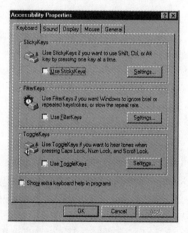

This hour approaches things a little differently from the others. Table 11.1 contains a list of every accessibility option available in Windows 95. The rest of the chapter describes, using the task approach, how to access and use each of these accessibility options.

TABLE 11.1 THE ACCESSIBILITY OPTIONS

Option	Description
Accessibility TimeOut	When the computer sits idle for a preset period of time, the accessibility options revert to their default state.
Accessibility status	A graphical display of icons that describe which accessibility indicator options are turned on at any given time.
BounceKeys	Keeps users from producing double-keystrokes if they accidentally bounce keys several times in succession.
Customizable	You can change the mouse pointer to make the cursor easier to see. (Hour 4, "Understanding the My Computer Window," explained how to change the mouse cursor.)
FilterKeys	The group of keystroke aids that include RepeatKeys and BounceKeys.
High-contrast	By changing the Windows 95 color scheme to a different color scheme set, you can make the screen's color contrast more obvious and discernible for people with impaired vision. (Hour 7, "Manage Your Desktop," explained how to change the Windows 95 color schemes.)
High-contrast mode	In addition to offering adjustable high-contrast color schemes, Windows 95 can also ensure that applications adjust themselves to display the highest possible contrast so that visually impaired users will be able to distinguish between background and foreground screen elements.
MouseKeys	Lets you simulate mouse movements and clicks using the keyboard.
RepeatKeys	Users can turn on or off the repetition of keys so that holding down a key does not necessarily repeat that keystroke.
Scalable user	Each of the system fonts, scroll bars, title bars, and menu interface elements options can be set to a larger size.
SerialKeys	Lets the user use a nonkeyboard input device.
ShowSounds	Provides visual feedback on the screen when applications produce sounds.
SlowKeys	Windows 95 can disregard keystrokes that are not held down for a preset time period. This aids users who often accidentally press keys.
SoundSentry	Sends a visual clue when Windows 95 beeps the speaker (in the case of warning and error message dialog boxes).

11

continues

TABLE 11.1   CONTINUED

Option	Description
StickyKeys	Lets the user press the *modifier keys* (the Shift, Ctrl, or Alt keys) individually instead of having to press them using combined keystrokes. Therefore, the user can press Alt, release Alt, and *then* press C instead of combining the two for Alt+C.
ToggleKeys	Sounds a noise on the speaker when the user presses the CapsLock, NumLock, or ScrollLock keys to make them active.

Task 11.1: Controlling the StickyKey Actions

Step 1: Description

Users who need help with the keyboard can set the keyboard options to take advantage of the StickyKeys, FilterKeys, and ToggleKeys options. After you request the keyboard help, you then can use the modified keyboard to set the other options. This task explains how to set up and use the StickyKeys feature.

Step 2: Action

1. Display the Accessibility Properties tabbed dialog box by opening the Control Panel and double-clicking the Accessibility Options icon.

2. Make sure the tab marked Keyboard is selected.

3. Click the Settings command button inside the StickyKeys section at the top of the dialog box. You'll see the dialog box shown in Figure 11.2.

FIGURE 11.2

The settings available for StickyKeys

4. Click the top option to turn on the shortcut key for StickyKeys. After you set this option, you can turn on and off the StickyKeys by pressing the Shift key five times.

> If you share your computer with other users, both you and others can quickly turn on and off the StickyKeys feature by pressing the Shift key five times without having to return to the Control Panel again.

5. If you check Press Modifier Key Twice to Lock, Windows 95 activates the modifier keys if you press any of them twice in a row. For example, instead of having to press the Ctrl key and then P while still holding Ctrl, you can press Ctrl twice to lock the Ctrl key in place, and then press P by itself to simulate the Ctrl+P keystroke. This keystroke locking feature lets users who can type only one keystroke at a time issue combination keystrokes. (Some users must type by pressing the keys with a pencil.)

   After turning on StickyKeys, you need to decide how you want the StickyKeys feature turned off. As just mentioned, you can toggle the StickyKeys on and off using a multi-Shift keypress, but there's an even better way. If you check Turn StickyKeys Off If Two Keys Are Pressed at Once, the StickyKeys feature stays active as long as you press the modifier keys individually without combining them and their matching keys. In other words, the StickyKeys feature stays on as long as you keep pressing the modifier keys by themselves. If you (or someone else who comes along) press Ctrl+P (or any other modifier keystroke combination) at the same time using a single keypress, Windows 95 turns off the StickyKeys feature.

   There are two final options: Make Sounds When Modifier Key Is Pressed and Show StickyKeys Status on Screen. These options determine whether or not Windows 95 sounds a beep on the speaker when you press a modifier key and whether or not Windows 95 displays a StickyKeys icon next to the taskbar clock when StickyKeys is active. These signals aid users who want audible or visual StickyKeys feedback. The taskbar icon changes when you press a modifier key.

   For this task, check every option on the Settings screen so you can practice using the StickyKeys feature. Click the OK button to return to the Accessibility Options tabbed dialog box. Don't check the Use StickyKeys option now, but click the OK button. If you check the Use StickyKeys option, Windows 95 immediately turns on StickyKeys, but you're going to turn on the feature differently in the next step.

6. Press the Shift key five times. When you do, you see a dialog box that reminds you of the StickyKeys feature. Click OK to finish activating StickyKeys. Not only do you then hear an audible sound that indicates StickyKeys is active, but you also see a StickyKeys indicator on the taskbar.

11

If you right-click the taskbar's icon, Windows 95 displays a pop-up menu from which you can adjust the StickyKeys settings. If you select Show Status Window, Windows 95 displays a pop-up dialog box on the screen that displays the accessibility options icons using a larger icon size than what appears on the taskbar.

7. Start WordPad by clicking the WordPad icon on the Programs | Accessories menu.

8. Press the Shift key (either the left or right Shift) and release the key. You'll hear an audible signal. You've now locked the Shift key for the next keystroke. Press the A key. An uppercase A appears at the cursor's location. You have not locked the Shift key however. Press the A key again and you'll see a lowercase a appear. Press Shift again, release Shift, and press B to see the uppercase B appear. Press B again to see a lowercase b appear.

You can keep pressing any modifier key, Alt, Ctrl, or Shift, to lock that modifier key before pressing the next key.

9. Now press Shift+A using a normal, single, combination keystroke. Not only does an uppercase A appear, *but you also turn off the StickyKeys feature.* Remember that you earlier checked the option labeled Turn StickyKeys off if two keys are pressed at once. Therefore, when you press a normal combination keystroke using one of the modifier keys, Windows 95 turns off StickyKeys.

Two users can now share the StickyKeys feature. One can turn on StickyKeys by pressing Shift five times. A second user who does not need StickyKeys does not have to worry about turning off the feature; as soon as the second user presses a combined modifier keystroke as usual, Windows 95 automatically turns off StickyKeys.

If you find yourself needing to use StickyKeys only occasionally, *don't* check Turn StickyKeys Off If Two Keys Are Pressed at Once. Force yourself to turn on and off StickyKeys consciously by pressing Shift five times. If you don't, you'll find yourself inadvertently turning off StickyKeys the first time you combine a modifier key with another key.

Step 3: Review

StickyKeys determines how you want Windows 95 to recognize modifier keys. For users who can type only one keystroke at a time, the StickyKeys feature lets those users press and release Alt, Ctrl, or Shift *before* their counterpart keystrokes. Therefore, for example, to type a capital letter, these users can press Shift, release Shift, and *then* press the letter they want to be capitalized.

Task 11.2: Controlling FilterKey and ToggleKey Actions

Step 1: Description

Inadvertent errors can occur when users hold keys down too long or press keys using a bouncing motion that often doubles or triples keystrokes. Windows 95 supports the use of FilterKeys to control some of the extra keystrokes that result from certain unintended actions. This task explains how to set up and control FilterKeys.

Step 2: Action

1. Display the Accessibility Properties tabbed dialog box by opening the Control Panel and double-clicking the Accessibility Options icon.
2. Make sure the tab marked Keyboard is selected.
3. Click the Settings command button inside the FilterKeys section of the dialog box. You'll see the dialog box shown in Figure 11.3.

FIGURE 11.3

The settings available for FilterKeys

4. Check Use Shortcut so that you can turn on and off the FilterKeys aid by pressing and holding down the right Shift key for eight seconds.

5. The Ignore Repeated Keystrokes option requests that Windows 95 ignore bounced keys that sometimes result in two or three repeated letters appearing on a line, such as in *theese wooordss*. The feature that controls these repeated keystrokes is called BounceKey. Certainly, you don't want Windows 95 to prevent you from typing double letters, because many words, such as *book* and *puppy*, require double letter combinations. Windows 95 initially sets a fairly long pause rate between letters. Therefore, depending on your typing skills, you might need to adjust the setting to control Windows 95's interpretation of double letters (so that it recognizes them as double letters in a word rather than incorrectly repeated letters that occur due to bounced keys). You can press the Settings command button to change the delay between accidental double keystrokes.

6. The option labeled Ignore Quick Keystrokes and Slow Down the Repeat Rate controls the RepeatKeys and SlowKeys features. There might be some users who accidentally press keystrokes from time to time. By checking this option, you can keep Windows 95 from receiving these accidental keystrokes as actual keystrokes; if a key is accidentally held down too long, you minimize the repeated keystrokes that would occur.

The two options described in Steps 5 and 6 are *mutually exclusive*; meaning that you can set either one option or the other. Therefore, you can activate either the BounceKeys feature or you can activate the RepeatKeys and SlowKeys features.

7. If you check Beep When Keys Are Pressed or Selected, Windows 95 beeps whenever it recognizes a valid keystroke. If you select Show FilterKey Status on Screen, Windows 95 displays a stopwatch icon on the taskbar when the FilterKey option is active. Click OK to close the window.

If you right-click the taskbar's icon, Windows 95 displays a pop-up menu from which you can adjust the FilterKeys settings.

8. If you select the ToggleKeys feature, Windows 95 sounds a high beep when you activate the CapsLock, NumLock, or ScrollLock keys and sounds a low beep when you press these keys again to turn them off. Select the ToggleKeys feature now from the Accessibility Options dialog box. Press CapsLock once to turn on the CapsLock key and you'll hear a high beep. Press CapsLock again to hear the low beep meaning that the second CapsLock keypress deactivated CapsLock.

9. Some Windows 95 programs contain their own accessibility options keyboard features and display onscreen help related to their special keys. If you want to see this help in such programs, check Show Extra Keyboard Help in Programs. Windows 95 informs all Windows 95 programs you run that you've selected this option, and those programs will respond with appropriate help when available.

Step 3: Review

The keyboard accessibility options change the behavior and functionality of keystrokes. The three modifier keys receive the most attention because they often require a double keypress that some users are not able to perform. The other keyboard accessibility options control accidental keystrokes to keep Windows 95 from recognizing bad keystrokes as valid.

Task 11.3: Controlling the Sound Accessibility Options

Step 1: Description

The Accessibility Options icon's Sound dialog box controls the features of the SoundSentry and ShowSounds accessibility options. These options provide visual feedback that some users require to let them know that certain audible sounds occurred. For instance, if a user cannot always hear the usual warning sounds an application makes when the wrong key is pressed, the user can request that Windows 95 display a visual clue that a sound was made.

Step 2: Action

1. Display the Accessibility Properties tabbed dialog box by opening the Control Panel and double-clicking the Accessibility Options icon.

2. Select the tab marked Sound. You'll see the dialog box shown in Figure 11.4.

FIGURE 11.4

The Sound accessibility options dialog box provides visual sound clues

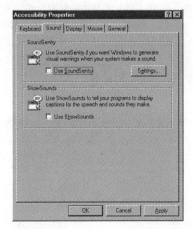

11

▼ After you activate the SoundSentry feature, Windows 95 flashes a title bar or
   another part of the screen when an application makes a sound.

> You can control which visual clue Windows 95 uses for sounds by clicking
> the Settings command button to display the SoundSentry dialog box.

3. If you click the ShowSounds check box, Windows 95 turns on the ShowSounds
   option supported by some Windows 95 programs.

> The SoundSentry and ShowSounds features can help you if you are hearing
> impaired, work in a quiet environment where sounds might disrupt others,
> or work in a noisy environment where you cannot always hear your comput-
> er's sounds.

Many applications produce sounds, such as music and speech, that some users cannot hear. By turning on the ShowSounds option, you request that Windows 95 produce visual clues whenever an application sounds from the speaker.

If you want to turn on the ShowSounds feature, now you can. Click OK to close
the dialog box and, if you have some kind of playback device such as a sound
card, double-click the Sounds icon inside the Control Panel. Select a sound and
click the playback button to hear an audible sound, as well as see a visual representation of that sound.

Step 3: Review

Use the ShowSounds and SoundSentry options when you need visual clues for the
sounds that applications produce. This task explained how to turn on and control these
▲ features.

Task 11.4: Controlling the Display

Step 1: Description

This task explains how to change the display to increase the contrast Windows 95 uses so
that people with vision impairments can see the screen more easily. Windows 95 can
change the contrast and letter size using the high-contrast mode.

▼ Step 2: Action

1. Display the Accessibility Properties tabbed dialog box by opening the Control Panel and double-clicking the Accessibility Options icon.

2. Select the tab marked Display. You'll see the dialog box shown in Figure 11.5.

FIGURE 11.5

FIGURE 11.5

The Display accessibility option dialog box provides a high-contrast view of the screen

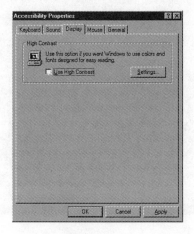

3. Click the Use High Contrast option to turn on the high-contrast feature. Windows 95 displays all dialog boxes, menus, and screen colors using a readable and legible display. Although you can click the Settings button to change the high-contrast settings, the default settings often suffice nicely. Windows 95 also turns on the scalable user interface elements to make icons, title bars, and text easier to read.

> The shortcut key for the high-contrast feature is Left Alt+Left Shift+PrtScr. You can turn the high-contrast feature on or off by pressing Left Alt+Left Shift+PrtScr.

> When you use the high-contrast option, Windows 95 increases the size of icons, menus, and screen elements. Although these elements are easier to decipher by reading the descriptions beneath icons and on title bars, the terms are often abbreviated because of their large size.

4. Click the OK command button. Windows 95 instantly changes the display to a high-contrast screen such as the one shown in Figure 11.6. The high-contrast mode stays on for subsequent startups of Windows 95.

▼

▼

FIGURE **11.6**

Windows 95 made this screen more readable using the high-contrast mode

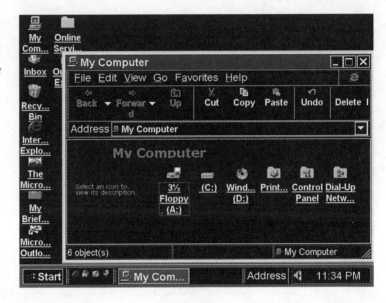

Step 3: Review

▲

If you need extra help reading the screen, you can turn on the accessibility options high-contrast option to increase the size of title bars, menus, and other screen elements, as well as change the color contrast to distinguish between screen elements more easily.

Task 11.5: Controlling the MouseKeys Feature

Step 1: Description

The MouseKeys feature lets you simulate mouse movements and mouse clicks using the numeric keypad on your keyboard. If you have trouble using the mouse or if you sometimes work with a laptop that has no mouse, you might want to turn on the MouseKeys feature.

> If your mouse quits working, you can still use Windows 95 effectively by turning on the MouseKeys feature and using the keyboard to simulate mouse movements.

Step 2: Action

1. Display the Accessibility Properties tabbed dialog box by opening the Control Panel and double-clicking the Accessibility Options icon.

▼

2. Select the tab marked Mouse. You'll see the dialog box shown in Figure 11.7.

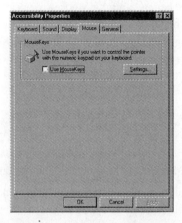

FIGURE 11.7

The Mouse accessibility option dialog box lets you simulate the mouse with keyboard action

3. If you want to use the keyboard to simulate mouse movements and mouse clicks, click the Use MouseKeys check box and then click the OK command button. If, before clicking OK, you want to see the setting values for the MouseKeys option, click the Settings button. The MouseKeys settings, shown in Figure 11.8, control the way the keyboard simulates the mouse actions.

11

FIGURE 11.8

You can change the MouseKeys settings

Click the Use Shortcut option to allow for the turning on and off of the MouseKeys feature from the keyboard shortcut (Left Alt+Left Shift+NumLock).

The pointer speed and acceleration options control the keyboard response rate when using the keyboard to simulate mouse movements. You probably do not need to adjust these default settings. The first option, Hold Down Ctrl to Speed Up and Shift to Slow Down, lets you make very large mouse movements by holding Ctrl when using a mouse cursor key and very small mouse movements (for precision) when holding down the Shift key along with a mouse cursor key. Keep this option checked so you can control the mouse speed when you need to.

▼ 4. Check On to Use MouseKeys When NumLock Is On if you want to use NumLock to control both the numeric keypad and the MouseKeys feature at the same time. When On, you can switch between using the numeric keypad for normal keyboard cursor navigation and using the numeric keypad for MouseKeys operation at the same time. If you set this option to Off, you can switch between using the numeric keypad for number data-entry and using the numeric keypad for MouseKeys operation at the same time.

Set the option to On if you normally use the numeric keypad for cursor movement and Off if you normally use the numeric keypad for the data-entry of numbers.

5. If you want visual feedback from a taskbar icon to show that MouseKeys is active, be sure to click the Show MouseKey Status on Screen option.

6. Click the OK command button to close the Settings dialog box and then click OK again to close the Accessibility Options dialog box.

7. Press NumLock and then press cursor-movement keys on the numeric keypad to move the mouse cursor. The keypad's number 5 simulates a single mouse click, and the plus sign simulates a double-click of the mouse. All other keys on the keypad move the mouse cursor in various directions.

Step 3: Review

The MouseKeys setting converts your numeric keypad to a mouse-controlling keypad when you press the NumLock key. If you have difficulty using the mouse, or if you don't have a working mouse attached to your computer, you can simulate all mouse move-
▲ ments by setting the various MouseKeys options.

Task 11.6: Controlling the Remaining Accessibility Options Features

Step 1: Description

The tab marked General on the Accessibility Options tabbed dialog box controls the remaining accessibility options. You can control the amount of time the accessibility options remain active and the notification of various accessibility options, and you can determine how Windows 95 recognizes a SerialKeys device that you might have attached.

Step 2: Action

1. Display the Accessibility Properties tabbed dialog box by opening the Control Panel and double-clicking the Accessibility Options icon.

▼ 2. Select the tab marked General. You'll see the dialog box shown in Figure 11.9.

FIGURE 11.9

The General accessibility option dialog box provides remaining accessibility options controls

3. The Minutes value determines how long Windows 95 waits before turning off the accessibility options. If you check the option labeled Turn off Accessibility Features After Idle, and then enter a Minutes value, Windows 95 turns off all accessibility options after the computer has been idle for the specified number of minutes.

   When set, a user can use the computer's accessibility options and then leave the computer to let someone else use the machine. After the specified number of minutes, Windows 95 turns off the accessibility options so that the next person to use the computer (after the time limit passes) will use the computer with no accessibility options in effect.

   Either click off the check mark from this option or change the minutes value to suit your working environment.

> If you know you will be alternating use of the accessibility options regularly, be sure to check all the shortcut options on each option so that when you return after the idle period, you don't have to go through each menu to turn the accessibility options back on.

4. The Notification section determines whether or not Windows 95 should issue the warning dialog box telling you that an accessibility option is turned on when you press the shortcut key for that option. If you want audible feedback when an accessibility option starts, be sure to check the second Notification option.

11

▼ 5. If you use an alternative input device that attaches to a serial port, check the Support SerialKey Devices option and click the Settings command button to inform Windows 95 which serial port the device is attached to and the baud rate of the device. The instructions for the alternative input device should contain information about the appropriate values.

Step 3: Review

The General section of the Accessibility Options dialog box determines the additional settings for the accessibility options. You can control how long the computer is idle before Windows 95 turns off any accessibility options. Also, Windows 95 can notify you of any accessibility options when you click the proper notification options. Finally, you can tell Windows 95 which alternative input devices you use through the SerialKeys
▲ options.

Summary

This hour explained how you can control the accessibility options inside Windows 95. Microsoft designed Windows 95 to be accessible to virtually anyone who needs to use a computer, even if that person requires extra help with the keyboard, video display, or mouse.

The primary keyboard accessibility options control the operation of the modifier keys (Alt, Ctrl, and Shift). If you have trouble combining a modifier key with another key, you can request that Windows 95 trap these keystrokes and lock them down when you press them. Other keyboard accessibility options control the repeat rate and help eliminate extra keyboard bounce.

All the accessibility options contain audible and visual clues that tell you when you set or reset these options. The high-contrast display options help improve the screen's visibility. In addition, you can set up the keyboard to control all mouse movements in case you're missing a mouse or cannot use a mouse.

Workshop

Term Review

Accessibility TimeOut   Turns off the accessibility options after a preset period of time.

BounceKeys   Keeps users from producing double-keystrokes if they accidentally bounce keys several times in succession.

FilterKeys   The group of keystroke aids that includes RepeatKeys and BounceKeys.

high-contrast display   A video option that makes your screen more readable by increasing the size of icons, menus, and text, as well as changing screen colors so that the items on the display are as readable as possible.

Modifier keys   The Alt, Ctrl, and Shift keys.

MouseKeys   Lets you simulate mouse movements and clicks using the keyboard's numeric keypad.

mutually exclusive   Two or more Windows 95 controls, such as option buttons, are mutually exclusive if you can set only one option at a time.

RepeatKeys   Users can turn off the repetition of keys, so that holding down a key does *not* necessarily repeat that keystroke.

Scalable user interface elements   The text, title bars, and icons enlarge to make them easier to see.

SerialKeys   Lets the user use a nonkeyboard input device.

SlowKeys   Windows 95 can disregard keystrokes that are not held down for a preset time period. This aids users who often accidentally press keys.

ShowSounds   Provides visual feedback on the screen when applications produce sounds.

SoundSentry   Sends a visual clue when Windows 95 beeps the speaker (in the case of warning or error message dialog boxes).

StickyKeys   Lets the user press the Shift, Alt, or Ctrl keys individually instead of having to press them with their combined keystrokes.

ToggleKeys   Sounds a high noise on the speaker if the CapsLock, NumLock, or ScrollLock keys are activated and a low noise when these keys are deactivated.

Q&A

Q How can users who have trouble using the default keyboard interface access the accessibility options?

A All someone has to do is get help the first time by having another user display the Control Panel's Accessibility Options tabbed dialog box. Click the option labeled Use StickyKeys. From that point forward, users can activate StickyKeys by pressing either Shift key five times in a row.

11

Q **How can I remember to turn off StickyKeys when my coworker is finished using the StickyKeys feature?**

A Make sure the Accessibility Options StickyKeys Settings dialog box has a check next to the option labeled Turn StickyKeys Off If Two Keys Are Pressed at Once. As soon as you press a modifier key in conjunction with any other key, Windows 95 turns off StickyKeys.

Q **Can I use the accessibility options if I don't have special physical needs that require accessibility option settings?**

A There are times when the accessibility options can benefit all people no matter what their physical needs are. For example, the SoundSentry and ShowSounds features are useful for those who work in noisy environments and cannot always hear the computer's speaker. If you forget your mouse when on the road with a laptop, you can turn on the MouseKeys option to simulate mouse movements and clicks with the keyboard.

Hour 12

Back Up and Squeeze Disk Space

This hour is for everybody and for nobody! Here's the reason for the paradox: *Everybody* wants more disk space, and *nobody* backs up often enough! This hour attempts to help you get more disk space and back up more often.

Windows 95 also contains a backup program that lets you back up your files. By making regular backups, and double-checking those backups, you help protect your files from accidental erasure later. If a disaster occurs, such as a disk drive failure (often called a *disk crash*), you can restore the backup by copying the files from the backup to a healthy disk drive. Be sure you've made a startup disk (as described in Hour 4, "Understanding the My Computer Window," so that you can boot from the disk drive and restore a hard disk that gets erased from an accident or a hardware failure.

Windows 95 contains the *DriveSpace* technology that compresses disk space by as much as 30 to 100 percent. Therefore, if you have a 200-megabyte disk drive, you can run DriveSpace, and you will have up to *400 megabytes* of space after DriveSpace finishes compressing the drive. DriveSpace compresses both hard disks and floppy disks.

The highlights of this hour include:

- Why backing up with Windows 95 Backup is simple to do
- When the best times to back up are
- Why the different kinds of backup are needed
- What precautions you can take to protect your backups
- How you can squeeze more data onto your disk drive

Back Up Often

The Windows 95 Backup program is a comprehensive backup program that you can use to save a copy of your disk files. The backup helps to protect you against data loss. If your hard disk breaks down, after you fix or replace that hard disk, you can then restore the backup and resume your work with much or all of your data intact. Without the backup, you have to try to re-create the entire disk drive, which is often impossible because you will not have a copy of every transaction and document that you've created.

The Windows 95 Backup program both creates and restores backups.

To ensure that your backup is accurate, you can run a comparison that compares every backed up file to your disk's files. Although the backup program does read, write, and compare as it makes your backup, the comparison gives you full assurance that your backup is completely accurate at the time of the comparison.

Many people back up regularly. Most of them do so because they once had a disk crash but did not have a backup. (The author is one of those guilty of losing a disk and all the data before learning to back up!) Please don't be one to learn the hard way. Learn to use the Windows 95 Backup program and back up your files regularly.

Put It in Reverse—Back Up!

The first time you back up you should back up your entire disk drive. After you back up the entire disk, you then can make subsequent daily or weekly backups and back up only the files that you've added or changed since the most recent backup.

The Windows 95 Backup program can often compress files while backing them up so that you can back up large disk drives to other disks or tapes that would not normally be able to hold all the data. If you turn on the compression option, the backup should take less time and make the backups easier to do.

The Windows 95 Backup program also lets you select which files you want to back up so that you can make a special backup of a few selected files. Windows 95 Backup can create a *full backup* of your entire disk drive or a *differential backup* (or *incremental backup*), which backs up only the files that have changed since the most recent backup. Backup also lets you direct restored files to a different drive or directory from where they originated.

Take your home computer's backup files with you to work every day and bring your work's backup files home each night. If a terrible disaster happens at home or at work, such as a fire, you can restore your data because the backups were not destroyed.

You must decide which *medium* you want to store the backup on. The Windows 95 Backup program creates backups on the following types of media:

- Network disks
- Hard disks
- CD-R recordable CD drives
- Removables such as Zip and JAZ disks
- Floppy disks
- QIC 40, 80, and 3010 tapes

12

Windows 95 Backup supports the tape-based QIC-113 format which means that Windows 95 Backup can back up and restore onto tapes and other backup media that many backup utility programs also can read and write. After you make a full backup, especially the very first time, you might also want to run Windows 95 Backup's comparison option to make sure that the backup matches the original data. The comparison ensures that your backup worked fully and accurately.

Not only can the Backup program back up your files to tape, but the Backup's Tools menu option supplies these common tape drive utilities:

- Erase Tape: Erases the tape in the tape drive so that you have access to all the tape's storage capacity.
- Format Tape: Writes the initial tracks needed when you purchase unformatted tapes for your backups.
- Redetect Tape Drive: Finds and configures a tape drive that you recently installed or changed. Generally, a fully plug-and-play compatible tape drive will not need redetecting.

As you back up, rotate your backup tapes or disks. Don't reuse the same backup set twice in a row. If something happens during the next backup, you not only lose your disk drive but the backup will not be accurate either. By keeping a second backup and rotating the backup medium that you use, you ensure that you have a full backup at all times. When you rotate, be sure to use the oldest backup set next.

Task 12.1: Backing Up Your Disk Drive

Step 1: Description

This task explains how to use the Windows 95 Backup program and its major features. This task describes how to back up a hard disk to floppy disks. Although a tape drive or network drive makes backing up easier than backing up to floppy disks because you don't have to keep switching disks in and out of the drive, most people today still back up to floppy disks.

> Backing up to disks can take a *lot* of disks! Even if you use Windows 95 Backup's compression option, a large hard disk backup consumes many disks. If you have a backup tape drive and want to back up to your tape drive (you should do this if you have the hardware), select your tape drive instead of floppy disks as you follow this task.

Step 2: Action

1. Display the Start menu.
2. Select the Programs command to display the next cascaded menu.
3. Display the Accessories menu.
4. Display the System Tools menu.
5. Click the Backup menu item. Windows 95 displays the Backup screen shown in Figure 12.1.

FIGURE 12.1

The opening Backup window for backing up a disk drive

The backup screen that you see is a Backup opening screen describing the backup process. Read the screen to get an overview of the backup process. If this is the last time you want to see the opening screen, click the option at the bottom of the page.

6. Click the OK command button after you finish reading the screen.

7. After a brief pause, Backup displays yet another descriptive window shown in Figure 12.2. Backup is informing you of the *full system backup file set*. A *backup file set* is a predetermined list of files to back up that you can create. If you back up only a certain group of files on a regular basis, you can create a backup file set that tells Backup to back up only those files. By creating a backup set, you only need to specify the group of files in that set one time. In the future, when you want to back up that same set of files, you open that backup file set and begin the backup without having to specify all the files again.

FIGURE 12.2

The full system backup file set should be your first backup

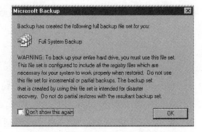

The Windows 95 Backup program supplies you with one backup file set called the full system backup file set. A backup set is a list of files that describe one backup. You can create backup file sets that tell Backup exactly how you want to back up and then select the appropriate backup file set when you want to back up. The Windows 95 Backup program supplies one starting backup file set, the full system backup file set, that instructs Backup to back up your entire hard disk.

12

▼   The window is suggesting that you use the full system backup file set the first time you back up. This task uses that backup file set to back up your entire hard disk (including programs, data, the Registry, and system files including the system files that are normally hidden from your view) to floppy disks. Later, you can create your own backup file sets that describe certain differential backups or backups that save only a certain set of files or folders.

If you want to follow this task but not take the time right now to back up your entire hard disk to floppy disks, you can cancel the backup process after it starts.

8. If you don't want to see the reminder window shown in Figure 12.2, you can check the option at the bottom of the screen to hide future displays of the window.

Click OK now to continue with the backup process.

At this point, you may or may not get a cautionary window telling you that either you do not have a tape drive or that Windows 95 did not detect a tape drive. Backup assumes that you want to back up to a tape drive, even though many people have no tape drives. If you have no tape drive, click OK. If you do have one, close the window and exit Backup. Select the Control Panel's Add New Hardware icon to install the tape drive.

9. The Backup program does not start backing up right away because Backup still does not know the kind of backup you want to perform or the type of media to which you want the backup to go.

Backup displays the window shown in Figure 12.3. The tabs at the top of the window let you select either a backup, restore, or comparison. For this task, you keep the Backup tab selected. You can look through the two other tabbed windows if you want to learn more about the other tasks Backup can perform. All three tabbed windows work virtually the same except that the direction of the data flow is reversed using Backup and Restore, and the Compare tabbed dialog box does not back up or restore, but compares a backup to its original set of files to make sure
▼   the backup worked.

▼

FIGURE 12.3

*The Backup window
where you describe the
backup details*

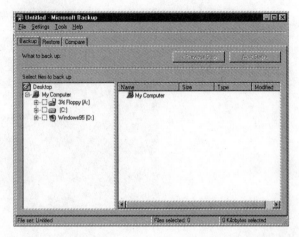

10. The Backup window contains two panes that work like the Explorer's screen. The window pane on the left describes the storage devices that you might want to back up. The right window pane describes the details of whatever device you select.

Although you are going to perform a full backup in this task, take a moment for a detour so you can learn something about creating a backup file set.

Select drive C by clicking on the square and wait while Backup collects a list of all files on your drive C. The collection takes a while. When finished, Backup displays a list of all files and folders from drive C with a check mark next to each. Backup assumes that you want to back up the entire drive C. If there are folders or files you don't want to back up, uncheck them.

11. Click the Next Step command button so that you can tell Backup what medium you want to use for the backup. Backup displays the screen shown in Figure 12.4. If Windows 95 still says no backup medium is detected, that's okay for this task because you are going to practice by starting to back up onto drive A, the disk drive.

12. Select drive A. Now that Windows 95 Backup knows the files to back up and the destination medium, you can save the backup file set that you've just designed (selected files from drive C backed up to drive A). To do so, select File | Save and enter a name for the backup file set.

Instead of backing up just the drive C, select the File | Open File Set command to display the backup file set open dialog box.

▼

12

FIGURE 12.4

Tell Backup the backup's destination medium

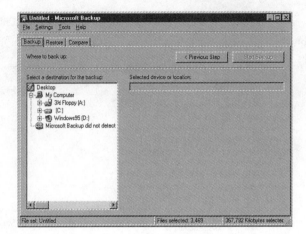

13. Select the Full System Backup. Backup then scans your computer and its files looking for everything to back up, as well as the hardware you can back up to. If you have only one hard disk, the full system backup file set is the same file selection as you would have if you'd selected all of drive C. If you have several hard disks, the full system backup file set selects every hard disk. Your only job left is to indicate the medium for the backup.

 When you want to make a differential backup, select Settings | Options and click on the Backup tabbed dialog box. Click the option labeled Incremental backup of selected files that have changed since the last full backup.

14. Click the Next Step command button and then select drive A for the destination floppy disk (or your tape drive if you have one).

15. Click the Start Backup command button. Backup displays the Backup Set Label dialog box shown in Figure 12.5. The *backup set label* is a descriptive name that labels this particular backup. For example, you could name this backup *My first full backup*.

FIGURE 12.5

Assign a label to this particular backup

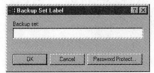

If you back up sensitive data, you might want to add a password to the backup so that others cannot get your backup files and restore the files onto their system. Before restoring a password-protected backup set, Windows 95 Backup asks the user for the password and refuses to restore without the proper password. Be sure to store your password in a safe place so you can find it (but nobody else can) if you forget the password.

Backup displays a dialog box that illustrates the backup procedure. Your entire hard disk probably cannot fit on a single disk. Backup asks you to insert the next disk in drive A after Backup fills the first disk. If you are backing up to a tape, the entire hard disk might fit on the tape without your intervening at all.

Select the Settings I Options menu and turn on the option, Turn On Audible Prompts in the General tabbed dialog box, so that Backup beeps when you need to insert the next disk.

16. When Backup finishes (click Cancel if you want to stop the backup early), select File I Exit. Put the backup disks (or tape) in a safe place and label the backup media so you know the backup is there.

Step 3: Review

The Windows 95 Backup program contains a complete set of backup, restore, and comparison features. The backup file sets make backing up regularly easy to do. You can create backup file sets that describe different backup settings and open whatever backup file set you want to use. (The Windows 95 Backup program supplies a full system backup set for you to use when you want to back up all hard disk drives.)

The Microsoft Windows 95 add-on product named *Microsoft Plus!* lets you preset a time for backing up your files. You can perform a hands-off backup if you back up to another hard disk, a network disk drive, a high-capacity disk such as a JAZ disk, or to a CD-R drive that has as much or more capacity as your hard disk. (When backing up to floppy disks, you have to be there to change the disks.)

12

▼

To restore your backup after a full disk drive crash, you should follow these general guidelines:

1. Replace the hard disk or disk controller that caused the problem. If your problem occurred due to operator error, such as an accidentally formatted disk, you don't need to replace the hardware.

2. Insert your startup disk in your disk drive.

3. Turn on your system. The computer boots to the disk drive's MS-DOS program.

4. Insert your Windows 95 CD-ROM in your CD drive and type *d:\setup* where *d:* is the name of your CD-ROM drive. Windows 95 reloads onto your system.

5. Run the Microsoft Backup program described in this hour's lesson.

6. Select the Restore option and choose the target disk you want to restore to (which is almost always your C: drive).

Depending on the nature of the problem, you might not have to replace a hard disk drive or reload your Windows 95 operating system. If you accidentally erased one or more files or folders, you might only need to restore a select number of files (you can select files and folders from within the Microsoft Backup program before you begin the restoration) without reloading Windows 95.

▲

Running DriveSpace

The DriveSpace program is easy to run. You only need to run DriveSpace once because after compressing the disk drive, the disk stays compressed. You also can reverse the DriveSpace compression if you want, as long as you have enough space on the uncompressed disk drive to hold all your files.

DriveSpace does not perform disk defragmentation. Whereas Hour 21, "Fine Tune with Advanced System Tools," explains how to defragment your disk space, DriveSpace takes the extra step and actually compresses your disk storage to give you almost twice as much room as you had previously.

Accessing Compressed Data

Some people mistakenly believe that compressing the disk drive with a program such as DriveSpace slows down disk access. In the majority of cases, a compressed disk drive is as fast or faster than an uncompressed drive.

Mechanical devices are slower than electronic devices. Memory access is much faster than disk access. When Windows 95 accesses a compressed disk drive, it has only to retrieve half as much physical data; Windows 95 then quickly decompresses that data in fast memory. The overall result is faster disk access.

After you compress a disk drive, Windows 95 and your computer act as if you've got more disk space. The free disk statistics show the extra drive space, and all programs access the disk as if the disk were originally designed to have the extra space.

DriveSpace uses the same compression technology previously used by MS-DOS 6. If you've already been working with a DoubleSpace or DriveSpace MS-DOS drive, you do not need to convert the drive to Windows 95 or compress the drive again. After it's compressed once, you can squeeze no additional disk space by trying a subsequent compression.

DriveSpace is incompatible with *FAT32*, an efficient disk storage scheme used by Windows 98 and by some users of Windows 95 who have Service Release Pack 2. (The Service Release Pack 2 is available only to some Windows 95 users who bought a PC with Windows 95 already installed.) You can see if you have it by selecting your Start menu's Settings | Control Panel option, opening the System icon, and reading your Windows 95 version number. If you see 4.00.950 B, you have Service Release Pack 2 and should avoid compressing your disk drive because you might want to convert your disk to FAT32 (see the Windows 95 help system for more information on FAT32) or you might already have a FAT32 disk drive.

12

Task 12.2: Compressing Disks Using DriveSpace
Step 1: Description

This task explains how to compress a disk drive using DriveSpace. The disk is to be a floppy disk. After you've compressed a floppy disk drive, you will more fully understand the process and can then compress a hard disk.

▼ To Do

You cannot compress a CD-ROM. DriveSpace must be able to write to a device before compressing that device. CD-ROM drives are read-only. (The term *ROM* means *read-only memory*.)

When compressing a disk drive, DriveSpace adds a *logical disk drive*, part of your existing disk drive partitioned off as if it were a new and separate drive, to your system called the *host drive*. DriveSpace names the new host drive *H*, or some other name that falls far down anyone's list of disk drives, so that you can determine which drive is a host drive and which drive is from your list of real disk drives. The host drive is not compressed, and you do not work with the host drive. DriveSpace and Windows 95 use the host drive to hold descriptive information about the compressed drive. All you really need to know about the new host drive is that the host is not an actual drive on your system, and Windows 95 uses the host drive to support the DriveSpace compression scheme. All open dialog boxes you see, as well as the My Computer window, will display the host drive now that you've compressed.

Step 2: Action

1. Display the Start menu.
2. Select the Programs command to display the next cascaded menu.
3. Display the Accessories menu.
4. Display the System Tools menu.
5. Click the DriveSpace menu item. Windows 95 displays the DriveSpace window shown in Figure 12.6.

FIGURE 12.6

The opening DriveSpace window for compressing a disk drive

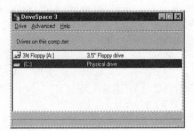

If your computer has additional disk drives, your DriveSpace window displays those additional drives in the list of drives.

▼   6. Insert a formatted disk in the disk drive. The disk can have data on it but it should
        contain about 30 percent free space. Before you can compress a disk, the disk
        should contain some free space so that DriveSpace can write some temporary files
        during the compression process. If the drive does not have enough free space,
        DriveSpace tells you before starting the actual compression so that you can free
        some space.

> If, while saving a file from an application during a regular work session, you
> receive an error message telling you that you are out of disk space, you
> must remove some files from the disk (using Explorer) before there is room
> to save the file. If you then want to compress the disk, you have to copy or
> move some of the disk's files to another disk drive to free enough space so
> that DriveSpace can compress the disk. It is always a good idea, when you
> think a disk is getting full, to check the amount of free space still available
> so that you can compress it before it no longer has enough free space for
> DriveSpace to work.

Obviously, DriveSpace cannot physically make a disk larger, but DriveSpace does
make the disk appear larger to Windows 95 and MS-DOS programs.

   7. Select the floppy disk drive from the list of drives.

   8. Select Drive | Compress. DriveSpace analyzes the disk and displays the Compress
      a Drive dialog box as shown in Figure 12.7.

12

FIGURE 12.7

*The before and after
effect of the disk's
compression*

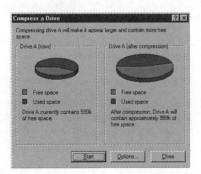

Depending on your disk's contents and original size, you can gain a little or a lot of
extra space by the compression. DriveSpace only compresses the disk shown in
Figure 12.7 by approximately 400,000 kilobytes, as you can see in the right-hand
▼   window labeled Drive A (After Compression).

If you want to decompress a compressed drive, you repeat these steps and choose Drive | Uncompress instead of Drive | Compress.

9. Click the Options command button. Windows 95 displays the Compression Options dialog box shown in Figure 12.8. The Compression Options dialog box describes the host drive's name (you can select a different name if you want) and free space (usually there is no free space). Click the OK command button to close the Compression Options dialog box and return to the Compress a Drive dialog box.

FIGURE 12.8

The Compression Options dialog box explains how the compression operates

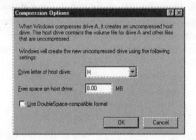

10. Click the Start command button to initiate the drive compression. Before compressing, DriveSpace gives you one last chance to cancel the compression. Also, DriveSpace offers the option of backing up your files. Although there is rarely a problem during the compression, it is possible that a power failure during the compression could interrupt the process and cause DriveSpace to corrupt the disk drive (so that the drive would need reformatting). By backing up the drive, you ensure that you can return to an uncompressed drive if needed.

If you choose to back up before completing the drive's compression, DriveSpace runs the Microsoft Backup program described in the previous section.

After the compression begins, DriveSpace checks the disk for errors and then compresses the disk. The compression can take a while. After finishing, DriveSpace displays a completion dialog box. Close the dialog box and look at Explorer's status bar to see the increased disk space available on the disk.

▼ Step 3: Review

After you compress a disk drive, Windows 95 recognizes the compressed drive and stores up to 100 percent more data on that drive. There is actually a second disk added to your drive letters called the host disk, but you can ignore the host disk because DriveSpace uses the host disk to store data tables used for accessing the compressed drive.

> If you want to format a compressed disk, you must run DriveSpace and select Drive | Format. The Explorer Format command does not format compressed disks. The disk stays compressed during the formatting procedure.

Summary

This hour described the DriveSpace compression program and the Windows 95 Backup program. Both of these programs are new to Windows 95 and take advantage of the Windows 95 32-bit architecture and multitasking capabilities.

The DriveSpace compression program can almost double your disk drive space. By compressing your files and the free file space, you effectively squeeze more data into the same amount of disk space. You can compress both your hard disk drives and floppy disk drives.

The Windows 95 Backup program lets you back up, restore, and compare backups to their original files. The Backup program is the most full-featured backup program that Microsoft has offered. You can create backup file sets that quickly initiate specific backup descriptions. If you purchase a copy of the new Microsoft Plus! program, you can schedule backups so that Windows 95 backs up files while you are away from the
▲ computer.

12

Workshop

Term Review

backup file set   A description that contains a specific list of files that you want to back up. For example, you might have a backup file set that backs up your accounting data files only, as well as a full backup file set that backs up your entire hard disk.

compression   The process of squeezing your disk drive so that almost 100 percent more data fits on a disk.

differential backup   A backup of only the files that have changed since the most recent backup. Also called an *incremental backup*.

disk crash   A disk drive failure.

DriveSpace   The name of the Windows 95 utility program that condenses the disk space so that more data fits on a disk drive.

FAT32   Stands for *32-bit File Allocation Table* and refers to an efficient disk-storage scheme used by some release versions of Windows 95 and Windows 98.

full backup   A complete backup of your entire disk drive.

full system backup file set   A backup file set supplied by Backup that performs a full backup.

host drive   A logical, uncompressed new drive that DriveSpace creates to hold compression information.

incremental backup   See *differential backup*.

logical disk drive   A drive created by partitioning space from an existing physical disk drive, but that is treated as a separate disk drive by the operating system.

media   The types of storage on which you store and back up data. Examples of media are a disk, a tape, and paper.

Microsoft Plus!   A Windows 95 add-on product you can purchase that can automate the backup process (as long as you back up to tape, a network drive, or another hard disk) so that you can request a backup at any time of day or night.

ROM   Stands for *read-only memory* and refers to devices or memory that you can read from, but not write to, delete from, or change.

Q&A

Q   Should I compress my disk as often as I defragment it?

A Compression is a one-time process but defragmentation is on-going and should be part of your regular maintenance. You should defragment every week or so. Depending on the amount of file access you do, you might need to defragment more or less often. If you notice your disk speed slowing down a bit, you'll often find that Defragment speeds the access process somewhat.

Only compress your disk drive (or each floppy disk) *once*. After the compression, the drive stays compressed. Unless you uncompress the drive, Windows 95 always recognizes the compressed drive.

Q Which kind of backup, a full or differential backup, should I perform?

A The first time you back up you should make a full backup. After you make one full backup, you can make subsequent differential backups of only those files that have changed. Be sure that you save the full backup, however, so that you can restore everything if you need to. If you have a disk failure, you'll restore the entire full backup and then restore each differential backup set of files.

Q Does a full backup take longer than a differential backup?

A Yes. As mentioned in the previous question, first perform one full backup and then, subsequently, you can perform the quicker differential backups.

After you've made several differential backups, you might want to make a full backup again. By making a full backup every once in a while, you can reuse your differential tapes or disks.

Q Other than full backups which I perform weekly, I want to back up only my three work folders every day. Should I take the time to create a backup file set that describes only those three folders?

A By all means, you should create a backup file set for those three folders. Although you must take a few moments to create the backup file set the first time, specifying exactly which folders you want to back up, subsequent backups will take less of your time. You'll thereafter only have to select the trio-folder backup file set and start the backup.

12

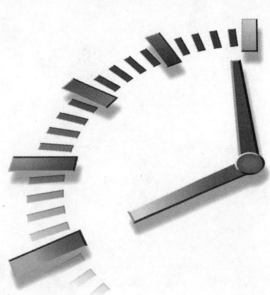

PART III

Windows 95's Evening Out

Hour

HOUR 13

Using the Online Services Window

This hour helps you locate an Internet Service Provider (ISP) using one of the services available in Windows 95's Online Services desktop folder. Although you can sign up for Internet service through a local ISP, Windows 95 provides you with the software needed to try out several popular online services that provide Internet capabilities, as well as other kinds of online benefits.

The highlights of this hour include:

- Why use an online service for your Internet Service Provider
- What advantages a service gives you over a straight ISP
- How to sign up for an online service
- Why you should sign up for trial memberships
- How free portals compete with online services

Introduction to Online Services

Open your Windows 95 desktop folder labeled Online Services to see Figure 13.1's set of icons. Each of the services, with the exception of AT&T WorldNet, are more than just Internet providers; the services offer unique advantages for the Internet user who wants more from an Internet provider than straight Internet Web access. If your Online Services window does not contain all of Figure 13.1's icons, run Windows Setup from the Control Panel's Add/Remove Programs dialog box.

FIGURE 13.1

You can sign up with any of these service providers

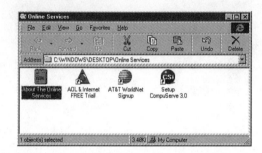

If you do not see the Online Services on your desktop, you might need to run the Control Panel's Add/Remove programs and add the Online Services from the Windows Setup dialog box page. In addition, your Online Services folder (often available as an icon on your Windows 95 desktop) will likely differ in content from the one in Figure 13.1. For example, you might see an icon for the Prodigy online service.

All of the services charge a fee for their access. Although they all offer somewhat different pricing plans, most services compete with one another so you must decide which is right for you based on your needs, the service reliability and capabilities each provides, and recommendations from others.

Don't discount recommendations; if most of your co-workers and friends subscribe to a service, such as Prodigy, you should consider Prodigy because you'll communicate with the others without problem and they can help you get started quickly.

All of the online services offer *flat-rate pricing plans*. With a flat-rate plan, you pay one monthly fee no matter how much (or how little) you use the service each month. In addition, the services provide local numbers in most areas so you don't have to pay long distance charges.

Windows 95–supplied online services traditionally offer unique content available only to subscribers. A local Internet service generally does not offer value-added services and are more of a generic Internet connection.

The growth of the Internet, with all its millions of Web sites, takes much of the uniqueness out of *unique content*. For example, CompuServe might offer movie reviews, but so does a plethora of Web sites—many of which offer as many or more movie reviews as CompuServe. Most daily newspapers and almost all magazines now offer Web sites, as well as almost all entertainment services. Therefore, if you want a specific reviewer's take on a new movie and you're willing to search the Internet, you can often get a good, or even a better, review somewhere other than your particular service provider's unique content.

Online services, such as Microsoft Network, offer more than just unique content—hence their success. Online services are sometimes used to utilize proprietary interfaces, although now the services start your Internet *browser* (a program, such as Internet Explorer, that enables you to access the Internet) pointing to a specific company Web page. These start pages are often called *portals* because they provide an entrance to the rest of the Internet.

Figure 13.2 shows CompuServe's opening screen. From this screen, you can access one of several categories easily, whereas you would need to know the Web locations to find such information using Internet Explorer with a more generic Internet Service Provider. The screen is actually a specialized Web portal site to the rest of CompuServe's services, forums, and the general Internet.

Newcomers to online technology often prefer the organized content available through an online service. Setting up Internet Explorer or another browser is not always a trivial task with generic ISPs. In addition, the dedicated toolbar buttons and menu structure of the online services get the newcomer (as well as the pros in many cases) to her information destinations faster.

13

FIGURE 13.2

Online service providers offer their own managed interface to the Internet and its information

One of the benefits of using the supplied Online Service folder is that you might not have a standalone Internet provider or know how to contact one. With Windows 95, you've already got everything you need to set up America Online (AOL), CompuServe, and others shown in your Online Services folder, so you don't have to wait to get started.

> You must have a credit card handy when signing up for a service.

One of the benefits of using Windows 95 to set up an online service is that you can try a service free for a month before deciding if you want to keep the service. The services compete heavily with one another and you, the user, benefit from that competition. Try all of the services free for a month and explore their benefits before you decide which one is right for you. (The hour's section that follows this task compares and contrasts some of the services.)

Task 13.1: Setting Up CompuServe

When you decide which online service you want to try, you need to set up that service in Windows 95 and subscribe to the service. All of the online services require that you set up the service before you can use it. Each service is compressed to save disk space until you are ready to use the service. This task shows you how to set up CompuServe, but you can follow the same general setup guidelines to set up any of the services.

You only need to set up an online service once. Most of the services automatically download updates when needed. After you set up a service, if you need a new software update, the service will automatically download the update to your PC and update the software for you without you doing anything.

Step 1: Description

Each Online Services folder icon starts a wizard that sets up one of the services. The wizard walks you through the CompuServe setup instructions and adds the appropriate service icons to your Start menu.

Step 2: Action

1. Open your desktop's Online Services window.

2. Open the CompuServe icon. A dialog box makes sure that you want to continue by asking if you want to install CompuServe.

3. Click Yes to begin the wizard. After a brief pause the CompuServe setup wizard begins.

4. Select your country and click the Next button. Online services are international so the wizard needs to know your country to set up the appropriate service.

5. If you are setting your first online service, select the Express install from the window shown in Figure 13.3. If you already have an ISP and want to access CompuServe from your existing connection, select Custom. (You need to contact your ISP to determine which settings CompuServe needs before you can connect to CompuServe with this option.)

All of the online services provide fairly adequate levels of security. Although no online service can ensure that your every keystroke's privacy is guarded, online services do provide more security than regular voice calls, credit card purchases in stores, and purchases you make by mail. Therefore, the stories you might have heard about online privacy issues are generally overblown.

Use common sense when you provide information over an online service or over the Internet. If you order products from a reputable dealer, the odds are vastly in your favor that you'll have no security troubles. Almost every financial transaction made today over an online service uses a *secure connection* meaning that information you supply is encrypted on your end before being sent and then decrypted on the receiving end.

13

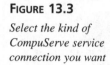

FIGURE 13.3

Select the kind of CompuServe service connection you want

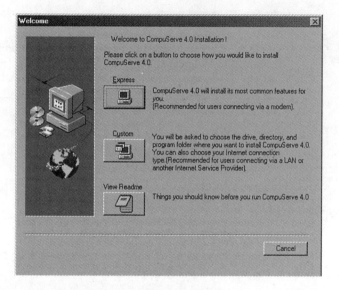

6. CompuServe displays the Create a Keyword dialog box.

   Enter a keyword, up to 16 characters, that acts as your security password. Although you need a password to sign in to CompuServe, the keyword security offers yet another level of security for those times when you must provide information, such as a credit card number. Any time an online CompuServe screen asks you for secure information, you are prompted to enter this keyword to help encrypt the information so it gets to CompuServe without any security violation along the way. Select a keyword you can remember such as your mother's maiden name.

7. CompuServe requires that you restart your PC after you set up the CompuServe files. Click the Restart button to do so now.

8. After your PC restarts, you can select your Start menu's Programs | Online Services menu to see a new submenu called CompuServe. Select the entry named CompuServe to complete your set up.

9. At the opening CompuServe screen, click Signup to sign up for a new CompuServe account. CompuServe requires a sign-in name, password (one that differs from your security keyword), and personal information such as your name, address, and credit card information. Unless you cancel the service, CompuServe bills your credit card monthly for the service. This is also true when you set up a free trial month account. CompuServe continues to keep your account active and bills you monthly, until you cancel the service.

▼ 10. When you first sign in, CompuServe lets you select which phone number you want to use. If you've elected to use CompuServe in conjunction with an existing provider, you don't need to enter phone number information. When you select any service, CompuServe dials the Internet using your existing dial-up provider.

Step 3: Review

This task walked you through the preliminary steps needed to set up and access CompuServe, one of the online service providers available through Windows 95. After you set up a service, you can access that service's specialized areas as well as surf the Internet using the service's Internet browser. Some of the services let you use your own Web browser, such as Internet Explorer, if you don't want to use the proprietary browser

▲ that comes with the service.

Comparing the Online Services

Which online service is right for you? Only you can answer that question, but the following sections briefly explain advantages of each of Windows 95's online services so you can better choose which is right for you.

In comparing the services, keep in mind that competition makes all of them worthwhile contenders, and they each provide some advantages over the others. All of the services provide the typical Internet-based online service features described in Table 13.1. Each online service, however, goes about implementing the features in different ways.

TABLE 13.1 LOOK FOR THESE FEATURES IN YOUR ONLINE SERVICE PROVIDER

Feature	Description
Chat	Lets you interactively communicate with others who are signed on at the same time you are. All online services, including a straight Internet connection, provide text-based chats where you type messages back and forth to others who have joined your *chat room*. Chat rooms are areas of interest, sorted by topic such as PC Support, Teen TV, Religious Talk, Windows Troubleshooting, Politics, and Movies.
Email	Stands for electronic mail and describes the service with which you can transfer messages and files to other users on your online service and across the Internet. The receiving user does not have to be logged in to receive mail you send.

continues

13

TABLE 13.1   CONTINUED

Feature	Description
FTP	Stands for File Transfer Protocol and lets you transfer files to and from other Internet-based computers. Online Services almost always provide their own FTP alternative when you want to retrieve files from the service. Generally, a service offers a file-search section where you can search for files of particular interest and download those files by clicking a button.
Internet Calling	If you have a multimedia PC (and who doesn't these days?) with a microphone and speaker, you can speak to others anywhere in the world. You are not charged for long distance connect charges but only for your regular online service (some exceptions apply). Internet calling is not all peachy, however, because the quality is low and both you and the other party must be connected to the Internet at exactly the same time; you both must also know which Internet location the other is at to connect. Internet calling holds promise, but for now not too many people use it despite its initial appeal.
Mailing Lists	Free (usually) subscription-based Internet services that send to you, as email, any and all new messages and files posted to the mailing lists you choose.
Newsgroups	An area of the Internet accessed through your online service that contains files and messages, organized by topic, that you can read, download, and send. (Newsgroups have nothing to do with Web pages that contain world headline news.)
Web	Web pages you browse from your Windows 95 desktop and Internet Explorer and online service.

Keep in mind that you get Table 13.1's standard Internet service no matter which online service provider you subscribe to. In addition, if you prefer to subscribe to a local ISP that offers nothing but an Internet connection, you can access any of the services listed in Table 13.1. Remember, however, that most online services put a friendly interface in front of these Internet services making them much simpler to use. In addition, online services provide you with support, news and current events, and entertainment areas that are more complete than you'll find with a straight Internet connection.

Most online services provide nice, friendly interface layers between you and the Internet. In addition to the interface, each service provides unique content such as online magazines that you cannot get elsewhere. Generally, an online service costs more than an Internet-only connection you can get locally, but you'll see a cost in another area as well: disk drive space. Most of the online services require between 30 and 50 megabytes of disk space. The unique content and interface requires a presence on your disk.

America Online (AOL)

AOL is the number one online service in use today. Its sheer number of users makes AOL a mixed blessing. Although AOL's content is some of the most complete, and its service offers perhaps the largest selection of specialized benefits, some users have a difficult time getting onto the service during peak hours. In addition, AOL throws a lot of advertising at you while you use the service. This advertising keeps your costs down and the content massive.

AOL is considered to be one of the easiest online services to use.

AOL's opening page, shown in Figure 13.4, offers a pushbutton topic selection throughout its entire interface. When you want to access the Internet, you have to use AOL's provided browser, which does not support the active desktop features that Internet Explorer supports unless you use a recent version of AOL that supports the Internet Explorer 4 active desktop.

AOL provides a wide variety of daily news, periodicals (newspapers and magazines), local weather, movie reviews and previews, and health forums.

13

AOL lets you sign on up to five members in your household. Each member can have his own distinct account and can send and receive email separately from the primary account holder. You don't pay extra for the extra users, but only one user can be signed in to AOL at one time.

FIGURE 13.4

AOL is one of the easiest online services to use

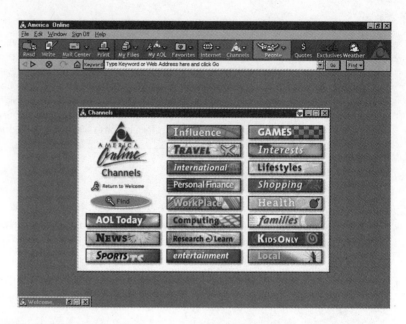

AOL lets you send and receive email between AOL and every other service and Internet user. When you hear, "You've Got Mail!" you know that at least one message awaits you. The email area is simple to use and you are nicely reminded, verbally through your speakers, when you have new email (you can turn this off). Another AOL service that should weigh into your online selection is that AOL offers you up to two megabytes of storage for your own personal home page. You'll have your own URL address and be registered so that others on the Internet (both AOL and non-AOL users) can access your Web page.

AT&T WorldNet Service

AT&T WorldNet service is not a true online service with unique content but is the only standalone Internet Service Provider (often abbreviated as *ISP*) available from within Windows 95. Billing is simple for most customers because AT&T WorldNet Service bills through AT&T long-distance service, if you use AT&T. (If you have a credit card that offers extras such as airline miles, you might opt not to bill through your AT&T long-distance carrier but select a credit card billing option to rack up those miles.) In addition, AT&T WorldNet is available wherever AT&T access is available around the world. AT&T WorldNet offers nothing fancy. You'll use Internet Explorer or another Web browser to surf the Internet, and Microsoft Outlook email and newsgroup reader works fine for AT&T WorldNet access. AT&T WorldNet also offers free storage space for your personal Web page.

CompuServe

CompuServe has been around the longest of all the online services listed in Windows 95's Online Services window. Due to its maturity, CompuServe offers more depth of information and a wider selection of forums than any other service. Want information on travel to Jakarta? CompuServe probably has more information than the other services. Do you need help locating a replacement disk drive door for your 1983 IBM-PC? CompuServe's hardware forums probably have the address where you can buy one.

As Figure 13.5 shows, you can easily access CompuServe's areas of interest by selecting services similar to the way you traverse AOL's pushbutton interface.

FIGURE 13.5

Access CompuServe's primary services through a selection interface similar to that of AOL

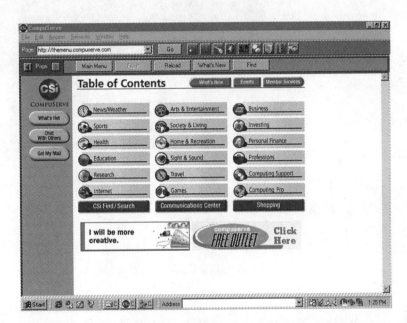

CompuServe provides members with the ability to subscribe to various email services that let you access your email with a pager or listen to your CompuServe messages over a voice phone. Such services are vital if you travel without a laptop and need your messages. Although a CompuServe signin name and email address is often cryptic (such as 420120,23433), you can request a customized name such as Casper and people can get email to you by sending your email to Casper@compuserve.com.

If you want a Web page, CompuServe gives you 5 megabytes, more than twice AOL's 2-megabyte storage limit, for the Web page you desire. For those who prefer Internet Explorer 4.0's active desktop features, CompuServe lets you use Internet Explorer.

13

Microsoft Network (*MSN*)

Microsoft Network offers the largest assortment of Microsoft-related sites and tools and seems to integrate more fully into Windows 95 than the other online services. (One might expect this because both Windows 95 and MSN are Microsoft products.)

MSN is known for its attempt to be *hip*. *MSN* sounds out jazz music and a video when you install the software to support the service. Figure 13.6 shows MSN's opening screen that appears after you sign on to the service.

FIGURE 13.6

The Microsoft Network screen offers several organized services and Internet connections. MSN uses Internet Explorer for its interface

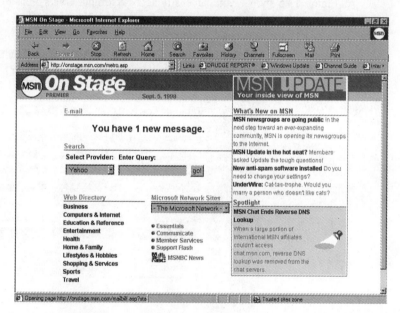

MSN takes advantage of the Windows environment and places an MSN icon on your taskbar when you install the MSN software. As Figure 13.7 shows, you can click on the taskbar to display an MSN menu at any point during your MSN session, or even when you aren't signed in.

As you use MSN, a timer pops up from the taskbar every few minutes to let you know how long you've been using MSN in that particular session. You can change the interval between timer pop-ups or remove the pop-ups altogether if you want to by selecting from the MSN Options entry. If you routinely chat with others, you can designate a list of online friends and the taskbar icon pops up to let you know which of your friends are online during your MSN session.

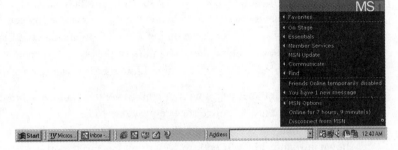

FIGURE 13.7

The Microsoft Network provides a taskbar icon you can click to display a menu

Prodigy

If you see Prodigy online service in your Windows 95 Online Services folder, you can sign up for Prodigy. Prodigy's online service, now called *Prodigy Internet*, provides more unique content than you'll find on just the Internet, and Prodigy's interface takes place entirely within Internet Explorer 4.

Prodigy does add a Prodigy-based toolbar to Internet Explorer so you have quick access to Prodigy's unique content.

Prodigy does give you two megabytes of storage for your own Web site, but you must use tools you find elsewhere to create your Web page. Prodigy supplies no Web site creation programs. Internet Explorer 4 comes with a Web page creation program called *FrontPage Express* that you can use to create a Web page. You can also use Word 97 to create Web pages or any number of Web page development programs on the market.

Prodigy's Internet Explorer interface lets you use Microsoft Outlook, Windows 95's newsreader and Internet mail program, as do the other online services, so you don't have to learn new commands to access newsgroups and email. Hour 15, "Email and Newsgroups" explains how to use Microsoft Outlook to access email and newsgroups from the Internet.

13

Why Online Services Are Less Critical Today

In the past, online services provided a unique interface so you had to learn specific commands and controls for each service you used. Today, the services are entirely Internet-based, so their distinctions are less important. Although they each organize content from their opening screen differently, they all provide access to the entire Internet, which is where the vast collection of data resides.

If you sign up for Internet service through a local Internet Service Provider, which is often available at a discount over national online services, you can access the Internet, but you won't have access to the online services' organized content or special information features. Nevertheless, the availability of the organized content is not as important as it used to be before the Internet matured into the consistent entity that it is today.

Many portals, Internet pages with organized content, are available free to anyone on the Internet and not just to online service providers. The online service providers are finding it more difficult to compete with the major portals such as *Excite* and *Yahoo!* (Yahoo! is shown in Figure 13.8). Therefore, you don't have to use an online service to reap the same benefits.

FIGURE 13.8

Portals such as Yahoo! offer organized access to Internet content

Organized Categories

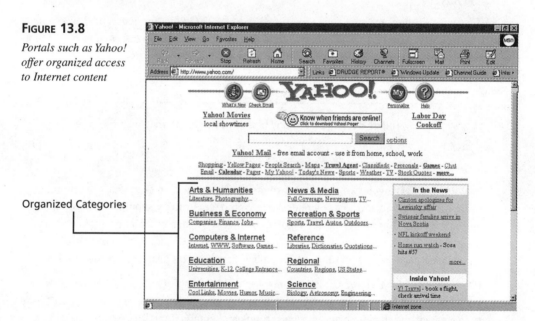

Prepare for an Internet Introduction

This hour concentrated on signing up for online services but did not describe the Internet in great detail. If you are brand new to the Internet, the next hour, "Windows 95 and Internet Explorer 4," explores the reasons why the Internet is so popular, describes how to traverse the Internet, and explains how to integrate the Internet into your Windows 95 desktop.

Summary

This hour explains how you can use one of the Windows 95 online services to access the Web, newsgroups, and email—if you don't already have access to an online service. Online services, with the exception of AT&T WorldNet, provide unique content that you cannot get from a Web ISP alone. You'll have access to forums, news, entertainment, and other links that offer a more structured content than a more generic Internet-only ISP. In addition, online services offer a simpler interface to Web services than you can get from an ISP and a Web browser alone.

Workshop

Term Review

chat   An online keyboard-based conversation you have with others in the chat room you've selected.

chat room   An area of interest where people can meet to discuss a particular topic. Different online services offer a different assortment of chat room topics.

email   Electronic mail service that lets you transfer files and messages to others who have an online account.

flat-rate pricing plan   An Internet Service Provider (ISP) payment plan where you get unlimited usage for the same monthly rate.

Internet calling   The process of using a program so that you and another computer user can speak to each other over your Internet connection.

mailing lists   Services organized by topic you can subscribe to, and receive free (usually) messages and files for the topics that interest you.

newsgroups   Areas of the Internet, organized by topic, that contain files and messages you can read and send.

portals   Web pages that offer standardized, organized connections to the rest of the Internet.

secure connection   An online connection with controls in place to protect the current transaction.

13

Q&A

Q Should I subscribe to more than one service?

A No, although you might want to sign up for multiple services for a trial month to try them out. The services compete with one another greatly and, although they differ, every one of them offers vast content as well as standard Web capabilities such as email and newsgroup access. If you find that your service frequently is busy when you dial in, a secondary service offers a backup number so you can get to the Web when you need access. Nevertheless, a few dial-in attempts usually get you through the busy signals if you're patient.

Q Do I have to provide my credit card number if I want to try the trial period?

A Unless you use AT&T WorldNet and bill to your AT&T long-distance carrier, you must provide a credit card number even if you sign up for a trial one-month period. The online service wants your business, and at the end of the trial period they also want your money. By providing a credit card when you first sign up, the service can ensure that they'll get paid for each month you stay on the service. All of the services offer email to their customer support so you can let them know if you ever want to cancel the service.

HOUR 14

Windows 95 and Internet Explorer 4

In today's world, the Internet is much more a part of computer users' lives than ever before. All but the earliest versions of Windows 95 include Internet Explorer 4, an Internet *browser* that enables you to access information on the Internet from Windows 95. If you happen not to have Internet Explorer 4 on your system, you can obtain it at your local software retailer for a small cost. In designing Internet Explorer 4, Microsoft kept your Windows 95 desktop firmly in mind by giving you access to the Internet throughout Windows 95 and not just from the separate Internet Explorer browser as in the past. You can access the Internet or your desktop from almost anywhere in Windows 95.

This hour explains the Internet in detail and shows you just some of the ways Internet Explorer 4 integrates itself with Windows 95.

The highlights of this hour include:

- Why the Internet has become such an important tool
- How modern Internet access techniques, such as Web pages, make the Internet more manageable

- How to surf the Internet
- How to specify search criteria so that you can locate the exact Internet information you need

The Internet

The Internet is a world-wide system of interconnected computers. Whereas your desktop computer is a standalone machine, and a network of computers is tied together by wires, the Internet is a worldwide online network of computers connected to standalone computers through modems. Hardly anyone understands all portions of the Internet because the Internet is not just a single system.

The Internet began as a government- and university-linked system of computers, but it has now grown to a business and personal system that contains almost an infinite amount of information. The Internet is so vast that nobody would be able to access all of its information today.

 There is no central Internet computer anywhere. The Internet is a system of connected computers. *Internet* is the term given to the entire system. The term *Web* (from *World Wide Web*) is given to the interconnected system of Internet information pages that you can access to read specific information.

The Internet's vastness almost caused its downfall. How can you access or find information on the Internet? Fortunately, Internet technicians began standardizing information when it became apparent that the Internet was growing and becoming a major information provider.

The WWW: World Wide Web

The *WWW*, or *World Wide Web*, or just *Web*, is a collection of Internet pages of information. Web pages can contain text, graphics, sound, video, and applet programs (see Hour 7, "Manage Your Desktop," for information on applets) that come to your PC from a remote Internet site. Figure 14.1 shows a sample Web page from the popular FoxNews site. As you can see, the Web page's graphics and text organize information into a magazine-like readable and appealing format.

Generally, a Web site might contain more information than fits easily on a single Web page. Therefore, many Web pages contain links to several additional extended pages, as well as other linked Web pages that might be related to the original topic. The first page you view is called the *home page*, and from the home page you can view other pages of information.

FIGURE **14.1**

Web pages provide Internet information in a nice format

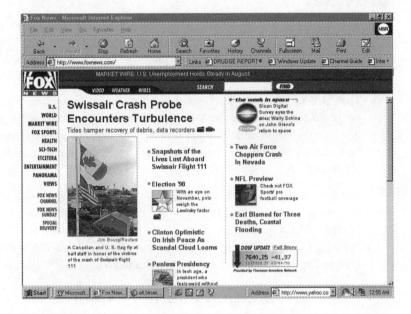

 Each Web page has a unique location that includes the source computer and the location on that computer. Such locations would be difficult to keep track of, however the Internet has standardized Web page locations with a series of addresses called *URLs*, or *Uniform Resource Locator* addresses. You can view any Web page if you know its URL. If you do not know the URL, the Internet provides a number of *search engines* that find Web pages when you tell them to search for topics.

 Surely you've run across computer addresses that look like this: www.microsoft.com and www.mcp.com; these are URLs that access Web pages. These two happen to be the URLs for Microsoft Corporation and Macmillan Computer Publishing, respectively.

14

Introducing the Internet Explorer Web Browser

Before you can access and view Web information, you need a program that can display Web page information including text, graphics, audio, and video. The program you need is called a *Web browser*—or just a *browser*. Although several companies offer browsers, Microsoft designed Internet Explorer 4 to integrate with Windows seamlessly.

This 24-hour tutorial uses Internet Explorer 4 in the figures and descriptions. Some people prefer to use a competing Web browser, such as Netscape Navigator, and you can use that browser from Windows 95 to access Web pages. Internet Explorer 4 integrates the best with Windows 95 (because Microsoft wrote both products) and fully supports the active desktop.

The previous hour, Hour 13, "Using the Online Services Window," describes how to connect to the Internet through one of several services available to Windows 95 users from the Windows 95 Online Services desktop folder. If you want Internet access through another ISP, such as a local Internet provider in your town, your provider will tell you how to use Internet Explorer or your other Web browser to access the ISP's Internet system.

Task 14.1: Starting Internet Explorer

Step 1: Description

Internet Explorer is easy to start. You literally can access the Internet with one or two clicks by running Internet Explorer. This task explains how to start Internet Explorer. Keep in mind that you must already have Internet access and you must know the phone number to that provider. (Your provider will have to give you the specific access and setup details.)

Step 2: Action

1. Double-click the Windows 95 desktop icon labeled The Internet. If you get an Internet Connection Wizard dialog box, you must contact your service provider to learn how to hook up Internet Explorer to the Internet.

> You can also click the taskbar's Internet Explorer button if the button appears on your taskbar. If not, Hour 16, "Activating Your Desktop," explains how to add the browser button to your taskbar.

2. If you access the Internet through the Microsoft Network provider, you see Figure 14.2's dialog box. If you use some other provider, you see a different dialog box.

▼   Some providers, including some versions of Microsoft Network, don't require that you wait for such a dialog box when you indicate you want access to the Internet. Some providers log you in to the Internet automatically if you've already entered login information.

Figure 14.2

You might need to log in to your Internet provider to use Internet Explorer

If required, enter your Internet ID and password and click Connect to dial up the Internet.

3. Assuming that you do have Internet access and you've been set up with a provider, Internet Explorer dials your provider and displays the page set up to be your initial browser's *home page*. Depending on the amount of information and graphics on the page, the display might take a few moments to load or might display right away.

Internet Explorer's Home toolbar button displays your browser's opening home page. At any time during your Internet browsing, you can return to Internet Explorer's home page by clicking this Home button. You can change your browser's home page address by entering a new home page address within the View | Internet Options dialog box's General page. When you enter a new home page address, Internet Explorer returns to that page whenever you click the Home toolbar button or when you start Internet Explorer in a subsequent session.

Step 3: Review

14

Using Internet Explorer to access the Internet and Web pages requires just one or two clicks. Internet Explorer automatically displays an initial start Web page from which you then can access additional Web pages and surf the Internet!

▲

Task 14.2: Managing the Internet Explorer Screen

Step 1: Description

Internet Explorer makes it easy to navigate Web pages. Before looking at a lot of Internet information, take a few minutes to familiarize yourself with the Internet Explorer screen.

Step 2: Action

1. Study Figure 14.3 to learn the parts of the Internet Explorer screen. Internet Explorer displays your home page and lists the home page's address in the address area.

FIGURE 14.3

Learn the Internet Explorer screen so that you can make the most of your time with the Internet Explorer browser

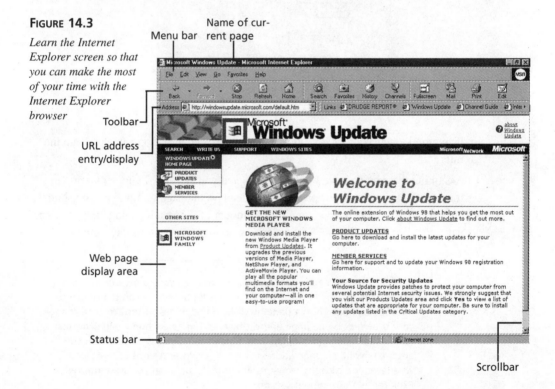

Menu bar • Name of current page • Toolbar • URL address entry/display • Web page display area • Status bar • Scrollbar

 You probably recognize Internet Explorer's toolbar. Windows 95 intentionally puts similar buttons throughout all of its windows (in Web view) so that you can navigate the Web from Windows 95 Explorer, My Computer, and other locations.

▼   2. Some Web site addresses are lengthy. Drag the Address text box left or right (giving more or less room to the link buttons) to adjust the address display width. The more room you give to the Address text box, the less room for the other toolbar buttons. You can maximize and minimize the Address text box by double-clicking its slider control.

3. Click the down arrow at the right of the address entry to open a list of recently traversed site addresses. If this is the first time you or anyone has used your computer's Internet Explorer, you might not see sites other than the current start page site. The toolbar's History button opens the left window pane shown in Figure 14.4 that lets you return to previous sites you've gone to in past Internet visits. If you click any of the sites (you can click other day names to open that day's sites), the display area (now at the right of the screen) updates to show that site. You can return to a single-page view by clicking the left window pane's Close button.

FIGURE 14.4

Internet Explorer uses the left side of the screen for various Internet functions such as the display of this history list

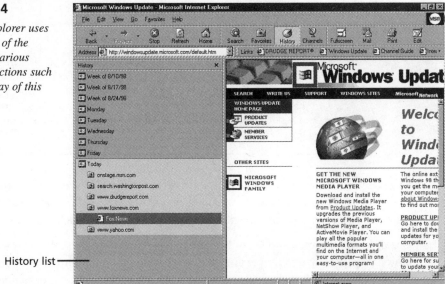

History list

4. Click the scrollbar to see more of the page. Most Web pages take more room than will fit on one screen.

5. Select View | Full Screen to dedicate all of your screen to the Web page except for a part of the toolbar at the top of the screen.

6. When looking at a full screen view, your menus still work, so you can again
▼   change the view by clicking Alt+V to display the View menu.

14

▼ **Step 3: Review**

Familiarize yourself with Internet Explorer's screen elements. As you traverse the
Internet, Internet Explorer helps you—as you'll see throughout the rest of this hour. By
adjusting the screen's elements, you can see more or less of large Web pages you
▲ encounter.

Surfing the Internet

Remember that the Web is a collection of inter-connected Web pages. Almost every Web
page contains links to other sites. These links (often called *hot links* or *hypertext links*)
are often underlined. (That's why, for consistency, the Windows 95 Active Desktop
underlines icons and provides one-click access to these icons.) You can locate these links
by moving your mouse cursor over the underlined description. If the mouse cursor
changes to a hand, you can click the hand to move to that page. After a brief pause, your
Web browser displays the page.

> A link is nothing more than an URL address to another Web site. Traverse
> related Web pages without worrying about addresses; just click link descrip-
> tions to move to those sites. In Hour 16, "Activating Your Desktop," you'll
> learn that if you change the display properties of the Windows 95 desktop,
> you can make your desktop act like hot links and view areas on your own PC
> inside Internet Explorer's Web page.

Suppose you view the home page of your financial broker. The page might include links
to other related pages, such as stock quotation pages, company financial informational
pages, and order-entry pages in which you can enter your own stock purchase requests.

One of the most useful features of Internet Explorer and every other Web browser is the
browser's capability to return to sites you've visited both in the current session and in
former sessions. The toolbar's Back button takes you back to a site or page you just visited, and you can keep clicking the Back button to return to pages you've visited this session. The Forward toolbar button returns you to pages from where you've backed up.

Keep in mind that you can click the Address drop-down list box to see a list of URL
addresses you've visited. In the History pane, you can find addresses from the current as
well as previous Internet Explorer Web sessions. If you know the address of a Web site
you want to view, you can type the site's address directly in the Address text box. When
you press Enter, Internet Explorer takes you to that site and displays the Web page.

Internet Explorer 4 fully integrates into Windows 95 and Windows 95 applications more than any previous browser. Most of the Microsoft Office products, for example, include an Internet Explorer-like interface in many areas, and they link directly to Internet Explorer when you perform certain Internet-related tasks from within an Office product. In some cases, you can bypass Explorer when you want a file listing or when you want to view a file while surfing Internet Web pages. From Internet Explorer's own Address text box or the File | Open dialog box, instead of entering a URL address, type a disk, pathname, and filename. If Internet Explorer recognizes the file's registered type, you'll see the file's contents.

If you find a location you really like, save that location in Internet Explorer's Favorites list. For example, if you run across a site that discusses your favorite television show and you want to return to that site again quickly, click the Favorites toolbar button and add the site to your Favorites list. The Address history does not keep track of a lot of recently visited addresses; you can, however, store your favorite sites in the Favorites folders so that you can quickly access them during another Internet session.

Many non-browser products, such as Microsoft Office, let you add Web links to non-Internet documents such as Word documents. When you type an URL address in Word, Word underlines the address. If you—or someone who reads your document from within Word—clicks on the URL link, Word automatically starts Internet Explorer (or whatever browser you use); as soon as Internet Explorer locates the page, it appears onscreen.

▼ To Do

Task 14.3: Moving Between Pages

Step 1: Description

This task lets you practice using the Internet Explorer browser to move between Web pages. After you visit a site, you can return to that site very simply.

Step 2: Action

1. If you have not started Internet Explorer, start it and log on to the Internet.

2. Click the Address list box to highlight your start page's URL address.

3. Type the following Web page address: `http://www.mcp.com`. Macmillan Publishing's home page appears, as shown in Figure 14.5. (Depending on the changes that have been made to the site recently, the site might not match Figure 14.5 exactly.)

▼

14

FIGURE 14.5

*Macmillan
Publishing's home
page*

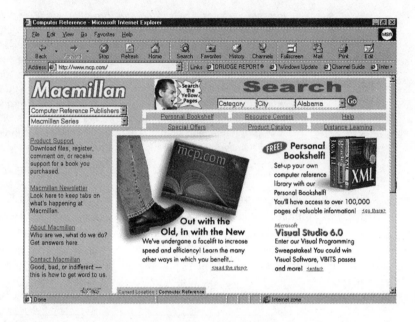

Often, you see Web addresses prefaced with the text http://. Internet
Explorer does not require the prefix before URLs.

Most Web addresses follow the format www.*SiteName*.com. If you type only
the *SiteName* in the Address text box and press Ctrl+Enter, Internet Explorer
converts the address to the full format and searches for the site.

4. Click any link on the page. After a brief pause, you see the linked Web page.
5. Click the toolbar's Back button. Almost instantly, the first page appears.

Internet Explorer (as well as most browsers) keeps a history of Web page
content in memory and on your disk, so the page appears quickly because
your browser actually reloads the page from buffered memory and not from
the original site. While waiting on non-buffered sites, the Internet Explorer
status bar shows you the progress as the page loads.

6. When you're back at Macmillan Publishing's home page, practice building a favorite site list by clicking the Favorites toolbar button.

7. Select the Favorites | Add To Favorites menu option. Internet Explorer displays the Add to Favorites dialog box.

8. Enter a description for the page. Make the description something you will remember the page by (such as `Macmillan Computer Book Publishing`) and click OK.

9. Click the Favorites toolbar button again. You'll see the new entry. When you select the favorite entry, Internet Explorer looks up that entry's stored URL address and goes to that Web page.

Step 3: Review

The toolbar makes it easy to visit and revisit Web sites that interest you. You can return to previous sites and move forward again.

> If you add too many favorites, your Favorites list becomes unmanageable. Create folders from the Add to Favorites dialog box's Create In button. By setting up a series of named folders named by subjects, you can group your favorite Web sites by subject.

Task 14.4: Refreshing and Stopping the Display
Step 1: Description

As you saw in the previous task, Internet Explorer saves recent Web page contents in a memory buffer. Therefore, even if a Web page contains lots of information and requires a minute or longer to load, if you return to that page in a subsequent session, your browser often displays the in-memory Web page. Although the memory buffer speeds things up, you might not want to see the buffer's Web page. You might, instead, want to see the original page in case the site has changed since your last visit.

Step 2: Action

1. Return to Macmillan Publishing's Web site again (`http://www.mcp.com`, in case you did not save the site).

2. Click on a link from that site.

3. Click the Back button to go right back. The site should appear almost instantly because you are actually viewing the site from your stored memory buffer.

4. Suppose you suspect that data has changed on the site and you want to see the real site again. Click the toolbar's Refresh button. Internet Explorer reloads the Web

To Do

14

▼ page from its original location. After the page loads, you see the page again with any updates that might have been applied since your last visit.

5. Click the Refresh button again to redisplay the page, but then immediately click the toolbar's Stop button. Instantly, Internet Explorer stops refreshing the page. Any graphic images not yet loaded remain as placeholders and do not appear no matter how long you view the page. The Stop button is useful for stopping the loading of a slow-loading Web page. If you have no need to see the images but you're only interested in the text that quickly appears, you can reduce the Internet traffic by stopping the page before it completely loads. Obviously, you do not want to stop the loading process unless you are familiar with the page's contents. Some Web pages contain videos and sound files that can take awhile to load.

6. You can limit the type of content sent from the Internet to Internet Explorer to speed your Web page surfing. To do this, select View | Options and click the Advanced tab. Uncheck the options under the Multimedia entry to limit pictures, animations, videos, or sounds from coming into your browser when you reach a Web page.

Step 3: Review

Use the Stop and Refresh buttons to control the loading of Web pages. The Stop button keeps Web pages from fully loading. You can click Stop as soon as you see as much of the page as you want to see. Click Refresh if you view a Web page from your memory buffer but want to reload the page from its URL address. If you suspect that a Web page has been updated since you last visited the page, click Refresh so that you can be assured you've seen the most recent version. In addition to controlling individual pages with Stop and Refresh, you can set options that prevent certain time-consuming Web page ele-
▲ ments, such as videos and sounds, from arriving at your browser.

Search for the Information You Need

How can you expect to find any information on a vast network of networks such as the Internet? Web pages offer linked sites in an appealing format that lets you comfortably view information and see related pages, but you must know the location of one of the site's pages before the links can help.

Fortunately, Internet Explorer (and other Web browsers) offers a searching mechanism that helps you locate information on the Web. By clicking the Search toolbar button, you select one of several search engines and enter your search value.

The Search Web page offers the benefit of multiple *search engines*. A search engine is a Web page that lets you enter words and phrases to search for, and then the search engine scans the vast information on the Web to locate sites that contain the phrase. The accuracy of the search depends on the words and phrases you enter, as well as the capability of the search engine. For example, some search engines you can choose from search only Web pages whereas others search *newsgroups* (discussion areas that hold files and messages related to topics).

After the search page concludes the search, Internet Explorer displays from zero to several address links on which you can click to find information about your topic. For example, Figure 14.6 shows the result of one search after dragging the search window edge to the right to read more of the search results. By scrolling down the page (and by clicking the additional pages of links if your search turns up a lot of sites), you can read the descriptions of the pages (the descriptions often contain the first few lines of the located Web page text). When you click a search result, that result's URL appears in the right window pane's Web browser.

FIGURE 14.6

The results of a search might produce several pages of Web sites

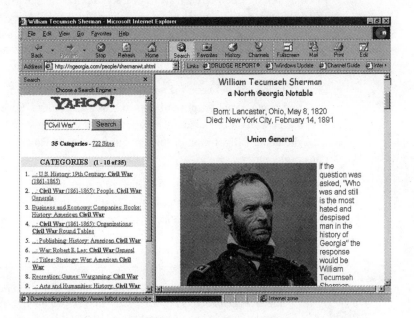

Each search engine locates information differently, and each search engine has its own rules for the words and phrases you enter. Keep in mind that the more specific your search phrase is, the more accurately the search engine can find information that will help you.

14

If your search failed to locate information you think is on the Web, or if the search turned up too many sites and you want to narrow the search, you

> can often click the search engine's Options or More Information button to read the search criteria rules for that search engine.

Generally, you can use these guidelines with most search engines:

- Enclose a multiple word phrase in quotation marks if you want the search engine to search for those words in the order you list. For example, if you enter `"Bill Clinton"`, the search engine searches for that specific name. If, however, you enter `Bill Clinton` (without the quotes), most search engines locate every site that contains the word Bill and every site that contains the word Clinton, most of which would have nothing to do with the man you originally wanted to locate.

- Place a plus sign before each word or quoted phrase when you want to search for Web sites that contain every word and phrase in the list. For example, entering `+"Rush Limbaugh" +Congress` would find only those sites that contain the name Rush Limbaugh and the word Congress, but would not find sites that listed only one or the other.

- Place the word `OR` between the words or quoted phrases if you want to search for sites that contain one or more of your words and phrases. For example, entering `"Bill Clinton" OR "Rush Limbaugh"` would locate any and every site that contains the name Bill Clinton or that contains the name Rush Limbaugh or that contains both names.

Remember that these search criteria rules are only guidelines that often work. Some search engines follow slightly different rules. You have to look up that search engine's help references for specific information if the previous rules do not seem to work the way you expect.

Most of the search engines are case sensitive when you mix uppercase and lowercase characters in your search; that is, you need to type words and phrases exactly as you expect them to appear if you want the search to match your search case exactly. Otherwise, if you enter a search criteria in all lowercase letters, the search engines generally do not base the match on case. Therefore, if you want to locate the city named Flint (in Michigan), enter `Flint`. Otherwise, if you enter the name in all lowercase letters, the search engine will probably search both for the city name as well as the rock.

Summary

This hour explained what the Internet is all about and how to access the Internet using Internet Explorer 4. Although Internet information appears in many forms, the most useful Internet often appears on Web pages that contain text, graphics, sound, and video.

Windows 95 supports Internet Explorer 4 with which you can view Web pages. Internet Explorer includes searching tools as well as a history system that keeps track of recent Web pages. Not only can you view Web pages with Internet Explorer, but you can also view other kinds of files on your computer. As the Internet becomes more organized and as Internet access gets faster and cheaper, you will make the Web browser more and more of your daily computing routine. One day, you'll find that you do most of your work from Web browsing software such as Internet Explorer.

Workshop

Term Review

browser   Software that searches for, loads, and displays information from Internet Web pages. Browsers display the text, graphics, sound, and even video that appear on modern Web pages.

home page   A Web site's foundational page from which all other pages connect. Often, your browser's starting page is the home page of a Web site such as Microsoft's home page.

hot links   (Also called links and hypertext links) Web page items with descriptions that you can click to display other Web pages. Often, a Web page contains several links to other sites that contain related information.

Internet   A collection of networked computer systems that contain a vast assortment of information, accessible by using a modem.

Internet Explorer   The Web browsing software that Microsoft provides with Windows 95.

search engine   A program that locates information on the Web.

Site   The location of a Web page or set of related Web pages.

URL address   (Stands for Uniform Resource Locator) The technical address of a Web page's location. When you enter the URL address in your browser's address text box, the browser locates that address's Web page and displays the Web page's contents.

14

Web   A system for formatting Internet information into readable and manageable pages of text, graphics, video, and sound.

WWW (Stands for Wide World Web)   See Web.

Q&A

Q I've clicked the Internet icon but I don't see Web pages. What do I have to do to get on the Internet?

A Do you have Internet access from Microsoft Network or from another Internet Service Provider? Generally, unless you work for a company that offers Internet access to its employees, you have to sign up for Internet access, get the access phone number, pay a monthly fee (most Internet Service Providers offer unlimited access for a flat monthly rate), and set up your browser, such as Internet Explorer, to access that provider.

If you want to use one of the services inside the desktop's Online Services folder, Hour 13, "Using the Online Services Window," tells you how to access the services by following wizards that sign you up for a subscription.

Q How do I know if I'm viewing a Web page from the memory buffer or from the actual site?

A If the page appears almost instantly after you enter the address, the chances are great that you are looking at the page from your browser's memory. In most cases, the memory's page matches the actual Web site. Nevertheless, if you want to make sure you're viewing the latest and greatest version of the Web page, click the Refresh toolbar button. Refresh forces Internet Explorer to reload the page from the actual site's address.

Hour 15

Email and Newsgroups

Internet Explorer 4 includes a program called *Outlook Express* that manages both email as well as newsgroup information. Outlook Express replaces older Windows messaging programs called *Windows Messaging* and *Windows Exchange*. By combining a newsgroup reader with email capabilities, you can manage more information easier than before.

Email plays as big or bigger role in today's communications as regular mail. Email's paperless aspect keeps your desk less cluttered, and email generally arrives at its destination within a few minutes to a few hours. Newsgroups offer a different kind of messaging center for messages you want to communicate publicly on a topic. You can post newsgroup topics, answers, and questions as well as read responses from others interested in the same subject.

The highlights of this hour include:

- How Outlook Express lets you view and send email messages
- When to attach files to email messages you send
- How to set up a signature file
- How to post and read newsgroup messages

The Email World

It is common for computer users to access more than one online service. Perhaps you work on the Internet as well as on America Online. Each morning, you might log on to the Internet to get incoming messages and send your outgoing Internet messages. When finished, you might log on to America Online to send and receive those messages. The burden of managing that electronic mail grows as more people sign up for more than one online service.

Are we living in a *paperless society*, as promised by the Management Information System gurus of the early 1970s? Not a chance. Computers help us use more paper and at a *faster* rate than ever before. It's often said in the computer industry that, despite the prevalence of electronic mail, we'll have paperless bathrooms before we'll have a paperless society!

Wouldn't it be nice to tell your computer to send and receive all your electronic mail without any intervention on your part? The computer could store all received mail in a central location; you could then manage, sort, print, respond to, or delete from there. Outlook Express provides the one-stop answer.

Outlook Express is not the same program as *Outlook* that comes with Microsoft Office 97 and later. The Microsoft Office's Outlook has more features than Outlook Express. With the Office Outlook, you can keep track of contacts, appointments, to-do lists, and plan meetings.

Managing Email with Outlook Express

Outlook Express offers benefits over previous email programs because Outlook Express supports several formats within an email message. Although you could send text data, *binary data* (compressed data such as programs and graphics), sound files, and video as email in previous programs, Outlook Express lets you store HTML code inside your message so that you can customize the look of your message. A message you send might look like a Web page. You can even send complete Web pages as email inside Outlook Express. If you embed a URL inside an email message, the recipient of your message can click that URL and go straight to that site on the Web.

Here are some of the additional features of Outlook Express's email capabilities:

- View email as text only to speed performance at the loss of seeing formatted messages
- Attach files to your messages
- Check spelling before you send a message
- Reply to messages and forward messages to other recipients
- Connect to Web-based email address search engines, such as Four11, to find people's addresses
- Connect to the Windows Address Book program. Address Book is compatible with several other address programs such as Microsoft Office's Outlook
- Send and receive mail to and from multiple Internet accounts

You can start Outlook Express from Internet Explorer (as this hour generally suggests) or open your taskbar's Email icon to start Outlook Express. If you use a more comprehensive email program, such as Office's Outlook, that email program begins instead of Outlook Express when you click the taskbar's email icon.

Task 15.1: Setting Up Outlook Express

Step 1: Description

This task explains how to set up Outlook Express for use within Internet Explorer.

If a wizard begins when you start Outlook Express the first time, you need to answer the wizard's prompts to set up your email account. Most of the online services, such as Prodigy, automatically set up Outlook Express. If you see the wizard, you might need to contact your ISP to determine which settings are needed for Outlook Express to recognize your ISP-based email account.

Step 2: Action

1. Start Internet Explorer and log in to your Internet account.
2. Select View | Internet Options and click the Programs tab to display Figure 15.1's the Programs page of the Internet Options dialog box.

FIGURE 15.1

Make sure Internet Explorer knows about Outlook Express

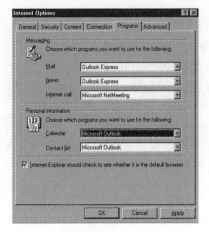

3. Select Outlook Express from the first two options labeled Mail and News, as Figure 15.1 shows. (Microsoft NetMeeting lets you contact other Internet users and set up chat and even voice-based meetings.)

4. Click OK to close the Internet Options dialog box. When you send or receive mail, Internet Explorer now uses Outlook Express as your email program.

> Outlook Express is smart and recognizes if you've already set up another email program before installing Internet Explorer. If you see Figure 15.2's dialog box the first time you use Outlook Express to send or receive a message, Outlook Express offers to use your previous email program's messages and addresses so you don't have to re-enter them in Outlook Express. Follow the wizard to load any or all of your previous program's options.

Step 3: Review

After you've told Internet Explorer that you want to use Outlook Express as your email program, Internet Explorer remembers your setup and uses Outlook Express every time you send or receive email.

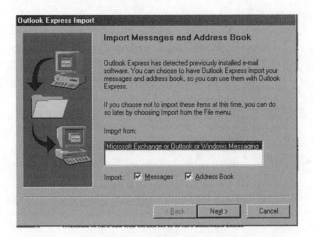

FIGURE 15.2

Outlook Express imports your messages and addresses from your former email program

15

Task 15.2: Sending Mail with Outlook Express

Step 1: Description

This task explains how to send various forms of email to recipients. Outlook Express has many options, but you can send email messages and files to others very easily without worrying too much about what else is under Outlook Express's hood.

Step 2: Action

1. Start Internet Explorer and log in to your Internet account.

2. Click the toolbar's Mail button and select New Message from the menu that drops down. The New Message dialog box opens as shown in Figure 15.3.

3. Enter your recipient's email address in the To field or click the file card icon beside the To field. If you know the name under which you stored an email address in the Windows Address Book, you can type the name instead of the email address in this field.

4. Use the Cc field to send copies of your message to another recipient. The recipient will know that the message was copied to her. If you enter an email address in the Bcc field, your recipient will not know that others received the message because the Bcc address is hidden.

5. Enter a subject line. Get in the habit of entering a subject so your recipients can file your messages by subject.

FIGURE 15.3

You can now send a message to one or more recipients

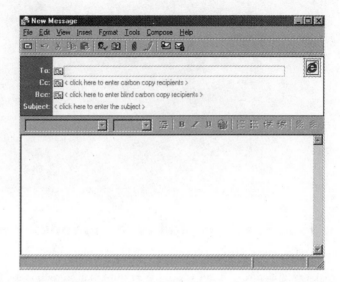

6. Press the Tab or Shift+Tab key to move from field to field. When you type the message in the message area, the scrollbar appears to let you scroll through messages that don't fit inside the window completely. Use the formatting toolbar above the message area to apply formatting, color, and even numbered and bulleted lists to your message.

7. If you want to attach one or more files to your message, click the Attach toolbar button (the one with the paper clip) and select your file from the Insert Attachment dialog box that appears.

8. To send the message, click the Send button (the toolbar button with the flying envelope), and the message goes on its way to the recipients.

Step 3: Review

Sending email messages and files requires only that you know the person's email address or that you've stored the address in your Windows Address book. Attach files of any type to your message and the recipient will receive the message and the files.

Task 15.3: Sending Web Pages as Email

Step 1: Description

This task explains how to send Web pages to email recipients.

Step 2: Action

1. Start Internet Explorer and log in to your Internet account.

▼   2. Display the Web page that you want to send to somebody. (You can send the page
        to your own email account for a test.)

     3. Click the toolbar's Mail button.

     4. Select Send Page. If the Web page is complicated, it might be considered a *read-
        only Web page* that cannot be edited. If so, Internet Explorer displays a message
        telling you that your recipient can receive the message as an attached file or as a
        read-only file. In this case, if you are sending the page to yourself or to someone
        who you know has Internet Explorer, send the page as a read-only page.

     5. The email window opens so that you can select a recipient and add copies to others
        if you like. You can see the Web page at the bottom of the window as shown in
        Figure 15.4. Now *that's* quite a fancy email message!

FIGURE 15.4

*The recipient sees the
Web page when view-
ing this email*

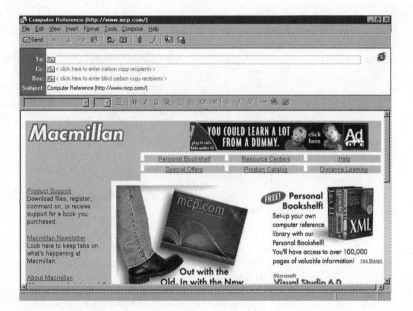

     6. Click the Send button to send the Web page.

Your recipient must also use an email program, such as Outlook Express, that
can display HTML code or else the recipient gets a lot of garbage in the message. Your recipient can still read the mail's text but the email contains a lot
of HTML formatting codes that are normally hidden. You can convert HTML
pages to straight text from the Format menu.

▼

▼ Step 3: Review

If you locate a Web site you want someone else to see, send that site to the person via email. Internet Explorer's Mail toolbar button contains a menu option that makes sending
▲ Web pages to others a breeze.

Task 15.4: Receiving Email

Step 1: Description

This task explains how to receive the email that people send to you.

Step 2: Action

1. Start Internet Explorer and log in to your Internet account.
2. Click the toolbar's Mail button.
3. Select Read Mail. Figure 15.5's mail center window appears.

FIGURE 15.5

Check your email from this window

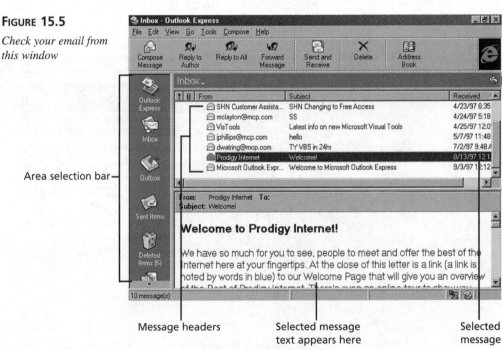

Area selection bar

Message headers   Selected message text appears here   Selected message

Outlook Express checks for new mail every few minutes depending on how often you set up the interval. You can, at any time, manually check for new mail and send any that has yet to be sent by clicking the toolbar's Send or Receive buttons. You don't have to be logged on to the Internet to create email, but you must be ▼ logged on to the Internet to send and receive email.

15

> Select Tools | Options and enter a new time value for the option labeled
> Check for new messages every *10* minutes if you want Outlook Express to
> check for incoming email more or less often than the 10-minute default.

The *Outbox* area (you can click on the Area selection bar to see your Outbox contents) holds items that you've readied to send but that have not actually gone out yet. When your Outbox contains unsent mail, the icon changes to show mail in the Outbox.

4. As you click on the headers in the Inbox, a preview appears for that message in the lower pane. (Drag the center bar up or down to make more or less room for the headers.) If you double-click on an Inbox item, a window opens so you can view that message from a larger window without the other screen elements getting in the way.

5. Delete mail you don't want by selecting one or more message headers and dragging them to the Deleted Items icon or selecting the item and pressing your delete key. The Deleted Items icon acts like the Windows 95 Recycle Bin. Mail does not really go away until you delete items from the Deleted Items area by clicking on the Deleted Items icon and removing unwanted mail.

6. You can easily reply to a message's author, or to the entire group if you were one of several who received the email, by clicking the Reply to Author or Reply to All toolbar button. In addition, when reading email, you can compose a new message by clicking on the toolbar's Compose Message button.

> Create new folders in the Area selection bar column so that you can orga-
> nize your email the way you want it. Right-click over the bar and select New
> Folder. For example, you might want to create a new folder that holds busi-
> ness correspondence and another for personal email. You can drag messages
> to either location to put mail together with others that match the same pur-
> pose.

Step 3: Review

Receiving email with Outlook Express is easier than going to your front porch mailbox! From Internet Explorer, you click the Mail icon and read your Inbox message *headers*. (A header is the message's sender ID and subject that you see from the Inbox.)

When you're in Outlook Express, click the Area selection bar's icon labeled Outlook Express to see the one-click Outlook Express window as shown in Figure 15.6. From this window, you can easily read and compose email, modify your Microsoft Address Book entries, locate people, and check newsgroups. (The next section describes newsgroup access.)

FIGURE 15.6

The Outlook Express folder shows this one-step usage screen

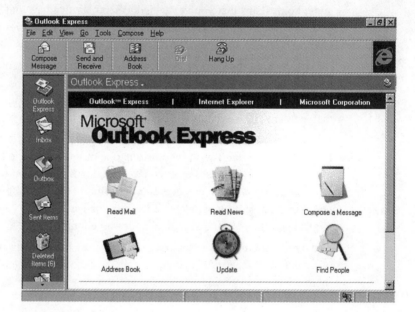

Using Newsgroups

In a way, a newsgroup acts like a combination between a slow email program and a community bulletin board. Newsgroups have little or nothing to do with the daily news. Instead, they are thousands of lists, arranged by subject, that hold messages and files that you and others can post and read.

Suppose you are interested in rollerblading and want to trade information you have with others who are interested in the sport. You could find one of the several newsgroups related to rollerblading and read the hundreds of messages and files posted to that newsgroup. Depending on the Internet service you use and the newsgroup filing rules, you can find messages months old or only from the past few days. Often, the larger newsgroups can keep only a limited number of days' worth of messages and files in the newsgroup.

This is how newsgroups act like slow email services: If someone has posted a question you know the answer to, you can post a reply. Your reply is seen by all in the newsgroup who want to read the reply. There is no guarantee that the person who submitted the question will ever go back to the newsgroup to read the answer, but the postings are for anybody and everybody who is interested.

Each ISP provides access to a different number of the thousands and thousands of newsgroups in existence. To see newsgroups available to your service, click Internet Explorer's Mail button and select Read News. Although your ISP might give you access to thousands of newsgroups, you'll want to subscribe just to those that interest you. Click Outlook Express's Newsgroups button to display the Newsgroups listing dialog box shown in Figure 15.7.

FIGURE 15.7

Select the newsgroups you want to subscribe to

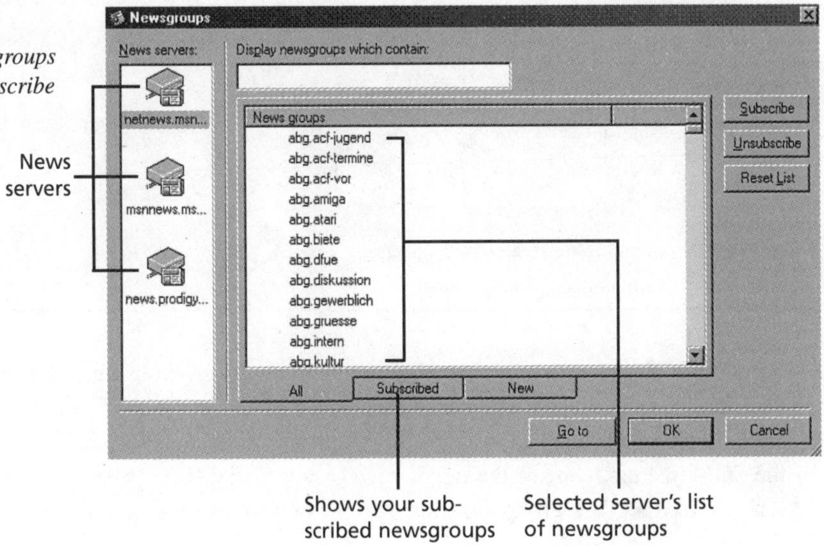

News servers

Shows your sub-
scribed newsgroups

Selected server's list
of newsgroups

You might see one or more news servers in the left column. Each news server contains a different set of newsgroups. Your ISP determines the number of servers that appear in the news server column. When you click on a server, the list of newsgroups that reside on that server appears in the center of the window.

Bear in mind that some servers contain thousands of newsgroups, and the first time you access a news server, that list downloads from the server to your PC so you can quickly scroll through the list in subsequent sessions. This download process might take a few minutes as indicated by the dialog box that appears during the download.

The newsgroups have strange names such as `rec.pets.dogs` and `alt.algebra.help`. Table 15.1 describes what the more common newsgroup prefixes stand for. Somewhere else in the newsgroup name you can often glean more information about the newsgroup's primary topic; for example, a newsgroup named `rec.sport.skating.roller` would probably contain skating news and `alt.autos.italian` would contain files and messages pertaining to Italian cars (*i macchina l'italiani!*).

TABLE 15.1 COMMON NEWSGROUP PREFIXES DESCRIBE THE NATURE OF THE NEWSGROUP

Prefix	Description
alt	Groups that allow for informal content and are not necessarily as widely distributed as the other newsgroups
biz	Business-related newsgroups
comp	Computer-related newsgroups
misc	Random newsgroups
rec	Recreational and sporting newsgroups
sci	Scientific newsgroups
soc	Social issue-related newsgroups
talk	Debate newsgroups

Scroll through the newsgroup list to find the newsgroups you want to see. When you find one or more newsgroups you want to see, subscribe to those newsgroups by double-clicking on the newsgroup name (or highlight the name and click Subscribe). If you click the Subscribe tab, you see the list of newsgroups you've subscribed to. Click the OK button to close the Newsgroups window and prepare to read the news.

> Enter a search topic in the text box at the top of the Newsgroups window to display newsgroups that contain that topic.

 To Do

Task 15.5: Reading and Posting Newsgroup News
Step 1: Description

This task explains how to read newsgroup messages and post messages to the newsgroups. Keep in mind that a message can be a short note or an entire file. As with email, if a news posting contains a file, the file will come as an attachment to the message.

Step 2: Action

▼

1. Start Internet Explorer and log in to your Internet account.

▼   2. Click the toolbar's Mail button.

     3. Select Read News. A list of your subscribed newsgroups appears as shown in Figure 15.8.

FIGURE 15.8

Your subscribed news-group messages appear when you first request newsgroup access

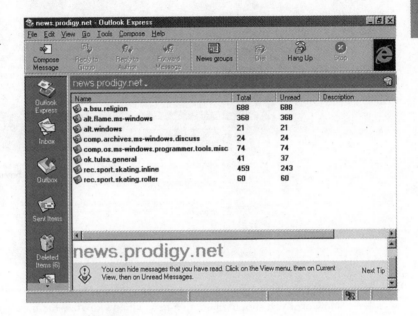

4. To read messages in a newsgroup, double-click that newsgroup name. Figure 15.9 appears showing the newsgroups in the upper window and the text for the selected newsgroup in the lower window. Some long messages take a while to arrive, and you don't see any of the message until the entire message downloads to your PC.

If a message has a plus sign next to it, click the plus sign to open all related messages. If someone posts a question, for example, and several people reply to that posting, all of those related messages group under the first question's message, and you can see the replies only after you click the plus sign. The plus sign becomes a minus sign when you expand the newsgroup item so that you can collapse the item again.

Some newsgroups are moderated better than others are. You'll often find unrelated messages throughout all newsgroups that don't belong within that newsgroup.

▼

FIGURE 15.9

Scroll through the news message headers and see the details in the lower window

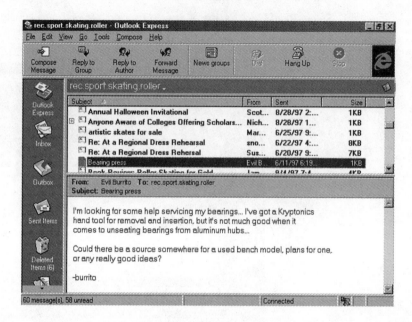

5. Check the Size column to determine if you can read the message in the lower window or if you should open up a new window to view the message. If a message is over 2K or 3K in size, you should probably double-click the message header to view the message inside a scrollable window. The window contains a menu that lets you save the message in a file on your disk for later retrieval. If a message has an attachment, you must open the message in a separate window to save the attachment as a file on your disk.

   After you've read a message inside the preview pane, you can click another message header to preview a different message. If you view a message in a separate window, you can close the window and choose a different message to view.

6. If you want to reply to a message, you have two options: Reply to the group, in which case everybody who subscribes to the newsgroup can read your reply (which is the general idea of newsgroups), or you can reply to the author privately via email. The Reply to Group and Reply to Author toolbar buttons accomplish this purpose. Each copies the original message at the bottom of your reply.

   You don't have to reply to existing messages. You can also start a new message *thread* (related postings) by clicking the Compose Message button and typing a new message. Your message appears in the newsgroup as a new post and not part of a chain of previous postings.

▼ **Step 3: Review**

Probably the biggest problem with newsgroups is the time you waste in them! You might hop over to a newsgroup to see if the group contains an answer you need and two hours later you find yourself still reading the postings there. Newsgroups can provide a wealth of information on thousands and thousands of topics. Although the Web is great for organizing information into collections of pages, newsgroups are useful for the straight mes-
▲ sages and files that people want to share with each other.

Summary

This hour explained how to use Outlook Express, Internet Explorer's email program and newsgroup manager. Email is a major part of the Internet user's life these days, and you'll appreciate Outlook Express's advanced support and email management simplicity.

If you want detailed information on a subject, you can search the Web for all kinds of data, but remember to look for related newsgroups as well. Whereas some Web sites are often consumer-related collections of merchandise and hype, newsgroups often contain thousands of messages from people such as yourself who have questions and answers to provide others with the same interest.

Workshop

Term Review

binary data   Compressed data such as programs and graphics as opposed to text files.

Deleted Items folder   The Outlook Express folder that holds email messages that you delete from other folders. When you delete items from the Deleted Items folder, the items completely go away and you cannot recover them.

Header   The Inbox's one-line display that shows an incoming message's sender, subject, and date received.

Inbox   The Outlook Express folder that holds your incoming email.

Outbox   The Outlook Express folder that holds your outgoing email that has yet to be sent. After Outlook Express sends the message, the Sent items folder holds a copy of the message.

Outlook Express   An Internet Explorer 4 program that manages both your email and newsgroup access.

read-only Web page   A Web page that contains frames and other advanced HTML code that cannot be changed.

Sent Items folder   The Outlook Express folder that holds all messages that you have sent over the Internet.

Thread   A set of postings that go together such as a question and the answer replies.

Windows Exchange   A pre-Windows Messaging program used by earlier versions of Windows to manage email.

Windows Messaging   A program used by earlier Windows versions to manage email.

Q&A

Q How can I get email from my multiple Internet accounts?

A If you subscribe to multiple online services or to multiple ISPs, you can set up Outlook Express to send and retrieve email from all your Internet accounts. Select Tools | Accounts to display the Internet Accounts dialog box. Select Add | Mail and follow the wizard to add your accounts to the email list. You almost surely have to contact your ISP to get the wizard's requested information. After you set up the accounts, Outlook Express checks each one when you request new mail.

Q I read a newsgroup message last month that I can no longer find in the newsgroup. How can I see old messages?

A Often you cannot. Each news server holds a limited number of messages (your news server has only so much disk space!). Often, Outlook Express downloads at most 300 messages at any one time. Sometimes, the server has more than 300 messages that are available. To request that Outlook Express retrieve additional messages, select Tools | Get Next 300 Headers. If more than 300 messages are available, Outlook Express downloads up to 300 more.

HOUR 16

Activating Your Desktop

Some of Windows 95's biggest differences over its predecessor, Windows 3.1, are a snazzy new interface, new menu structure, new hardware support, and new ease of use. Windows 95 also offers increased ease with connecting to the World Wide Web. If you aren't connected to the Web, you probably soon will be. Windows 95 makes that connection simple.

Actually, Windows 95 and active desktop seem to blur the line between online and desktop computing. With active desktop turned on, it's difficult to tell in parts of Windows 95 if you're working on the Internet, on a local disk file, or using a combination of both. You'll find Web-related features throughout all areas of Windows 95. Even the Windows desktop, for years the local PC's wholly-owned area, now might contain live content being sent there from the Internet.

The highlights of this hour include:

- How the Web-like Internet Explorer 4 interface works to eliminate desktop and Internet access differences
- How your taskbar gives simple access to the Internet

- How to set up a Web page element as wallpaper
- What push technology is all about
- How to place push content on your desktop
- Why channel technology gives you more specific information than push technology
- How to subscribe to channels you want

Your Desktop and the Web

In Hour 3, "Take Windows 95 to Task," you learned how to add Web-like selection and execution to your desktop icons. Internet Explorer 4 provides the mechanism for the Web-like Windows 95 interface. On the Web, when you click once on an icon that links you to another spot, the single click takes you to that remote spot, and the one-click access of Windows 95 icons helps blur the distinction between your desktop and the connected Internet.

Microsoft is pushing this desktop/Web blur for good reason. The Internet is part of today's computing environment. Although millions of PC users still don't use the Internet, the Internet's growth has outpaced all expectations, and the sheer number of current users, plus the expected number of users in the next five years, make the Internet the most important component in the computing world.

Why should the desktop be distinct from the online world? You access files on your disk drives, perhaps on networked drives, and also on the Internet. Shouldn't you use the same browser to access all of them? Should your interface for any file, no matter where that file resides, be the same so that you don't have to learn two separate programs to manage your data?

Online via Modems and Faster Connections

The tight Web and desktop combination does fall apart in one respect—at least for the time being. If you access the Internet through a company's *T1 connection* (a high-speed wired Internet connection that gives you constant Web access), or through cable-modem access provided by your local cable company, you will more likely understand how the desktop and Web can be blurred and work together. If, however, you use a modem to access the Internet, as millions do each day, the desktop and Web distinction can be blurred as much as possible but you'll still face two real walls: *speed* and *connection*.

If you have a quick Internet connection such as a T1 and if you don't have to fight busy signals to log in, moving from a one-PC desktop to a connected desktop is not a leap. Your own files as well as those on the Internet are available when you want them. A Web

16

page that you traverse appears almost as quickly as a word processor file you stored yesterday on your hard disk. If, however, you must fight busy signals, log in, and use a fairly slow connection (as you have to do even with the fastest of today's modems), you are painfully aware that even though Windows 95's desktop provides access to a seamless Internet connection, the reality is that you always must make some effort to get on the Internet.

Perhaps you can be reassured that such Internet connections are probably not going to last forever. The Internet's slow modem speeds are being worked on. Although more and more people use the Internet each day, your speed should never get *worse* than today's speed, and many companies are working on getting the Internet faster for all. Therefore, the seamless desktop is worth the trouble even if you still use a modem for Internet access. Although you'll still face the modem connection woes that often arise, your Windows 95 desktop is prepared for the day when that fast Internet connection will arrive.

Taskbar Web Access

If you've set up the taskbar's Quick Launch toolbar, you can get to your Internet browser's start up home page by clicking one of the Internet Explorer icons on your taskbar. In addition, if you add the Address toolbar to your taskbar, you can type Web addresses directly on your taskbar and explore Web sites.

Your desktop is not the only place that you can put icons to launch programs quickly. You can add icons to your taskbar. Sometimes, the taskbar is called a *Quick Launch* bar due to its capability to hold program icons that you can click at any time to start the programs.

Special taskbar additions appear after you've installed Internet Explorer 4. To access these additions' configuration properties, right-click over a blank area of your taskbar. Figure 16.1 shows the pop-up menu that appears. Along with displaying the Taskbar Properties dialog box and the managing your desktop windows, the taskbar's right-click pop-up menu includes a Toolbars entry that lets you do the following:

FIGURE 16.1

Modify your taskbar from the right-click menu

- Address: Display or hide the address text box in which you can enter Internet addresses to view without having to start your Internet browser first.

- Links: Display or hide buttons that hold Internet sites. (You can add to the buttons from within your Internet browser program or by dragging Internet Web page icons to the Links taskbar area.)

- Desktop: Place or remove all your desktop icons on the taskbar so that you don't have to minimize your open windows to launch any desktop program.

- Quick Launch: Display or hide buttons from which you can start your Internet browser, retrieve email messages, minimize all open windows (with the Show Desktop button), or view your *Internet channels* (special Internet sites that send to your browser Web content).

- New Toolbar: Create your own toolbar of buttons that correspond to any folder on your system, including your Printers folder. The toolbar you create subsequently appears on the taskbar's right-click menu. By placing shortcuts, such as a shortcut to Windows Explorer, in your new toolbar's folder, you can enable one-click launching of any program on your PC.

> If your taskbar gets too cluttered with icons, you might have to drag the top edge up to give the taskbar more room.

Task 16.1: Setting Up the Taskbar for the Web
Step 1: Description
This task shows you how to set up your taskbar for Web exploration. Your taskbar is always present, so if you make your taskbar Web accessible, you've made it possible to get to the Web whenever you want.

> If you use a dial-up Internet Service Provider and you are not logged on to the Internet when you use a Web-based taskbar component, your Internet login window appears temporarily while you log in to the Internet. After you are logged in, your task will complete.

Step 2: Action
1. Right-click over your taskbar and select the Toolbars menu.
2. If Address has no check mark next to it, select Address to add the Address bar to your taskbar.
3. If Quick Launch has no check mark next to it, select Quick Launch to add the Quick Launch toolbar to your taskbar. Your taskbar now looks something like the

▼ one in Figure 16.2. As always, you can drag the taskbar's slider control left or right to give more room to any of the elements there. The Internet Explorer icon launches Internet Explorer and takes you to your browser's home page. The Show Desktop icon minimizes all open windows. The View Channels button gives you access to your push content as explained in this hour's final section.

FIGURE 16.2

Your taskbar provides quick Internet access

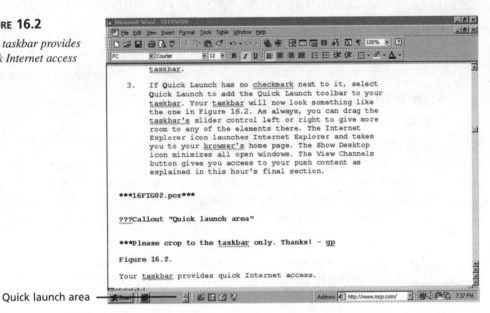

Quick launch area

4. Click the Internet Explorer icon to log in to the Internet if you're not already logged in and to view your home page.

5. Although you can use your browser to enter an URL, click your taskbar's Address field and enter a Web address such as www.microsoft.com to see its page. Even if you are not on the Internet and even if you do not have your browser running from Step 4, the page appears when you enter its address on the taskbar.

Step 3: Review

▲ The taskbar provides easy access to the Web when you work within Windows 95.

Active Desktop

One of the newest desktop features is the active desktop. The active desktop is so simple, you might not realize the power behind it right at the beginning. You can use *anything* that appears in your Web browser on your desktop as wallpaper. If you access a Web

16

page with a graphic, with a link to another page, with an *ActiveX* or *Java applet* (ActiveX and Java applets are miniature programs that arrive in your browser with a Web page), or with straight text, you can place that Web page element on your desktop for later reference.

Task 16.2: Sending Web Page Information to Your Desktop

Step 1: Description

This task shows you how to send Web page information to your desktop as wallpaper.

Step 2: Action

1. Display a Web page on your browser.

2. Right-click on a graphic or title on the Web page.

3. Select Set as Wallpaper. After a brief pause, click your taskbar's Show Desktop button to see your new wallpaper. Depending on your Display Properties settings, your wallpaper might be centered, *tiled* (repeated to cover your entire desktop), or stretched to fill your whole screen.

> If you open your Display Properties dialog box (by right-clicking over the desktop area) you will see your new wallpaper listed in the Background page's Wallpaper list.

4. Display your Web browser again.

5. Locate a link to another site.

6. Drag that link to your desktop. After a brief pause, your desktop will hold a shortcut to that page. You can subsequently go to that link simply by clicking the new desktop icon.

Step 3: Review

You can set any Web element such as a graphic or active applet as wallpaper by right-clicking on that element on a Web page. Your new wallpaper either fills your entire screen (if you've set up a proper tiled or stretched display property) or sits in the middle of your desktop.

> If your wallpaper element changes on its original Web site, your wallpaper will not reflect the change until you right-click over the wallpaper element and select Refresh.

Add Desktop Components

You can add active *components* to your desktop. A component is any Web-based document. A Web document generally has the filename extension *HTML* after the *HyperText Markup Language* used for Web page layout. You can create your own HTML files and place them on your desktop or use Web pages as a component.

16

> The difference between a component and wallpaper is that you can place as many components on your desktop as you have room for and resize them. You can activate one and only one element to be used as your desktop's wallpaper background at any one time.

The desktop components form the basis of the *push technology* that you'll learn about in this hour's final section.

Task 16.3: Adding Desktop Components

Step 1: Description

Almost any program written recently for Windows 95, such as Microsoft Word, can save data as an HTML file. These files can serve as desktop components as you'll see in this task. If you have wallpaper, the components do not replace the wallpaper but sit atop the desktop wallpaper. In this task, you'll create your own HTML file and use that file on your desktop as a component. You don't have to limit yourself to an HTML file, however. You can save virtually any document as a component on your desktop.

Step 2: Action

1. Select your Start menu's Programs | Programs\ Accessories | Notepad program. Notepad, a text editor, appears on your screen.

2. Type the following: **I want to activate my desktop!**

3. Select File | Save As to open the Save As dialog box.

4. Click the Up One Level button until the Save In field shows only your C: drive without a pathname after it.

5. Type **Trial** in the File Name field. Notepad saves the file as a text file under the name Trial.txt.

6. Exit Notepad.

7. Right-click over your desktop.

8. Select Active Desktop | Customize My Desktop.

▼ 9. Click the Web tab to display the dialog box shown in Figure 16.3. (Your dialog box might differ slightly in the items you see in the list box.)

FIGURE 16.3

Set up active desktop items from the Web page

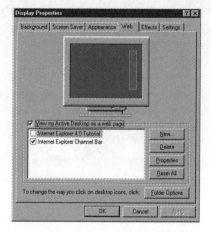

10. Click New to create a new component. If Windows 95 asks if you want to connect to the Active Desktop Gallery, select No.

11. Click the Browse button. You now must enter the name of the Notepad file you created.

12. Type **C:\Trial.txt** in the Filename text box and click OK twice. Windows 95 adds that file to the list of components that you can place on your active desktop. A check mark should appear next to the Trial.txt file, but if one does not, click the filename to add the check mark.

13. Click OK. After a brief pause, your desktop shows a new box with your Notepad file in it, as shown in Figure 16.4. If you move your mouse over the new component, the note turns into a window with resizing handles and a Close button so that you can move, close, and resize the window as you can with any window.

Step 3: Review

You can place any file on your desktop as a component. As you saw in this simple task, you can turn any document into a component. When you add HTML-based Internet files to your desktop, your desktop will contain several active elements that update as long as you stay connected to the Web, which is what the next task demonstrates.

You don't have to create a new file to place a component on your desktop. You can place virtually any existing document on your desktop as a component.

▼

FIGURE 16.4

Your Notepad file now appears as a desktop component

Task 16.4: Adding Active Components

Step 1: Description

If all Web pages are created as HTML files (and they are) and if you can use any HTML file as a desktop component (and you can), why not make for a more active desktop and place a complete Web page or two on your desktop? This task shows how you can make a component out of any Web page due to the Web's adherence to HTML files.

Step 2: Action

1. Right-click on your desktop.

2. Select Active Desktop | Customize My Desktop.

3. Click the Web tab. You see the Trial.txt file that you created in the previous task in the window. (Delete removes any items you no longer want to use as components.)

4. Click New to create a new component.

5. Type **http://** followed by whatever Web address you want to use such as **http://www.microsoft.com**.

6. Click OK. Windows 95 asks if you want to customize a subscription, but you should ignore such a request until you learn more about push content in this hour's final section. Windows 95 downloads the Web page to your desktop. A check mark

▼ should appear next to the Web page address you just added, but if one does not, click the filename to add the check mark. (Uncheck the Trial.txt check box if the check mark is still there.)

7. Click OK. After a brief pause, your desktop shows a new box with the Web page component in it, as shown in Figure 16.5. When you rest your mouse over the top edge of the Web page component, the component turns into a typical window with resizing handles so that you can resize or close the component if you want to change it.

FIGURE 16.5

Your desktop is getting busy!

Web page component

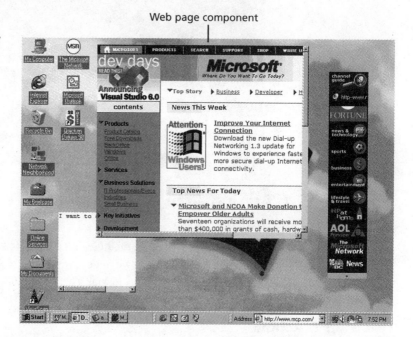

Step 3: Review

You can now place Web pages on your desktop as components. Resize and move the components as needed. The components act like regular windows with one exception: ▲ When you click the Show Desktop taskbar icon, all open windows minimize but the components stay open. Therefore, live Web pages remain on your desktop. Keep up with the latest scores or stock ticker if you access Web sites with such information.

Push and Channel Content

The Internet is a vast collection of data, much of it random. When you want something, you have to locate it. Even when you know the location of a Web site or information you need, you must traverse the Web to get to the information. All that is changing. Instead of going after Internet data, you can now get that data sent to you.

Internet Explorer 4 introduced new *push technology* to get Internet data to your desktop. Push technology refers to information that comes to your desktop from the Internet without your having to first locate the data. Push technology is much more than getting regular email (although some push technology-based sites incorporate email).

When you receive push technology, information comes from the Web to your desktop or Web browser. Several forms of push technology exist. In its simplest form, you can receive regular email, such as the morning news, so that when you get to your PC the information is waiting on you.

Internet Explorer 4 and Windows 95 offer more advanced push technology than regular email, however. You can pull Web pages and specific content on your desktop or in your Web browser automatically. In addition, you can view only changed information from the last time you visited a Web site. The push information might appear on your taskbar (such as a scrolling stock ticker with your personalized stock quotes) or in a screen saver during your PC's lull times. Internet Explorer contains special window panes in which you can view push technology information.

Active Desktop Push

By selecting the push content you want, you can be assured of getting the Web sites you need to track. Without having to go to your favorite sites, you can, after you subscribe to these sites, keep them refreshed automatically when you click your taskbar's View Channels button.

Task 16.5: Getting Push Content

Step 1: Description

This task explains how to capture content as it relates to push technology. Microsoft provides active content sites you can access. The desktop links stay active as long as you're logged in to the Internet.

Step 2: Action

1. Right-click on your desktop.
2. Select Active Desktop | Customize My Desktop to display the Desktop Properties window.
3. Click the Web tab.
4. Click the New button. The Display Properties dialog box offers to visit Microsoft's Active Desktop gallery as shown in Figure 16.6.

▼

FIGURE 16.6

Microsoft gives you lots of active desktop options on its Web site

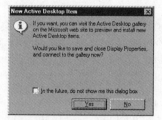

5. Click Yes to visit the site. If needed, your Internet login window appears so you can log in to the Internet. After a brief pause, the Web page shown in Figure 16.7 appears. The page offers active content that you can place on your desktop.

FIGURE 16.7

Microsoft gives you a gallery of active desktop choices to select

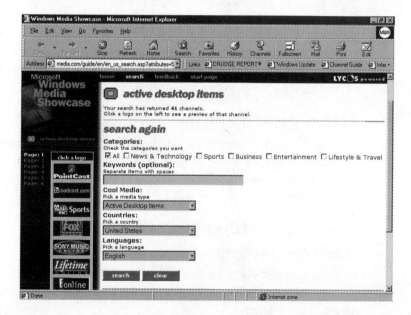

The active desktop Web site you see might differ from Figure 16.7 because Microsoft adds to and changes the Web site often; you should visit the site often to see if new active content that you want appears.

6. Select one of the left pane's active components and the Web site displays a description for you.

7. If you want the content (click your browser's Back button to return to the previous page for a different item), click the description page's button labeled Add Active Channel.

▼

▼   A dialog box appears describing the item, its origin URL address, and explains how the item notifies you when the content changes and howyour desktop notifies you when new content updates the item. (Generally, the item's desktop icon changes during one of these processes.) You can click the Customize button to select how you want the item updated.

8. Click OK to begin the download of your channel selections. Your Internet channel bar now includes the new channel, and you can click that channel any time to see the latest version of that Web page.

 If you don't see your Internet channel bar, right-click on your desktop and select Active Desktop | Customize My Desktop and click the box next to Internet Explorer bar. When you click OK, the channel bar returns to your desktop.

16

FIGURE 16.8

Customize channels from your taskbar's View Channels button

Pre-set channel previews   Additional channel features

 You can add other content to your Internet channel bar quickly by clicking the View Channels taskbar button to display the channel-selection Web page shown in Figure 16.8. Select one of the topics or specially-previewed channel sites to see the current content and decide if you want to add the

▼

> content to your current channel selection. In addition, you can view your channel content directly from within Internet Explorer 4 by selecting Favorites | Channels and selecting one of your channels.

Step 3: Review   Select active push content to receive, and your browser, treating that Web site's content as a channel, keeps the site refreshed on your
▲ system.

Channels and Windows 95

Perhaps the best way to experience the power of channels is to use them. Before you can access a channel, you must subscribe to that channel's content as you did in the previous task. As with other active Internet activities, Microsoft has designed a series of pre-tuned channels you can subscribe to.

> Some of the channel content comes to you via audio and even video. You can listen to the channel content and watch moving video when you select such content.

Turn Push Technology into a Screen Saver

Some channel content can be made into screen savers. When you subscribe to the content's channel guide, you'll learn if a screen saver is available. You can request that push technology only appear when your screen saver activates. Screen savers have changed a lot over the years as you learned in Hour 7, "Manage Your Desktop." Not all channel sites are available as screen savers, so you have to check with the specific channel content provider to see if a screen saver option is there.

Summary

This hour shows how Windows 95 integrates so well with the Internet. Although your Internet connection can somewhat hamper the true invisible marriage between Windows 95 and the Internet, Windows 95's desktop does open itself up to full Internet integration so that you can access the Internet as easily as you access files on your own disk. As you saw in this hour, you can even place live Web pages on your desktop as wallpaper elements or as components so you can view information when you need it.

This hour also described how you can access push technology. Why should you search the Internet every time you want information? Let the Internet come to you! You can request that the Web send information directly to your channels. You might want to be notified by email if something changes, or you might always want certain Internet information to appear on your screen when you click your taskbar's Show Desktop button.

Workshop

Term Review

ActiveX   Web page controls that enable designers to place small active programs, called applets, in a Web page to perform work such as showing a video or interacting with the Web page user.

Applet   A miniature program, often found on a Web page, that comes to the Web page viewer's PC and activates the Web page with graphics or an interactive program such as a question-and-answer application.

Channels   Specific areas of Web content you can subscribe to.

FrontPage Express   An HTML file editor that lets you customize your desktop windows.

HTML   Stands for *HyperText Markup Language* and refers to the language that programmers use to create Web pages.

Java   A language that Web page designers use to place small applet programs on Web pages.

push technology   Receiving information automatically from the Internet without having to traverse the Web each time you want the information. Push technology data comes to you.

Quick Launch   An area of the taskbar that has the capability to hold program icons that you can click at any time to start the programs.

T1 connection   A high-speed constant Internet connection available to people who work in companies that install T1 lines.

tiled wallpaper   Desktop wallpaper that repeats until your entire desktop is covered.

Q&A

Q I use the Internet for email and nothing else; can the active desktop help me?

A Perhaps not right now. Nevertheless, you probably will be using the Web before long. As the Web gets faster and as more content is put on the Web, such as live video, the Web should become more of a staple item for all PC users. At that time, your desktop and Internet relationship will be critical.

Q Do I have to pay for push content that I subscribe to?

A Not at this time. Push content arrives free. Many sites do throw in advertisements to defray the costs of the push material. Keep in mind that as push content grows and more and more material is available, in the future, you might have to pay for some kind of premium push content. If, however, you don't have to pay to access a Web page, you don't have to pay to retrieve push content from that site.

Q I've added a Web page as a desktop component. Everything works fine, but why can't I click on a link to see a different page?

A Although a Web page component looks and acts like a Web page inside your Web browser, the component does not let you open a Web site link directly. Nevertheless, you can right-click on a component's link and select Open in New Window. Internet Explorer automatically opens and displays that link's Web site.

Hour 17

Make Web Pages with FrontPage Express

Not only does Internet Explorer 4 add push content, the active desktop, Outlook Express, and the quick launch taskbar to Windows 95, but another auxiliary program called *FrontPage Express* comes with Internet Explorer 4. With this program, you can create and edit your own Web pages.

FrontPage Express works like a word processor and graphics controller for any Web page you want to develop or edit. Not only can you create and edit your own Web pages, but you can edit Web pages of others that appear on the Internet (you cannot put the edited content back on another's Web site, however).

The highlights of this hour include

- How FrontPage Express hides the job of HTML coding from your Web page designing job
- Where to store Web pages
- How to use FrontPage Express's tools to edit Web pages

- When the FrontPage Express wizard can lessen your Web-page design workload
- What other products you can get to help you work with Web pages

Introduction to FrontPage Express

FrontPage Express is a program that graphically enables you to edit Web pages. Behind all Web pages is the HTML language. HTML is a language that contains commands to format the text, graphics, video, sound, and applets that you place on your Web page. Listing 17.1 shows a partial HTML listing of a Web page. As you can see, the HTML language can get tricky.

LISTING 17.1   HTML COMMANDS CAN BE DIFFICULT TO DECIPHER

```
<!DOCTYPE HTML PUBLIC "-//W3C//DTD HTML 3.2//EN">
<HTML>

<HEAD>
<META HTTP-EQUIV="Content-Type" CONTENT="text/html; charset=iso-8859-1">
<TITLE>Computer Reference</TITLE>
<LINK REL="stylesheet"
HREF="/includes/stylesheets/maize_corporate.css"></HEAD>
<BODY TEXT="#000000" BGCOLOR="#FFFFFF">
<TABLE BORDER="0" CELLPADDING="0" CELLSPACING="0" WIDTH="765">
<form>                                        <TR>
<TD VALIGN="TOP" ROWSPAN="2" BGCOLOR="#FFCC66"><A HREF="/"><IMG
SRC="/images/logos/corporate/compref_you_glow_girl.gif" WIDTH="220"
HEIGHT="55" ALIGN="BOTTOM" ALT="Macmillan Computer Reference"
BORDER="0"></A>
<BR>
```

When an HTML page comes to your browser, your browser interprets the HTML formatting commands and displays the resulting Web page in a format useful for the person viewing the page. Figure 17.1 shows the resulting Web page from the HTML commands in Listing 17.1. The Web page, when formatted, is easy to work with. The HTML is for the browser to interpret, not for the person viewing the Web page.

Before Web page editors such as FrontPage Express, you had to master the HTML language before you could create or edit a Web page. Fortunately, FrontPage Express and other similar programs let you bypass HTML by putting a buffer between you and the underlying HTML code. If you want to draw a line or place a graphic image in a particular location on the Web page you're designing, you can drag that item onto the page with your mouse and with a little help from FrontPage Express.

FIGURE 17.1

After your browser interprets all the HTML commands, the resulting Web page looks nice

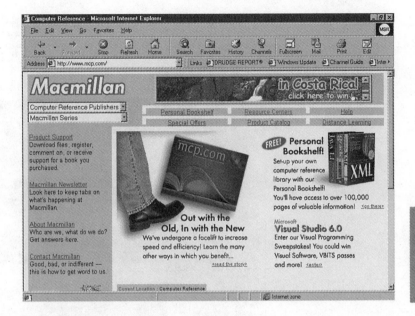

Task 17.1: Starting FrontPage Express

Step 1: Description

This task shows you how to start FrontPage Express and load a sample Web page so that you can see how FrontPage Express lets you edit or create a Web page graphically.

▼ Step 2: Action

1. Select the Start menu's Programs | Internet Explorer | FrontPage Express menu option. Depending on the setup of your Start menu, you might find the Internet Explorer menu group on a menu different from the Accessories menu. FrontPage Express loads and displays a blank editing area.

2. Select File | Open and a dialog box appears that lets you select a file from your disk or from the Internet.

3. Click the From Location option and type www.mcp.com in the text box to inform FrontPage Express that you want to edit that site's Web page.

In subsequent FrontPage Express sessions, the File menu keeps track of pages you've recently edited and displays the most-recent four Web pages at the bottom of the File menu for quick access. Therefore, you can then select File | 1, File | 2, File | 3, or File | 4 to open any of your four most recently-edited Web pages.

▼

▼ 4. Click OK and FrontPage Express loads the Web page from the Internet. After a brief pause, you'll see the Web page inside FrontPage Express's editing area as shown in Figure 17.2. The Web page appears similar to the way it looks in your browser to simplify editing.

FIGURE 17.2

FrontPage Express works graphically with Web page content

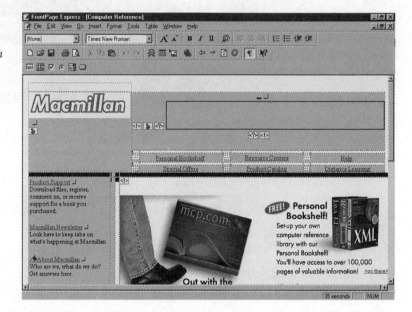

5. You can select File | Exit to close the Web page and leave FrontPage Express for now.

Step 3: Review

FrontPage Express lets you edit Web pages located on your own PC or on the Web. In addition to offering a graphical interface, FrontPage Express supports the View | HTML menu option. This option opens a separate text-editing window on top of the graphical page you are editing so you can edit or write HTML code (if you know HTML well enough to do so). Some Web page designers prefer to have the HTML option because some tasks, such as framing a Web page, require more exact control than FrontPage Express can provide.

▼
FrontPage Express does not actually edit Web pages in place; the changes you make reside only on your own PC unless you have server access to the Web page you change.

PREPARING FOR WEB PAGE PUBLISHING

Before you can publish pages on the Web, you must have access to a *Web server*. Perhaps your company uses a Web server for its site; if so, you can store your Web pages on that computer. If you have access to an online service, such as America Online, it might offer an area for one or more Web pages that you can copy to the online site's Web server. Many Internet Service Providers also offer storage for Web pages.

If you want to publish a personal Web page for fun, you will enjoy telling the world your stories and sharing your family photos with others. If, however, you want to start a business on the Internet or offer timely information that you want others to visit often, you need to be aware that Web page *maintenance* is time-consuming. You don't just create a Web page, load the page on the Web, and expect to keep people's interest if you don't keep the material up-to-date. Use FrontPage Express's tools to maintain your Web pages and keep the viewers' interest.

17

FrontPage Express supports both the Internet and *intranets*. Intranets are networked computers that use Internet protocol, such as Web page technology, to communicate. Therefore, if your company maintains an intranet, you can create, edit, and save Web pages to that intranet as easily (and sometimes more easily) as to the Internet.

Work with FrontPage Express

A full hour is not enough time to master FrontPage Express, but you can gain a quick understanding of the product in this section by learning some of the fundamental parts of the program.

When you want to create a Web page, you can select File | New, and the New Page dialog box shown in Figure 17.3 appears. Here are the options available from inside the dialog box:

- Normal Page: Creates a blank Web page
- Confirmation Form: Acknowledges the receipt of user input from an Internet source
- Form Page Wizard: Helps you create a Web page that collects information from the user
- Personal Home Page Wizard: Walks you through the design of a home page

- Survey Form: Enables you to create a Web page that gathers information from the user and stores that information on your Web server

FIGURE 17.3

FrontPage Express requires you to select a template or wizard

All Web pages you create with FrontPage Express contain basic HTML editing tags that let the Web page operate in an Internet browser. You'll find the basic, HTML-based, blank Web page contents in Listing 17.2. As you can see, many HTML commands, called *tags*, are enclosed in angled brackets. Often, a command begins with an opening tag (such as <HEAD>) followed by a closing tag (such as </HEAD>) indicated with a forward slash before the closing tag.

LISTING 17.2   ALL WEB PAGES CONTAIN THESE FUNDAMENTAL HTML COMMANDS

```
<html>

<head>
<meta http-equiv="Content-Type"
content="text/html; charset=iso-8859-1">
<meta name="GENERATOR" content="Microsoft FrontPage Express 2.0">
<title>Untitled Normal Page</title>
</head>

<body bgcolor="#FFFFFF">
</body>
</html>
```

Although HTML is rather simple compared to major programming languages such as C++, HTML is cryptic, and you already see that working in a graphical environment such as FrontPage Express is much simpler than mastering HTML commands.

The initial tags shown in Listing 17.2 are only sufficient to define a blank Web page, and it's your job to fill in the page with text, graphics, and other elements. To get an idea of how FrontPage Express hides the underlying tags from you, select New Page from the

New Page dialog box and you'll notice that the FrontPage Express editing area is blank (even though the tags from Listing 17.2 do reside under blank Web page you are viewing).

Select File | Page Properties and click the Title field to enter a title. Type **My Home Page** in the field and click OK. The title bar of FrontPage Express's program window should show your new title. Select View | HTML to view the HTML window shown in Figure 17.4. FrontPage Express places your title between two <TITLE> tags even though you entered the title using the Properties dialog box. Although you could have typed the HTML <TITLE> information, selecting from FrontPage Express's menus is easier.

FIGURE 17.4

Your title appears in the HTML window even though you did not type HTML code

Your title —

The title is not the only property that the Properties dialog box can help you manage. If you select File | Properties again and click the tabs to see the other dialog box property sheets, you'll find these tabbed sheets that help you quickly place Web page elements on your page:

- Background: Select an image or colors to form your Web page's background
- Margins: Specify the top and left margins of your Web page
- Custom: Advanced Web-page designers can create variables that hold content that is placed in the variables when the Web page is displayed on the Internet

As you add to your Web page, watch your status bar at the bottom of the FrontPage Express window. FrontPage Express estimates the amount of time required, in seconds, for your Web page to load on an Internet user's PC using a 28.8K modem connection. As you add elements to your Web page,

> the estimated download time increases. You want your users to see your
> Web page as quickly as possible without sacrificing quality or attention-get-
> ting graphics and other Web page components.

FrontPage Express's toolbars go a long way towards helping you create and edit Web
pages. Figure 17.5 shows one of FrontPage Express's toolbars that enable you to send
special controls to your Web page without bothering with HTML.

FIGURE 17.5

*Use the FrontPage
Express toolbar to add
controls to your Web
page*

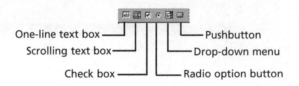

One-line text box ————— Pushbutton
Scrolling text box ————— Drop-down menu
Check box ————— Radio option button

To add one of the controls anywhere on your Web page, double-click the control.
FrontPage Express places the control on the Web page. You then can drag the control to
its proper location and size the control to the size you require. Unlike desktop-publishing
programs and visual programming systems such as Visual Basic, FrontPage Express does
not initially place the control in the center of the form but places each control side-by-
side as you choose them. You then can drag and resize them as needed.

Here is a description of each control that you can add:

- One-line text box: An area where the Internet user can type and edit information
  on the Web page.

- Scrolling text box: A multiline text box the user can scroll left, right, up, or down
  to read the full contents.

- Check box: An option the user can click to add (select) or remove (deselect) a
  check mark.

- Radio option button: An option the user can click to select or deselect the option;
  only one radio option button can be selected in a single page frame, not unlike the
  old car radios that allowed for only one radio station button to be pressed in at any
  one time.

- Drop-down menu: A menu that opens from its one-line station on the Web page

- Pushbutton (sometimes called a command button): A button the user can click to
  trigger an action, such as the playing of a sound clip

FrontPage Express requires that you master some programming skills to operate command buttons and respond to the option selections properly. This hour does not go into the advanced processing required for more complex Web pages that include interactive applets and multimedia segments.

Without programming in HTML, you can place tables, graphics, and hyperlinks (links to other Web pages that the user can click to select) by clicking the Insert Table, Insert Graphic, and Create or Edit Hyperlink toolbar buttons that appear on the toolbar beneath the menu. More advanced Web page components, such as animation and sound clips, still require that you master HTML or upgrade to a more powerful Web page editor. More FrontPage Express limits are discussed in the next section.

17

FrontPage Express's Limits

Despite its impressive array of features, FrontPage Express is not a full-fledged Web page editing package. More powerful Web page editors exist that contain some of the following features not found in FrontPage Express:

- Extra wizards and templates that provide help for specialized Web pages that contain multimedia content
- Built-in browsing capabilities so that you can locate the pages you want to edit
- The ability to include special kinds of elements and controls such as multimedia controls
- A Web site collection feature that lets you collect all the pages you design for a Web site and transfer those pages to the Internet (or intranet) as a collection of sites
- A Web server that lets you serve Web pages to other Internet (or intranet) users directly from your PC

Microsoft sells a more complete version of FrontPage Express called *FrontPage*. FrontPage contains all the features that FrontPage Express lacks but retains the familiar FrontPage Express interface.

Task 17.2: Using a FrontPage Express Web Page Wizard

Step 1: Description

This Task begins your exploration of FrontPage Express by walking you through the screens of one of FrontPage Express's Web page wizards.

Step 2: Action

1. Select File | New to open the New Page dialog box.

2. Select Personal Home Page Wizard to start the wizard that walks you through the creation of a home page. FrontPage Express displays the opening window shown in Figure 17.6.

FIGURE 17.6

Select the items you want on your home page

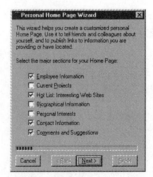

3. Click Next to accept the defaults and move to the next dialog box.

4. You can now enter your home page's address and name. The address typically includes just the page address (not your server's Web site), and the default URL is home1.htm. The page title is Home Page 1 but you should change that to something else, such as My Home Page so you can see how FrontPage Express uses the name.

5. Click Next to select the job-related items that you want to appear on the page. The home page is obviously geared toward the career-minded, professional home page designer. You can, however, through your selections throughout the wizard, select other items to appear, such as more personal information.

> The home page that the wizard generates is only the beginning. After the wizard creates the page, you can use FrontPage Express's editing tools to modify the page and add other elements. You can even add HTML command tags if you know HTML.

▼ 6. Click Next to display the next dialog box. You can select the way the wizard puts listed items on your Web page. Accept the default, Bullet list, for this example.

7. Click Next to display Figure 17.7's contact information window. Select and enter the information you want to appear on your home page (the wizard formats the information on the final page to look nice).

FIGURE 17.7

Add the contact information that you want to appear on your home page

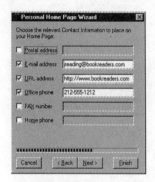

17

8. Click Next to display a dialog box from which you can select one of the following choices to keep track of the home page viewer's comments and suggestions:
   - Use Form, Store Results in Data File: Saves user's comments and suggestions in a separate data file.
   - Use Form, Store Results in Web Page: Saves the user's comments and suggestions in the Web page so that others can view the results.
   - Use Link, Send EMail to This Address: Saves the user's comments and suggestions in an email message that is sent to you from the user's email client program such as Outlook Express.

   Keep the first option, the default.

9. Click Next to display the window that lets you adjust the order of your home page sections. These are the sections you selected earlier. If you've accepted the defaults to this point, here are the sections you can order:
   - Employee Information
   - Hot List
   - Contact Information
   - Comments and Suggestions

10. Click Next to move to the final wizard window where you can click Finish to terminate the wizard and generate your new home page. Figure 17.8 shows the resulting home page that appears.
▼

FIGURE 17.8

Although your new home page is simple, you now can edit the elements on it

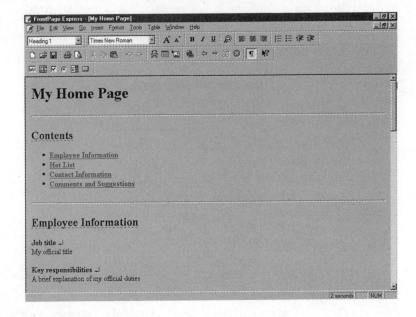

Step 3: Review

Scroll through your new home page to see the elements on it. You can add text boxes, check boxes, and options to the page, rearrange elements of the page, add graphics, and other elements. You can select View | HTML to see the HTML code that you might want to edit as well.

Publishing Your Web Page

After you finalize your Web page with FrontPage Express, FrontPage Express can help you publish your page on the Web or on your local network server as an intranet using the Web Publishing Wizard. The wizard translates your Web page from the FrontPage Express format to HTML format to be compatible with Web browsers.

To start the wizard, select File | Save. The wizard begins and collects information that your Internet provider needs about your Web pages and sends that information, along with your Web pages, to your provider. (You need proper Internet access and a browser to use the wizard.) After you complete the wizard, your Web page should be available for use.

Although the Web Publishing Wizard helps gather information and makes publishing your Web page fairly simple, you still might have to contact your Internet provider (the provider sponsoring your Web page) to determine some of the answers to the Web Publishing Wizard's questions. For example, you need to tell the wizard the URL where your Web page will reside and the type of provider you use.

Summary

This hour explained how to use FrontPage Express to create and edit Web pages. Although FrontPage Express is a simple program, you can use FrontPage Express's wizard to create common Web pages and then edit those pages to add your own graphics and other components to the page.

FrontPage Express makes it unnecessary to master HTML commands. The HTML language was the original formatting language of Web pages. Although all Web pages contain HTML code, programs such as FrontPage Express hide the underlying HTML code from you so that you can create Web pages from the graphical elements.

Workshop

Term Review

hyperlinks   Links to other Web pages that the user can click to select.

intranet   A local area network of computers whose users communicate with each other on the network through Web pages and Internet technology instead of dialing up an Internet Service Provider and accessing the Web pages from another location.

FrontPage Express   An HTML file editor that comes with Internet Explorer 4.

tag   An HTML command that appears inside angled brackets.

Web page maintenance   The process of modifying and updating Web page information.

Web server   A computer dedicated to presenting Web pages on the Internet.

Q&A

Q Can I use my Windows 95 PC as a Web server?

A You *can*, but you probably don't want to tie up your PC by using it as a Web server. Windows NT computers are better equipped to be Web servers. If you want to try, however, you need to ensure that you've upgraded Windows 95 to the Service Release 2 as described in Hour 24, "Windows 95 Tips and Traps," or get FrontPage which includes the FrontPage Server program that turns your PC into a server. In addition, you need to weigh the fact that your PC must be on 24 hours a day unless you want your customers screaming about an unavailable site. By dedicating a phone line and a server PC to your Web site, you help ensure that your site's viewers can always access your site. The constant up time required by Web sites also makes a good case for renting space for your site on your ISP's computer.

If you use a slow PC and a dial-up Internet connection, your PC offers slow Web page viewing. Therefore, no matter how effective your Web page content is and no matter how well you used FrontPage Express's tools to develop an attention-getting Web page display, your Web server is probably too slow to keep your viewers' interest.

Q How can users find my site?

A If you put a business on the Web, you certainly want to make it as easy as possible for users to locate your site. One of the best ways to do that is to register your site with search engines such as *Yahoo!* (www.yahoo.com) or *Excite* (www.excite.com). The search engine includes your site, indexed by keywords that you suggest, for a modest fee. You can find a list of current search engine sites by clicking the Search button on Internet Explorer's toolbar and selecting Choose a Search Engine. The search engine sites include contact information you can use to find out more about registering your site with them.

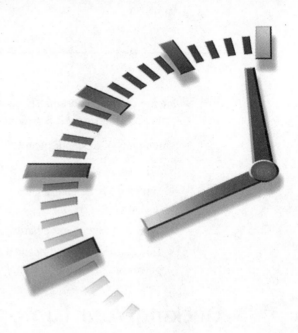

Hour 18

Using Windows 95 on the Road

This hour shows you how Windows 95 supports mobile computing environments. If you use a laptop, you'll appreciate the laptop features Microsoft included with Windows 95. Windows 95 recognizes when you change a laptop's configuration using sort of a *Plug and Play on-the-fly* because you don't even have to turn off your laptop when making common hardware changes such as docking the laptop into a docking bay.

Perhaps you use a laptop while on the road and a desktop computer at the office or at home. If so, you need to transfer files easily between them and, at the same time, keep those files in synchronization so that you always work with the latest file version. Whatever your situation, the Windows 95 *Briefcase* will help you synchronize your document files so they remain as current as possible.

The nature of laptop use is mobile computing. The number of cables you must plug in when connecting your laptop to a printer or to another PC makes the laptop somewhat cumbersome when you want to communicate with another device. Fortunately, most of today's laptops come with infrared ports so that you can access other devices without cables.

The highlights of this hour include:

- Why automatic configuration for mobile computing environments is so important
- Why the My Briefcase icon is one of the most important icons on the Windows 95 desktop for users of both portable and desktop computers
- Which common laptop hardware changes Windows 95 detects
- How infrared connections make communicating with peripherals and other computers simpler than using cables

Docking Your Laptop

The Microsoft programmers understood the need for mobile computing environments when they developed Windows 95. Mobile computing environments refer to those environments in which portable computers such as laptops are used. In the past few years, companies have begun developing *docking stations* for computer users who take a laptop with them on the road and then come home and plug the laptop directly into a docking station. The docking station is a connecting device that connects the laptop to a full-size color screen, printer, mouse, and keyboard. Therefore, the computer user uses the laptop on the road and then uses the laptop's system unit at home or in the office, with regular-size peripheral equipment.

But there are also other ways to find help while using UnInstaller. UnInstaller's online Help feature can help you out in any jam. But there are also other ways to find help while using UnInstaller.

Sitting at the Dock

Many devices known as *docking stations* are more accurately described as *port replicators* because they extend the laptop's expansion ports, such as the printer and serial port, to the docking station device on your desktop. Leaving all your peripherals plugged into the docking station is simpler than plugging each device into your laptop every time you arrive back at your desk. You only have to slide your laptop into the docking station to access those peripherals plugged into it.

Figure 18.1 shows a laptop connected to a docking station. Windows 95 can detect whether or not a computer is docked and make appropriate adjustments instantly and accordingly. When undocked, Windows 95 can use the laptop's screen, and when docked, Windows 95 can immediately adjust the screen to a larger and higher-resolution monitor.

FIGURE 18.1

A docking station lets you utilize full-size desktop peripherals from your laptop

18

If your hardware is not Plug and Play compatible, you have to reboot your computer before Windows 95 can reconfigure itself to the docking. If, however, you have full Plug and Play compliance, as most laptops sold since 1996 include, you don't have to reboot for Windows 95 to recognize the change in docking status.

Windows 95 often can recognize that a computer has been docked, but most hardware does not allow you to undock your PC without Windows 95 knowing about the undocking. If Windows 95 does not recognize the fact that you've undocked, you can select Eject PC from the Start menu, and Windows 95 will know to reconfigure for the undocking and use the laptop's own configuration. For example, if your laptop contains an internal modem, the laptop, when undocked, will no longer be configured to use the docking station's modem.

When undocked, the Eject PC option does not appear on your Start menu.

Using PC Cards

For several years, laptops have supported PC Cards (PC Cards are sometimes called *PCMCIA cards*), the small credit card–sized expansion peripherals that plug into the side of your laptops. These cards let you add a modem, memory, networking capabilities, and even another hard disk to your laptop.

Three card types exist:

- **Type I**　The original card soon replaced with Type II (Type I cards are no longer available)
- **Type II**　The most common PC Card you can purchase today primarily used for modems, memory, and networking
- **Type III**　A double-sized card used primarily for disk expansion (yes, you can fit several megabytes into the size of a couple of credit cards)

Most laptops in use today support two Type II cards at once, or one Type III PC Card due to its double width.

The Control Panel includes an icon labeled PC Card (PCMCIA) that contains the PC Card control you need as you work in Windows 95. When you select this Control Panel item, Windows 95 open the PC Card Properties dialog box shown in Figure 18.2.

FIGURE 18.2

The PC Card Properties dialog box lets you control your PC Card settings

Figure 18.2 indicates that the laptop has two PC Card sockets (as most laptops sold today have) and that both are empty. The first option at the bottom of the dialog box determines if the PC Card icon will appear on your taskbar, giving you quicker access to the PC Card Properties dialog box than going through the Control Panel. If selected, the second option warns you if you remove a PC Card before you stop the card. Although you can insert and remove most PC Cards during the operation of Windows 95 without stopping the card first, if you use a PC Card with a hard disk, you'll want to stop the card *before* removing it to ensure that all unwritten data is on the card's disk.

To start any card, simply insert the card into the appropriate PC Card slot. Your PC can be on or off for this operation, one of the only times you can modify PC hardware with the power on. Windows 95 senses the change, installs the modem support through Plug and Play, and adds the card to the list in the PC Card Properties dialog box that will no longer be empty. To remove the card, you only need to eject the PC Card from its slot and Windows 95 reconfigures itself accordingly.

> To stop a PC Card before you eject the card, open the Control Panel's PC Card Properties dialog box, click the PC Card you want to stop, and click the Stop button. Windows 95 then displays a dialog box telling you that you can remove the card and removes the PC Card icon from your taskbar.

Clicking the Global Settings tab on the PC Properties dialog box opens the tabbed page shown in Figure 18.3. You should only uncheck the Automatic selection option if your PC Card manual indicates the need to do so. You then can control the memory used by the PC Card as specified in your card's owner's manual. The second option lets you enable and disable sound effects that occur when you insert and remove a PC Card.

FIGURE 18.3

Control PC Card memory and sound effects through the Global Settings

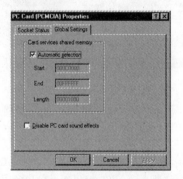

> The PC Card Properties sound effects option has nothing to do with the sounds your modem makes when you initiate a phone call. The option controls a sound that Windows 95 plays when you insert or remove a card.

> Some PC Cards are easy to eject—almost *too* easy! Therefore, check the sound effects option and you will hear if you accidentally eject the PC Card from its slot while your PC is in use.

The Windows 95 Briefcase

When on the road, you want to work with the most up-to-date data files possible. Therefore, users often copy the latest files from their desktops to portable PCs before leaving on a trip. The direct cable connection, described at the end of the last section, is a great way to copy those files. (Users also use floppy disks to transfer data between two computers.)

After they return, those users often have to reverse the process and copy their latest laptop data files over the ones on the desktops (via floppy disks) to refresh the desktop's files so that both computers stay in synchronization with each other. Until Windows 95, the only way to ensure that you were working with the latest data files was to look at the file date and time values and work with only the latest. At best, trying to maintain the latest files was a hassle, often causing confusion and errors as well.

The Briefcase application does all the nitty-gritty for you and synchronizes two computers that you have connected together via a network or by cable. You can find the Briefcase application on your desktop. When you open the My Briefcase icon, Windows 95 displays the My Briefcase window, shown in Figure 18.4.

FIGURE 18.4

The Briefcase is ready for your files

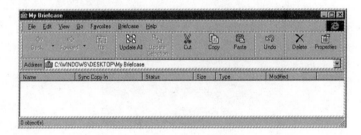

 The Briefcase icon appears on the desktop, not on the Control Panel or within the Start menu, so that you can drag files onto the Briefcase from Explorer or from an Open dialog box.

Briefcase acts just like a briefcase that you take between your office and home. Before leaving in the morning, you put important papers in your briefcase. In the Windows 95 environment, before going on the road with your laptop, you should drag all data files that you want to work with to the Briefcase.

Suppose you copy two files to the Briefcase icon by dragging the files from Windows 95 Explorer to the My Briefcase desktop icon. Figure 18.5 shows two files in the Briefcase window ready to be transferred to a laptop computer.

FIGURE 18.5

There are two document files in Briefcase at the moment

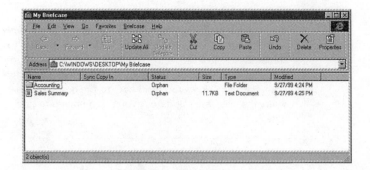

If you are using a floppy disk for the Briefcase intermediary storage medium, move the My Briefcase icon to the floppy disk. You can display the floppy disk by displaying the Explorer window or opening the My Computer window and dragging the My Briefcase icon to the floppy disk drive. You must have a formatted disk in the drive before you can copy the desktop's My Briefcase icon there.

Insert the floppy disk into your laptop's disk drive. While on the road, you can work with those files in the Briefcase. If you save a Briefcase file to the laptop's hard disk, be sure to return the file to the laptop's Briefcase before you reconcile the files on your primary desktop computer later.

After you get back to the desktop, insert the floppy disk into the desktop's disk drive and open the desktop's My Briefcase icon again. Select Briefcase | Update All (or click the toolbar button) or select only those files you want to update, and then select Briefcase | Update Selection (or click the toolbar button). Briefcase synchronizes the desktop's files by doing one of three things:

- If your desktop does not have one or more Briefcase files, then the Briefcase application copies those files to the desktop computer.
- If your desktop already has those files on its disk, then Briefcase transfers files from the Briefcase *only* if the Briefcase's files are newer than the desktop's.
- If your desktop already has one or more Briefcase files and the files are older than the Briefcase versions, the Briefcase application copies the newer versions over the old ones on the desktop.

If you want to update files using a direct cable connection, infrared connection (see the next section), or network instead of an intermediary floppy disk, make the physical connection first to the laptop with a direct cable or plug the laptop into your network. Then drag the files from the desktop computer to the laptop's My Briefcase icon. This sends the files to the Briefcase on the laptop. While on the road, work with the files inside the Briefcase icon. When you reconnect to the desktop or network, you can select the Briefcase | Update All menu command to bring the desktop up-to-date.

Going Wireless with Infrared

In the 1980s, IBM introduced the PCJr, a PC designed for home use and one that used an *infrared port* for its keyboard. (You cannot see infrared light, but infrared signals work well in remote control devices such as television remotes.) The user was not encumbered by a wire on the keyboard; the user could lean back in the chair and point the keyboard in the general direction of the PC to use the PCJr.

IBM was years ahead of its time and years behind the market. The computer's sales bombed.

Today, the home computer market has not only grown, it's far surpassed anyone's expectations. With the integration of the television and PC, along with wireless keyboards and other peripherals, we can see that the PCJr's demise was due to bad timing.

Interestingly, Microsoft got into the home software market with its Microsoft At Home applications just as the home market was beginning its tremendous growth. At the end of 1997, the height of home computer and software sales, Microsoft announced that they were pulling most of their At Home software off the shelves due to slow sales. The PC market is always fun to watch but never fun to predict!

Windows 95 fully supports infrared devices. At the time of Windows 95's release, the most common device that used infrared technology was the laptop PC. Infrared allows the laptop user to transfer files from one PC to another without the use of networks or even cables. As you will see in Hour 23, "Hardware and Windows 95," Windows 95's Direct Cable Connection makes transferring files simple, but you can get simpler if you use infrared transfer. Just point your laptop at your desktop and Windows 95 automatically senses the infrared devices and makes the connection you need.

Many manufacturers are adding infrared ports to peripherals such as printers and networks. Forget about cables, just point your PC in the direction of your printer to begin printing!

Although many vendors sell laptops with infrared ports built in, rarely does a desktop PC have an infrared port attached. You can purchase them for your desktop PC to help improve communications with a laptop or other peripheral.

Most infrared devices are truly Plug and Play. Turn on your printer and Windows 95 configures itself for the printer, emitting a sound to let you know that the infrared ports are communicating.

As with many Windows 95 features, including PC Card support described in the previous section, an infrared icon appears on your taskbar when your PC or laptop is ready for infrared communications. If you do not see the icon, you can add it to your taskbar.

18

Task 18.1: Enabling Your Infrared Port

Step 1: Description

You must enable your infrared port before you can use it. This task shows you how to let Windows 95 know that you want the port enabled for use.

Step 2: Action

1. Open the Start | Settings | Control Panel dialog box.
2. Open the Infrared icon's window to display the Infrared Monitor dialog box.
3. Click the Options tab.
4. Click the first option to enable infrared communications. Figure 18.6 shows the dialog box. You can determine how often your PC should search for infrared devices within range. The default is a scan that occurs every 3 seconds.
5. Click the Identification tab to locate your PC's name and description (created when you installed Windows 95). If you communicate with another PC with an infrared port, the other PC recognizes your PC and displays its name in the recognized device list that you can display.
6. After you click OK, your taskbar shows the infrared icon. The icon shows a blinking infrared indicator. If another infrared device comes within range, your taskbar

▼ To Do ▼

shows two icons blinking at each other indicating that another device is within range.

FIGURE 18.6

Enable your infrared device from the Infrared Monitor dialog box

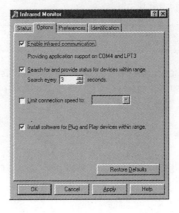

Step 3: Review

After you enable your infrared port, the icon appears on your taskbar and your PC is ready to search for another infrared device. Your PC sends out a signal every time interval that you specify in the Infrared Monitor dialog box. The icon will show a second icon if another device comes within range.

Task 18.2: Finding Infrared Devices

Step 1: Description

As your PC searches for an infrared signal, you can continue to work within Windows 95 as you always have. When you are ready to communicate with an infrared device, such as a printer or another PC with an infrared port, your PC will recognize that device.

Step 2: Action

1. Enable your infrared port, if you have not already, as directed in Task 18.1.

2. Bring the second infrared device within range of your PC. Generally, the devices must be within 3 feet, and you should aim their ports in the other's general direction. Windows 95 indicates the recognition of the other device.

3. You can now begin printing or sharing files between the two PCs. If you want to transfer files from your laptop to a desktop infrared port, use the Direct Cable Connector wizard (Hour 23, "Hardware and Windows 95," explains how to set up a direct cable connection) to set up a connection. The infrared port replaces the serial or parallel connection that you initiate.

▼   If you use an infrared printer, check the printer's manual to see which infrared port to use. Although you only have one physical infrared port on your PC, Windows 95 sets up the port as both a serial and a parallel infrared port to handle both kinds of data transmission and multiple infrared devices at one time. Although the printer might normally be a parallel printer, some printers require a serial infrared port connection.

4. Explorer and the File | Open dialog boxes now display the other PC if you connect to a PC's infrared device, and the Print dialog boxes display the infrared printer if you have connected to a printer device.

Step 3: Review

Connecting another infrared device to your laptop is simple. Windows 95 does all the configuration as long as you bring the second device within range. You have no need to hook cables between two PCs with infrared devices or between a PC and an infrared printer. The infrared port is especially helpful for laptop users who want to use a wireless connection to transfer files between the PCs using the Direct Cable Connection wizard.

> After you make the infrared connection between a laptop and another PC, you can use the infrared transmission to communicate between the two Briefcases on Windows 95 systems.

▲

18

Summary

This hour showed how laptop users can take advantage of Windows 95's special mobile support features. Windows 95 includes support for docked laptop computers, so the configuration changes whenever you dock and undock. In addition, infrared ports make communicating between two infrared devices simple and wire-free.

The easy interconnection possible in Windows 95 means that you'll be connecting more computers together than ever before. With those connections comes confusion, however. A desktop and laptop computers' files can get out of synchronization. Generally, you want to work with the latest version of a file, but comparing dates and times yourself is tedious and error-prone. The My Briefcase icon solves that problem by making the time and date comparisons for you and refreshing any laptop or desktop files that need refreshing to make sure both systems have the latest versions of document files.

> For the proper synchronization to occur, you must set your computer's time and date properly on both your laptop and your desktop PC.

Workshop

Term Review

Briefcase   The Windows 95 application that synchronizes the document files from two computers so that you can always have the most up-to-date files at any time.

docking station   A device, into which you can insert some laptop computers, that instantly connects the laptop to a full-size screen, keyboard, mouse, and printer.

I/O   Also known as *input/output,* referring to data flow to and from a device such as a disk drive or a PC card.

Infrared   Invisible light that works well for transmitting between digital devices such as television remote controls and infrared peripherals.

mobile computing environments   The computer environment that includes laptop computers and desktop docking stations for the laptops.

PCMCIA Cards   Also called *PC cards.* Small credit card–sized I/O cards that add functionality such as modems and memory to laptops and to some desktop systems.

Q&A

Q I often cross time zones and change my laptop accordingly. Will Briefcase be affected by the time changes?

A It is possible for Briefcase to make incorrect decisions when copying files using different time zones. You can do very little to make Briefcase happy when you move across time zones. The best thing you can do is resist the temptation to change the laptop's clock while on the road. Keep your laptop clock set the same as your desktop computer, so that when you return to the desktop, Briefcase will have no trouble reconciling your files.

Q I don't use a desktop PC, so do I need a docking station for my laptop?

A Actually, those without a desktop are the *best* candidates for a docking station. When on the road you can use your laptop, and when you return to your desk you can use the laptop's processor as your desktop PC. The docking station can connect to a full-screen monitor, keyboard, mouse, modem, and printer. To access these devices and to configure your laptop to use those devices, you only need to insert (*dock*) your laptop into the docking station, and Windows 95 reconfigures itself for the new devices.

Q **Can I add an infrared port to my older laptop that has none?**

A Probably, but doing so requires that you purchase a standalone infrared port. You have to plug the port into your laptop when you use the infrared communications. Such cabling probably defeats the purpose and makes infrared communications only slightly better than a wired file or printer connection.

18

PART IV
Into the Nighttime

Hour

Hour 19

Printing with Power

This hour explains the printing options available to you as a Windows 95 user. The printer is one of those devices that you don't want to think a lot about; you want to print a document within your word processor or from within your spreadsheet program and, a few moments later, grab the resulting printed output from the printer. Most of the time, you do not have to think about how Windows 95 relates to your printer.

The reason this hour spends time discussing the printing capabilities of Windows 95 is that after you understand the Windows 95 *printer subsystem* (the internal program that automatically controls all printing from within Windows 95), you will be better equipped to handle advanced printer management. There are times when you want to print something, but change your mind after you've issued the print command. The printer subsystem lets you rearrange, reroute, and redo printer output before that output gets to the printer.

The highlights of this hour include:

- When to use the Add Printers Wizard to set up new printers
- What advantages the print subsystem offers you

- How to use the Print dialog boxes to route output to a printer
- How to manage the Print job window's list of printed documents
- When to defer printing

Introduction to Spooled Printing

When you print documents, Windows 95 automatically starts the printer subsystem. The printer subsystem controls all printing from within Windows 95; whereas the MS-DOS environment sent data directly to the printer when you printed data, Windows 95 *spools* output through the printer subsystem as shown in Figure 19.1. When spooled, the print job goes to a disk file, managed by the printer subsystem, before being sent directly to the printer.

FIGURE 19.1

Windows 95 spools output to the printer subsystem disk file

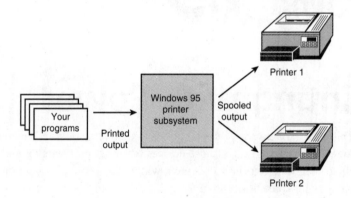

> Every document you print creates a unique *print job* that appears on the spooler. Windows 95 gives you access to these print jobs.

By routing printed output to a spooled disk file instead of sending the output directly to the printer, you can intercept it before that output goes to paper. Therefore, you have more control over how the output appears on the printer. You also can select which printer receives the output in case there are more than one printer connected to your computer.

Setting Up a Printer

If you add a printer to your system, remove a printer from your system, or set up Windows 95 to use a printer for the first time, you have to inform Windows 95. But that's not always a problem because Windows 95 offers Plug and Play as well as gives you the *Add Printer Wizard* to help you each step of the way.

> As mentioned in Hour 6, "A Call for Help," a *wizard* is a step-by-step procedure that Windows 95 uses to guide you through a series of dialog boxes typically for installation and setup.

Turn off your PC before you plug a new printer into your PC's parallel printer port. When you turn your PC on again, Windows 95 responds in one of the following ways:

- Automatically recognizes the printer and installs the drivers for you
- Recognizes that you've changed the hardware and starts the Add New Printer wizard so that you can select the new printer
- Does not realize that you added a printer and you have to run the Add New Printer wizard yourself

A special Printers folder available from the Start | Settings menu contains all information about your computer's printer hardware. If you have yet to set up a printer, you have to open the Printers folder and walk through the Add Printer Wizard so that Windows 95 knows exactly what printer to use.

Task 19.1: Using the Add Printer Wizard

Step 1: Description

Windows 95 needs to know how to format the printed output that you want. Almost every printer supports different combinations of print functions, and almost every printer requires unique *print codes* that determine how the printer interprets specific characters and character-formatting options. The Add Printer Wizard configures the necessary details and asks you appropriate questions that determine how printed output eventually appears.

> If you use a network and you need to set up a network printer in Windows 95, use the Network Neighborhood window to open the network printer; you can browse the network to find the printer. Then set up the printer following the instructions that appear on the screen.

Step 2: Action

1. Connect your printer to your computer using a printer cable. Most printers connect to the computer's *parallel port*.

▼ To Do

19

▼ 2. Click the Start button to display the Start menu.

3. Select Settings | Printers to open the Printers window shown in Figure 19.2.

FIGURE 19.2

*The Printers window
controls the setup and
operation of printers*

If you have not yet set up any printer, you see only the Add Printer icon in
the Printers window.

The Printers window provides access to all of your printer subsystem capabilities.
It is from the Printers window that you can manage and rearrange print jobs that
you've started from Windows 95 applications.

4. The Printers window contains the icon, labeled Add Printer, that starts the Add
Printer Wizard. If you've not set up a printer yet, you should open the Add Printer
icon now. When you open it, you see the first screen of the Add Printer Wizard
shown in Figure 19.3.

FIGURE 19.3

*The Add Printer
Wizard walks you
through the setup of a
new printer*

▼ 5. Click the Next command button to start the Add Printer Wizard's operation. Select
either the Local printer or the Network printer.

> As you walk through a wizard, you can click the Back command button to back up a step and answer any previous prompt differently.

6. A list of printer manufacturers appears in the left scrolling window. When you choose a manufacturer, such as *Epson* or *HP*, that manufacturer's printer models appear in the right scrolling window.

   Over time, printer manufacturers update their printers and offer new models. There is no way that Microsoft can predict what a printer manufacturer will do next. Therefore, you might buy a printer that's made after Windows 95 was written. If so, the printer should come with a disk that you can use to add that printer to Windows 95. If this is your case, click the Have Disk button and follow the instructions on the screen.

   If your printer *is* in the list, find your printer's model on the right of the dialog box, highlight the model, and click the Next button.

> If you cannot find your printer's exact model, there is probably a printer in the list that closely matches your printer. You might have to check your printer manual for models that are compatible. Choose the printer that most closely matches your printer's model.

> Microsoft routinely adds new printer makes and models to their list of supported printers. You can often find *printer drivers* (printer description files that Windows 95 uses to talk to your printer) for new printers on the Internet, both on Microsoft's site (www.microsoft.com) as well as the printer manufacturer's sites. Your printer's manual should list the manufacturer's Web site. If it doesn't, you can always use a search engine to look for the manufacturer's site.

7. The wizard next needs information about the port that your printer is plugged into. The dialog box shown in Figure 19.4 requests this information.

   Most of the time, you click Next to select the default value of the parallel printer port. Perhaps before doing so, you should click the Configure Port command button. The Configure Port dialog box contains two options. The first option determines if the spooling should apply to MS-DOS programs in addition to Windows 95 programs. The second option determines if you want the printer subsystem to

19

▼ check the port before printing, to make sure that the port is ready for data. Unless you are using special printer hardware that requires extra control, you should leave both these options checked and click the OK command button to return to the wizard.

FIGURE 19.4

The Add Printer Wizard needs to know where your printer is

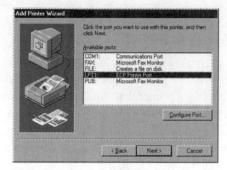

Select the port where your computer is connected and click the Next command button now.

If you want to route an image of the printed output to a disk file, you can select FILE:. Every time you print, Windows 95 then asks you for the name of a file that you want Windows 95 to use for collecting the printed output. After it is sent to a file, you can edit the file, view the file, or print the file. If you don't have a printer attached to your PC, as might be the case with a laptop while on the road, you can print to a file and then use the Windows 95 WordPad text editor (see Hour 8, "Desktop Accessories," for WordPad information) to browse the file at your leisure. In addition, while on the road, you can print your output to files and then print those files when you return home or to your office that has a printer.

Printer Ports

If you have more than one parallel printer port, you will see at least one additional port listed inside the wizard's list box. COM1: and COM2: are names for the first two *serial ports* on your computer.

Rarely do today's printers attach to serial ports because these ports are better used for modem and mouse connections. Nevertheless, there are some printers that use the serial ports. The name LPT1: (and possibly LPT2:) refers to the parallel port where most printer cables are connected.

▼

8. When you see the screen shown in Figure 19.5, you can enter the name you want to use for the printer when selecting among printers within Windows 95. If you like the default name, don't change it. If you want a different name, such as Joe's Printer (in case you're setting up a network printer), type the new name. If this is the only printer you are setting up, select Yes when the wizard asks about this being the default printer. Windows 95 then uses the printer automatically every time you print something. If you are setting up a secondary printer, select No.

FIGURE 19.5

You must tell Windows 95 how to refer to the printer

9. Click the Next command button to move to the next wizard screen.

10. If you click Yes on the next wizard screen, Windows 95 prints a test page on the printer. (Be sure your printer is turned on and that it has paper.) By printing a test page, you ensure that Windows 95 properly recognizes the printer. Click the Finish command button to complete the wizard.

> Windows 95 rarely has the proper printer setup file on the hard disk. You probably have to insert the Windows 95 installation CD-ROM so that Windows 95 can find the proper information for the printer you've selected. Windows 95 prompts you for this CD-ROM if needed. If your printer is a new model, it probably came with a disk or CD from which you can pull drivers for Windows 95 to use.

11. After Windows 95 completes the printer setup, a new icon with your printer's name appears in the Printers window.

Step 3: Review

Windows 95 must know exactly what kind of printer you have connected to your computer. Depending on the hardware you have, you might have more than one printer physically attached to your computer. If so, you have to run the Add Printer setup wizard for

▼ each printer you will print to. When running the Add Printer Wizard, you specify which
   printer Windows 95 should use for the default printer. (The default printer might appear
   with a check mark next to it in the Printers window, depending on your Windows 95
   installation.) Of course, any time you print documents, you can select a printer that differs from the default printer if you want output to go to a secondary printer source. You
   can also change the default printer by right-clicking on the printer you want to set as the
▲ default printer and selecting the Set As Default command from the right-click menu.

> If you use your computer for accounting or personal finance, you might
> have a laser printer for reports and a dot-matrix printer for checks. The
> default printer should be the printer that you print to most often. If your
> laser printer is the default printer, you have to route output, using the Print
> dialog box explained in the next section, to the check printer when you
> want to print checks.

The Print Dialog Box

When you print from an application such as WordPad, you'll see the Print dialog box
shown in Figure 19.6. The Print dialog box contains several options from which you can
choose. Most of the time, the default option values are appropriate, so you simply press
Enter to select the OK command button when printing.

FIGURE 19.6

*The Print dialog box
controls the way a
print job is routed*

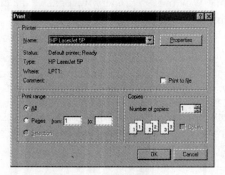

The Print dialog box contains a drop-down list box of every printer you've added to
Windows 95. The default printer is the printer you chose using the Add Printer Wizard's
final screen. To change the default printer so that Windows 95 automatically routes output to it, select a different printer at printing time and choose Set as Default from the
right-click's pop-up menu.

Even if you have not set up a file-based output device (see Task 19.1's description of the FILE: port), you can route the printer's output to a file by clicking the Print-to-file option. If you want output to go to a physical printer as soon as possible, as is most often the case, leave this option unchecked.

The Print range is All if you want to print all pages. For example, if you are printing 20 pages from a word processor, the All option sends all 20 pages to the printer. If you select the Pages option, you enter a starting page number and ending page number to print only a portion of the document.

The Copies section determines how many copies you want to print. The default is one copy, but you can request an additional number of copies. If you enter a number greater than 1, check the Collate option if you want the pages collated (you usually do). If you highlight part of the text before beginning the print process, you can click the Selection option button to print only the selected text.

For special print jobs, you can click the Properties command button to display a printer Properties dialog box such as the one shown in Figure 19.7. Each printer model supports a different set of options, so each printer's Properties dialog box contains different options as well. In the Properties dialog box, you specify the type of paper in the printer's paper tray, the *orientation* (the direction the printed output appears on the paper), and the printer resolution (the higher the printer resolution, the better your output looks, but the longer the printer takes to print a single page), among other options that your printer might support.

19

FIGURE 19.7

*A printer Properties
dialog box controls
your printer options*

Keep in mind that the output goes to the print spooler and *not* directly to the printer. The next section explains how you can manage the print spooler.

Some applications begin printing as soon as you click a printing toolbar button instead of displaying the Print dialog box before beginning to print. Be sure that you understand the way each of your applications handles printing. If you click such a toolbar button several times, you could inadvertently send many copies of output to your printer. Notepad and even Microsoft Word treat print jobs this way.

Some print jobs take a while to send their output to the spool file and, subsequently, to the printer. The taskbar displays a printer icon to the left of the clock during the printing process. If you rest the cursor over the printer icon, Windows 95 displays a roving help box that describes how many jobs are in line to print. If you open the print icon, Windows 95 displays the list of all print jobs (the next section describes the window of print jobs). If you right-click on the icon, Windows 95 gives you the choice of displaying a window containing a list of all print jobs or the print jobs for specific printers that are queued up waiting for printed output.

Explorer and Open dialog boxes all display documents, as you've seen already throughout this book. If you want to print a document, such as a bitmap graphic document file, a text document file, or a word processing document file, the right-click menu contains a Print command that automatically prints the selected document (or documents) that you right-click on. The right-click does *not* produce the Print dialog box described in this section; rather, Windows 95 automatically and instantly prints one copy of the document on the primary default printer.

Windows 95 cannot print all types of documents. For example, executable programs (such as those ending with the .EXE or .COM extension) are not printable. When you right-click over these non-printable files, the right-click menu does not contain a Print command.

There's yet one more way to print documents that works well in some situations. If you have the My Computer window open or if you are using the Explorer, you can print any printable document by dragging that document to any printer icon inside the Printers window. Windows 95 automatically begins printing the document that you drag.

If you copy a printer icon from the Printers window to your desktop (by holding Ctrl and dragging the icon to your desktop), you eliminate the need to open the Printers window every time you need to access your printer. You can drag files directly to the desktop's icon instead of first having to open the Printers window. In addition, you can access your printer's Properties page by right-clicking on the desktop's printer icon and selecting Properties from the pop-up menu.

Managing Print Jobs

When you print documents, Windows 95 formats the output into the format required by the default printer and then sends that output to a spool file. When the output completes, the printer subsystem routes the output to the actual printer, as long as it is connected and turned on.

Suppose that you want to print several documents to your printer in succession. Although today's printers are fairly fast, the computer's disk drives and memory are much faster than the relative speed of printers. Therefore, you can end up sending several documents to the printer before the first document even finishes printing on paper.

After printing one or more documents, go to the Printer window and open the printer icon that matches the printer you've routed all your output to. A scrolling list of print jobs, such as the one shown in Figure 19.8, appears inside the window.

FIGURE 19.8

You can see all the print jobs spooled up, waiting to print

Document Name	Status	Owner	Progress	Started At
Microsoft Word - Egypt.doc	Printing		0 of 1 pages	7:46:22 PM 9/27/99
Microsoft Word - EIB Institute.doc			1 page(s)	7:46:32 PM 9/27/99
Microsoft Word - Garydisk.doc			1 page(s)	7:46:34 PM 9/27/99
Microsoft Word - Home Office.doc			1 page(s)	7:46:37 PM 9/27/99
Microsoft Word - Sales Forecast....			1 page(s)	7:46:39 PM 9/27/99
Microsoft Word - Trip Expenses....			1 page(s)	7:46:42 PM 9/27/99

HP LaserJet 5P

Printer Document View Help

6 jobs in queue

19

Each line in the window describes one print job. If you've printed three documents, all three documents appear inside the window. The Progress column shows how far along your print job is by telling you how many pages of the print job have completed. The remaining print jobs on the list are awaiting their turn to print.

If you want to change the order of the print jobs in the *queue* (another name for the list of print jobs), you can drag a print job to the top or bottom. Dragging a print job around in the list changes priority for that print job. For example, your boss might be waiting over your shoulder for a report. If you had several jobs you had sent to print before your boss showed up, you could move the boss's print job to the top of the list so it would print next.

Right-clicking on a print job gives you the option of pausing a print job (putting it on hold until you resume the job) or canceling the print job altogether.

> If you select more than one print job by holding down the Ctrl key when you click on the print jobs, you can pause or cancel more than one print job at the same time.

Deferred Printing

There might be times when you print documents but *do not* want those documents to appear on a printer! Often people carry a laptop with them but not a printer. Even if you don't have a printer with you, you can create expense reports and other documents that you want to print as soon as you get back to your office.

Instead of keeping track of each document you want to print later, you can go ahead and issue a *deferred printing* request. When you do this, Windows 95 spools the document or documents to a file on your disk drive. The printer subsystem does not attempt to send the spooled data to a printer just yet. When you later attach a printer to your PC, you can release the deferred printing request and Windows 95 begins printing the saved print jobs.

Ordinarily, if you print a document to a printer but you have no printer attached to your computer, Windows 95 issues the error message shown in Figure 19.9. Although Windows 95 can spool the output properly and set up a print job for the output, Windows 95 cannot finish the job due to a lack of a printer, and so the dialog box lets you know about the problem.

FIGURE 19.9

Windows 95 cannot print if a printer is not attached to your PC

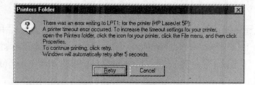

> If you do have a printer attached to your computer but you get the error dialog box shown in Figure 19.9, you probably forgot to turn on the printer or put the printer *online* so that it can accept output. You can correct the

problem and click Retry to restart the printing. If you do not click Retry, Windows 95 automatically retries printing every five seconds.

If you want to defer printing for another time, open the Printers folder and click over the icon that matches the printer you want to store print jobs for. After you highlight the icon, select File | Work Offline. When you return to your office or plug a printer into the printer port, you can repeat this process to uncheck the Work Offline option. As soon as you set the printer icon back to its normal online status, Windows 95 begins printing to that printer.

If your printer icon's File menu does not have a Work Offline option, you can select Pause Printing to achieve the same delayed printing effect. The actual printing begins when you click Pause Printing once more to turn off the pause. The Work Offline option is available only on certain laptop and networked computer configurations.

Separator Pages

If you share a network printer with others, you'll often send print jobs to the printer at approximately the same time as a co-worker. Windows 95 ensures that the first print job to arrive prints first, in its entirety, before the second print job. That means you don't have to worry about conflicting and shuffled output. Nevertheless, print jobs can sometimes be time-consuming to separate from a stack of printed pages that await you and others at the networked printer. Therefore, you might want to designate a *page separator* for the printer. A page separator is a page that prints between print jobs. You can place text or graphics on the page so that it helps you more easily locate where your job starts within a large stack of printer output.

19

After you turn on the separator page printing feature, Windows 95 prints a separator page before each print job. If your printer is rarely used by two or more people at once, or connected to a network, you always get a separator page before your print job even if yours is the only print job sent to the printer. Separator pages are especially wasteful if you print only one page to the printer because a separator page always appears with that one page. Therefore, designate a separator page only if you share a printer with other users and often print at the same time as them.

Task 19.2: Designating Separator Pages

Step 1: Description Separator pages do not have to be fancy. Designate a separator page, as this task demonstrates, if you and others send print jobs to the same printer often.

> If you don't use a network printer but you often send several documents to your printer before picking up the output, a separator page helps you find the division between the various print jobs. In other words, separator pages aren't just for networked printers.

Step 2: Action

1. Open your Printers window from the Start menu's Settings option or from the My Computer window.

2. Right-click on the printer that you want to add separator pages to. (You typically have only one or two printer icons in the window.)

3. Select Properties from the pop-up menu to display the Properties page.

4. From the Separator page list box, select the separator page you want. If you want to use your own file, you can type your file's full pathname and filename or click the Browse button to locate your file.

   The file you use for a separator page must end with the .WMF filename extension. .WMF files are named *Windows metafiles* and you must have access to a program that can create such files before you can supply your own separator pages. These .WMF files hold printer image output for your specific printer.

5. Click OK to close the Printers window.

Step 3: Review

By setting the separator page option on your printer's Properties sheet, you can designate a separator page that Windows 95 prints before each print job. The separator pages help you separate multiple outputs from one another. When you search through a large printed stack of output, you know you're at a new print job's output when you get to the next

 separator page.

Summary

This hour explored the printer options you have with Windows 95. Before using a printer for the first time, you must set up the printer using the Add Printer Wizard available inside the Printers folder. Windows 95 supports several hundred makes and models of printers so you stand a very good chance of finding your printer on the list.

Windows 95 does not send output directly to a printer. Instead, it spools output to a disk file and then, after the spooled output is completed, Windows 95 sends the output to a printer. It is possible for you to defer the printing if you do not have a printer hooked up at the time you issue the print command. For example, if you're away from your home or office with a laptop computer.

Windows 95 supports more than one connected printer at the same time. If you have two or more printers set up under Windows 95, you can, at the time that you print a document, direct that document to any printer on the system. In addition, if you share a printer with lots of users or if you print multiple jobs before you collect them from the printer, you can designate separator pages to make separating the output easier.

Workshop

Term Review

deferred printing   The process of issuing print commands but delaying the physical printing of those documents until later. Sometimes deferred printing is called *delayed printing*.

Offline   A printer is offline when the printer is turned off, or when it is on but not ready to accept output (you might turn the printer offline when you need to feed pages through the printer manually).

Online   A printer is online when the printer is turned on and ready to accept output.

Orientation   The position or direction of output on the printed page.

parallel port   A connector on your computer where most printer cables plug in.

print codes   Special characters that dictate how printers output and format characters.

print jobs   Every document that you send to a printer for output which appears on the print spooler.

printer drivers   Small descriptor files that allow Windows 95 to communicate properly with specific printers.

printer subsystem   A program automatically started by Windows 95 that controls the way output appears on the printer.

19

Queue   A list, such as the list of print jobs, that you see in the Printers window when you open a printer icon.

separator page   A page that prints before the first page of each print job and helps you identify your job in a stack of several print jobs that you or others might have sent to the printer.

spooled output   Output that is sent to a disk file before being routed to a printer.

Windows metafile   A special Windows 95 file that ends with the .WMF filename extension. You can use Windows metafiles for separator pages that you create yourself as long as you have a program that is capable of creating metafiles with the .WMF filename extension.

Q&A

Q Why should I care how my output gets to the printer?

A There are times when you'll send several documents to the printer and then change your mind about printing one or more of them. As long as the documents haven't actually printed on paper yet, you can stop the document from printing by utilizing the printer subsystem available within Windows 95.

All printer output goes through the print spooler instead of going directly to the printer. The spooler holds all print jobs and controls the order of the print jobs. After a job is on the spooler's list of documents, you can delete the documents or rearrange their printing priority. If you do not know how Windows 95 spools print-ed output, you cannot rearrange printer output.

Q Does the spooling of output slow down my printing?

A It's true that your output will not print as fast as it would if the output went directly to the printer. Nevertheless, the decrease in speed is minimal. The advantages you gain by spooling your output more than make up for the delay in printing.

Q When would I set up more than one printer?

A If you have more than one printer connected to your computer, you can choose one printer as the default printer and one as a secondary printer. Windows 95 prints to the default printer unless you override the default and route output to the secondary printer. You have to run the Add Printer Wizard for both printers before you use them the first time, so that Windows 95 knows how to format the output. Other times that you might want to set up more than one printer is if you're connected to a network that offers several printers for your use or if you have a laptop that you connect to different printer models at different locations.

Q Why does a right-click on some files produce a menu with a Print command whereas a right-click on others does not?

A Windows 95 knows that some files are printable and some are not. For example, you could not print a sound file. Executable programs are not printable either. Only document files that contain graphics or text are printable. Therefore, Windows 95 makes sure that the Print command appears only in the right-click menu for document files that Windows 95 can print.

19

Hour **20**

Fonts and Viewers

As you now know, Windows 95 is *document-centered*, meaning that Windows 95 manages files as if those files were documents stored inside folders. No matter what kind of information those documents contain, you can view the documents on your screen.

Windows 95 gives you several ways to manage documents. In previous versions of Windows, you often had to open documents to view their contents because the filename limitations simply didn't let you assign descriptive titles. The long filenames in Windows 95 help to eliminate some of this viewing, but there are still many times when you need to look up information in a document.

If you open a document from virtually anywhere within Windows 95, it tries its best to determine the nature of the document and opens a program that displays that document. At times, however, you might not have such a program available. For example, you might work on a desktop or laptop with limited disk space. If you don't have many programs on the computer, how can you view all the spreadsheets, word processor documents, and graphic documents on the computer's disk? The answer is explained this hour.

The highlights of this hour include:

- What's possible from the Fonts window
- How to add new fonts to Windows 95
- How to remove fonts from Windows 95
- When to use Quick Viewers to look at documents
- Why the document's orientation often makes a document easier to read
- How to display a page preview of documents inside the Quick Viewers

Font with Style

Due to the design of documents, the way that Windows 95 displays documents is critical to your viewing of them. The documents must be easy to read. If Windows 95 doesn't automatically display a document in a form that provides for easy viewing, you have to change the way the document appears. Perhaps the simplest way to make a document easier to read, no matter what tool you use to view those documents, is by changing the document's font. A font is the typeface Windows 95 uses to display a character. If you see two letter A's on the screen and one is larger, more slanted, bolder, fancier, or more scripted, you are looking at two different fonts.

Fonts from the same *font family* are the same typeface (they look alike) but they come in standard formatting versions such as italicized, boldfaced, and underlined text. Therefore, an italicized font named *Courier* and a boldfaced font named *Courier* both belong to the same font family, even though they look different due to the italicized version of the one and the boldface of the other. A font named *Algerian* and a font named *Symbol*, however, would belong to two different font families; not only do they look different, but they also come in various styles.

Before computers were invented, printer experts stored collections of typefaces in their shops. Each typeface contained every letter, number, and special character the printer needed for printed documents. Therefore, the printer might have 50 typefaces in his inventory with each of those typefaces containing the same letters, numbers, and special characters, but each having a different appearance or size.

Windows 95 also contains a collection of typefaces, and those typefaces are stored as fonts on the hard disk. If you want to use a special typeface for a title, you must make sure that Windows 95 contains that typeface in its font collection. If not, you have to purchase the font and add that font to your system. Software dealers sell numerous font collections. Several fonts come with Windows 95 and the programs that you use, so you might not even need additional fonts.

The Control Panel contains an icon labeled Fonts from which you can manage, add, and delete fonts from Windows 95's collection of fonts. When you open the Control Panel's Fonts icon, Windows 95 opens the Fonts window shown in Figure 20.1. Task 20.1 explains how to manage fonts from the Fonts window.

FIGURE 20.1

The Fonts window displays your fonts

Task 20.1: The Fonts Window

Step 1: Description

This task explains how to access your system's fonts by using the Fonts window. The Fonts window is the control center for the fonts on your system. You can add or remove fonts from this window, as well as learn more about the font details you already have.

Step 2: Action

1. Open the Control Panel.
2. Open the Fonts icon. Windows 95 opens the Fonts window.

   Each icon inside the Fonts window contains information about one specific font on your system. Some fonts are *scalable,* which means that Windows 95 can display the fonts in virtually any size.

Font sizes are measured in points. A font that is 12 points high is 1/6 inch high, and a font that is 72 points is one inch high.

20

> Change the view (using the View menu command) if you want to display the font information using a different format, such as the detailed or small icon view formats.

3. Open any of the icons inside the Fonts window. Windows 95 immediately displays a preview of that font, as shown in Figure 20.2. When you want to create a special letter or flier with a fancy font, you can preview all of the fonts by opening each one until you find one you like. After you find a font, you can select it from your word processor to enter the text using that font.

FIGURE 20.2

Get a preview before selecting a font

> Many fancy fonts are available to you. Don't go overboard, though. Your message is always more important than the font that you use. Make your font's style fit the message, and don't mix more than two or three fonts on a single page. Too many different fonts on a single page make the page look cluttered.

4. If you click the Print command button, Windows 95 prints the preview of the font. If you click Done (do so now), Windows 95 closes the font's preview window.

5. Another way to gather information about certain kinds of fonts is to right-click on a font and select Properties from the menu that appears. Figure 20.3 shows the resulting tabbed dialog box.

FIGURE 20.3

*You can view the prop-
erties of your fonts*

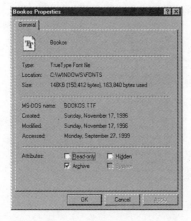

 Some font property dialog boxes contain more than one tabbed page.

The font icons with the letters TT are *TrueType* fonts. As you learned in Hour 10,
"MS-DOS and Windows 95," a TrueType font is a scalable font that Windows 95
prints using 32-bit technology so it looks as close to typeset characters as possible.
The remaining fonts, with the letter A or another icon, refer to screen and printer
fonts of more limited size ranges than TrueType fonts normally can provide.

 Some users prefer to work only with TrueType fonts, due to the rich look
associated with them and their scalability. If you want to view only TrueType
fonts in the Fonts window, select View I Options and click the TrueType tab.
Click the option to display only TrueType fonts.

20

6. Choose View I List Fonts By Similarity from the menu. Windows 95 searches
   through your fonts looking for all other fonts that are similar to a font you choose
   from the drop-down list box and displays the result of that search. Some fonts are
   very similar, some are somewhat similar, and some are not similar at all.

   Figure 20.4 shows a font similarity screen that shows how the other fonts compare
   to the *Arial* font.

FIGURE 20.4

Find fonts that are similar to other fonts

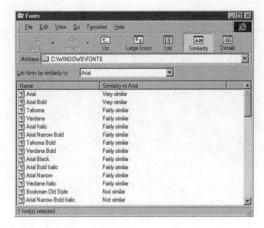

7. Choose View | Large Icons to return to the icon view.

8. Check or uncheck View | Hide Variations (Bold, Italic, and so on) depending on whether or not you want to see variations within font families. If the box is unchecked, Windows 95 displays a different icon for each font variation within the same family.

9. When you purchase new fonts, you cannot simply copy those fonts to a directory and expect Windows 95 to know that the fonts are there. When you want to add fonts, you'll probably obtain those fonts on a CD-ROM, disk, or by downloading to your hard disk from the Internet. Insert the disk or CD-ROM (or make sure you know where the file is located on your hard disk) and select File | Install New Font. Windows 95 displays the Add Fonts dialog box shown in Figure 20.5.

FIGURE 20.5

Add new fonts to Windows 95 using the Add Fonts dialog box

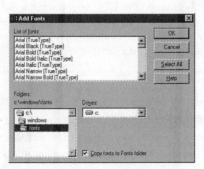

Select the drive with the new fonts inside the Drives list box, and Windows 95 displays a list of fonts from that drive in the upper window. Click on the font you want to install (hold Ctrl and click more than one font if you want to install several

▼   fonts) and click the OK command button to install the font to the Windows folder
      named Fonts.

   10. Close the Fonts window.

> After you install fonts, they are immediately available to all your Windows
> 95 applications.

Step 3: Review

Windows 95 provides a single location, the Fonts window, where you can view and manage all the fonts on your system. Due to the graphical and document-centered design of
Windows 95, your collection and selection of fonts is vital to making your documents as
▲ easy to read as possible.

Task 20.2: Removing Fonts from Windows 95

Step 1: Description

Fonts take up a lot of disk space. If your disk space is a premium and if you have lots of
fonts that you rarely or never use, you can follow the steps in this task to remove some of
the fonts. Often, today's word processing and desktop publishing programs add lots of
fonts to your system, and you might not need as many as you have at hand.

Step 2: Action

   1. Open the Control Panel.

   2. Open the Fonts icon.

   3. Scroll to the font you want to delete.

   4. Click the font that you want to delete; Windows 95 highlights the font. If you hold
       the Ctrl key while you click, you can select more than one font to delete. Figure
       20.6 shows several selected fonts. By selecting several at once, you can remove the
       fonts with one task instead of removing each one individually.

   5. Right-click over any highlighted font to display the pop-up menu.

   6. Select Delete.

   7. Click the Yes button to confirm the removal.

Step 3: Review

Remove unwanted fonts if you want to save disk space and make your fonts more man-
▼ ageable. The Control Panel's Fonts entry lets you easily select and remove fonts.

20

Figure 20.6

Select multiple fonts if you want to delete several at once

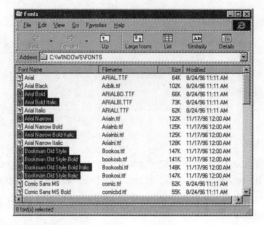

Viewing Documents

If you open any file that appears in Explorer or in any file dialog box, you now know that Windows 95 attempts to load and run the program that created the document so that you can view and edit it. Although this feature is a wonderful part of the Windows 95 environment, you might still face a major problem: You might not always have a program that can open that file.

For example, suppose that a friend of yours, a budding artist, gives you a new digital drawing that she wants you to study and critique. You copy the file to your hard disk using Explorer, open the file, and, instead of a graphics program that displays the image for your review, you see the dialog box shown in Figure 20.7. Windows 95 needs help! Windows 95 does not recognize the file's type, so it displays a scrolling list of programs, hoping that you can find and select a program from the list that can open the file.

Figure 20.7

Windows 95 does not recognize a file's format

What do you do when you do not have the application needed to view the file? You can buy a copy of the program you need to look at the file; you can *not* look at the file and tell your friend that you did look at it (you wouldn't tell a fib to a friend); or you can install the Windows 95 *Quick Viewers*.

The standard Windows 95 installation does not include the Windows 95 Quick Viewers, but you can easily install them by using the Control Panel Add/Remove Programs Windows Setup option. The Quick Viewers application is actually a collection of applets that display documents formatted in a variety of formats. If Windows 95 does not recognize a document's file extension or type, you cannot view the contents of the file, but the right-click menu contains an Open With option. When you select Open With, a list of all registered applications on your PC (which should be virtually all Windows applications installed) appears, and you can select the application that goes with the data document you are wanting to view. Instead of a viewer, Windows subsequently opens that application as well as the document and remembers that association in the future.

Microsoft is asking software developers to add viewers to their Windows 95 programs so that the collection of Windows 95 viewers is as current as possible. These programs will link their applications' Quick Viewers to Windows 95's own set.

Table 20.1 contains a list of most of the Windows 95 viewers available in the typical Windows 95 installation. Table 20.1 also contains a list of filename extensions that each Quick Viewers recognizes. (Even if Explorer does not display filename extensions, the Quick Viewers application recognizes the filename extensions and loads the proper viewer dialog box.)

The Quick Viewers application lets you look at files, but you cannot edit those files.

20

TABLE 20.1 THE AVAILABLE QUICK VIEWERS FORMATS

Extension	File Type
.ASC	ASCII
.BMP	Windows 95 bitmap
.CDR	CorelDRAW!
.DOC	Word for Windows and WordPerfect

continues

TABLE 20.1 CONTINUED

Extension	File Type
.DRW	Micrographix Draw
.EPS	Encapsulated PostScript
.GIF	CompuServe Graphics Interchange Format
.INF	Setup
.INI	Windows 95 Configuration
.MOD	Multiplan 3, 4.0, and 4.1
.PPT	PowerPoint
.PRE	Freelance for Windows
.RLE	Run-Length Encoding bitmap
.RTF	Rich Text Format
.SAM	AMI and AMI Pro
.TIF	TIFF graphics
.TXT	Text
.WB1	Quattro Pro for Windows
.WK1	Lotus 1-2-3 releases 1 and 2
.WK3	Lotus 1-2-3 release 3
.WK4	Lotus 1-2-3 release 4 spreadsheets and charts
.WKS	Lotus 1-2-3 and Microsoft Works release 3
.WMF	Windows metafiles
.WPD	WordPerfect demonstrations
.WPS	Works word processor
.WQ1	Quattro Pro for MS-DOS
.WQ2	Quattro Pro for MS-DOS release 5
.WRI	Windows 3.x Write
.XLC	Excel charts (older versions of Excel)
.XLS	Excel spreadsheets and charts (recent releases of Excel)

Task 20.3: Using the Quick View Viewers

Step 1: Description

To Do

This task explains how to use Quick Viewers to look at a document. If you have any application that creates one of the Quick Viewers extensions listed in Table 20.1, try to view one of those files. This task uses a standard text file for which you really only need

▼ the Notepad text editor to see and edit, but the text file lets you practice using the Quick Viewers.

Step 2: Action

1. Start Explorer.

2. Display the Windows folder in the left window and its contents in the right window.

3. Scroll to the file named Readme (the file's full name is Readme.txt, and you may or may not have set the Explorer's option to hide the filename extension).

4. Right-click the Readme file. You'll see the Quick View command on the menu (as long as you've installed the Quick Viewers).

5. Select the Quick View command. Windows 95 analyzes the Readme file, realizes that the file is a text file and that there is a viewer for text files, and displays the Quick View window.

6. Open the title bar to maximize the window. You see a window that looks something like the one shown in Figure 20.8.

FIGURE 20.8

Windows 95 finds the proper way to view a text file

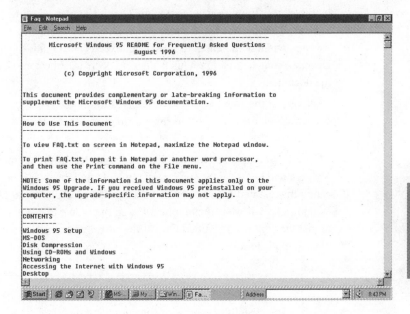

Depending on the date of your Windows 95 release, the text inside the Quick Viewers window might differ slightly from the text in Figure 20.8.

20

▼   7. Scroll through the file. If you were viewing any type of file from Table 20.1, you
       would be viewing the text or graphics from that file as if you were working within
       a program that created those files. For example, Figure 20.9 contains a maximized
       Quick Viewers window that's displaying an Excel worksheet.

FIGURE 20.9

*Quick Viewers is dis-
playing an Excel work-
sheet*

	A	B	C	D	E
1	Mountains	Cities	Countries	Lakes	Deserts
2	McKinley	Mexico	Canada	Athabasca	Chihuahuan
3	Logan	New York	United States	Erie	Colorado
4	Citlaltepec	Los Angeles	Mexico	Great Bear	Great Basin
5	St. Elias	Chicago		Great Salt	Mojave
6	Popocatepetl	Montreal		Great Slave	Painted
7	Foraker			Huron	Sonoran
8	Iztaccihuatl			Michigan	Vizcaino
9	Lucania			Nicaragua	Yuma
10				Ontario	
11				Superior	
12				Winnipeg	

WORLD - Quick View
File View Help

To edit, click Open File for Editing on the File menu.

   8. Two buttons on the toolbar have the letter A. The one with the large letter A
       increases the font size used inside the Quick Viewers window. Every time you
       click the Increase font size command button, the document's font inside the Quick
       Viewers window increases to make the text easier to read. Every time you click the
       Decrease font size button, Quick Viewers decreases the font size to show more of
       the document.

       Click one of the font buttons several times to see the effect of the button's font
       change. Click the other button several times to see the reversal of the font size
       change.

   9. The toolbar contains a Notepad icon at the far left of the toolbar. The Quick
       Viewers window's toolbar will normally contain whatever icon matches the appli-
       cation that created the file you're viewing. If you click that application's icon,
       Windows 95 will start that application, so that you can edit that document instead
       of just viewing it. (The File | Open File for Editing command also opens that docu-
       ment's application.)

> If you don't have the editing application installed on your computer's disk,
> you obviously cannot edit the document using that secondary application.
> You can only display the file using the Quick Viewers.

▼

▼ 10. Click the View | Page View command. Windows 95 displays a page preview of the document similar to the one shown in Figure 20.10.

FIGURE 20.10

Quick Viewers can display a page view

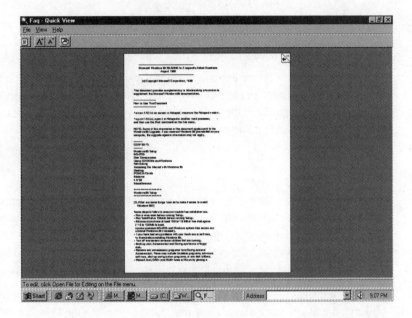

Click the arrow in the upper-right corner of the page preview to see a preview of the next page. You can scroll back and forth within the previewed document by clicking the arrows in the corner.

11. Click View | Landscape to see a landscape view of the document. If a document is wide (the Readme text file is not a wide file), landscape view shows how the document looks if displayed across the wide edge of the page. Click View | Landscape again to return to the portrait view where the document appears down the page (as a letter's text is often printed).

12. Close the Quick Viewers by selecting File | Exit.>

The page's *orientation* is the portrait or landscape mode.

▼

20

If you want to change the font used in the viewer's display, select View | Font from the menu.

Step 3: Review

The Quick Viewers are extremely helpful, especially if you work on a laptop or other computer that has limited disk space. The Quick Viewers allow only displaying, not editing, of documents, but the set of Quick Viewers consumes much less disk space than the separate applications themselves.

Summary

This hour discussed the viewing of documents, especially documents that display formatted text. The ease with which you can read text onscreen and in the printed document is often determined by the font used for displaying that text. The Fonts window contains a centralized location from which you can manage all the fonts used by Windows 95. When you purchase new fonts, you add those fonts using the Fonts window.

When displaying a list of document filenames, a simple right-click on a file produces a menu that lets you quickly view that document using the Windows 95 Quick Viewers. The Quick Viewers application is actually a collection of several individual viewer applications combined into one application. More viewers are being added to Quick Viewers all the time so that future software programs will offer viewers to the Windows 95 collection.

Workshop

Term Review

document-centered   The concept that Windows 95 promotes by maintaining that you work with a computer's files as if they were documents inside folders in a file cabinet.

Font   The typeface used for a document's character display.

font family   Characters that take on the same typeface, but that come in italics, boldfaced, and underlined versions, are all part of the same font family.

landscape view   Shows how the document would look if displayed across the wide edge of the page. Landscape view is helpful for wide documents.

Orientation   The way the document appears on the page. The orientation is either the portrait view (vertical) or landscape view (horizontal).

portrait view   Shows how the document would look if displayed down the page, as a letter's text is typically printed.

Scalable   A font is scalable if Windows 95 can generate characters from the font in any size.

Viewer   A Windows 95 accessory program with which you can look at documents.

Q&A

Q Why do I need to know how to preview fonts?

A If you are thinking about purchasing new fonts, you will want to display or print a preview of all your current fonts. The preview might show that you have more fonts than you originally thought. You might also want to preview a font before using it in a word processor or graphics program.

Q I just bought new fonts. What do I do?

A Open the Fonts windows and select File | Install New Font to display the Add Fonts dialog box. Windows 95 must run through a collection and verification procedure before it recognizes your new fonts. Luckily, this procedure is easy, thanks to the Add Fonts dialog box. Basically, you click on the disk or CD-ROM that contains the new fonts, select the font or fonts you want to install, and click the OK command button to let Windows 95 take care of the rest. Some fonts come with their own installer or setup program that you run just as you would run an installation routine to install many applications.

Q I don't have Microsoft Excel. How can I analyze my office spreadsheets at home?

A You don't need Microsoft Excel to look at Excel spreadsheets. All you need is Windows 95, because it provides the collection of Quick Viewers with which you can display virtually any type of document.

The Quick Viewers application lets you change the way you view documents. You can change the font type, the font size, and the orientation (whether or not the page appears in a landscape or portrait views). If you want to view the overall document, the Quick Viewers also support the use of a preview mode.

Q I use Quick Viewers often because it's always there when I right-click over a document's name. I often decide I want to change the document, and so I must exit Quick Viewers and start the application that created the document. Is there a faster way to edit a document from the Quick Viewers window?

20

A Yes. Click the first button on the Quick Viewers' toolbar and Windows 95 opens the document's parent application, and then you can edit the file.

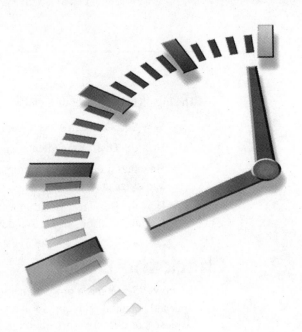

HOUR 21

Fine-Tune with Advanced System Tools

Windows 95 works well but, like a well-made automobile, you must tune it once in a while to optimize its operation and keep Windows 95 running at top speed. (Who wants a sluggish operating system?) When your operating system slows down, your entire computer system slows down because the operating system controls everything else that happens.

Periodically, you can run tune-up programs that Microsoft provides with Windows 95 to keep your system running smoothly. Most of a system's slowdown is due to the disk drive's mechanical design. The disk, being a mechanical device, can experience problems. The disk's magnetic surface wears down and files can get lost as a result. Windows 95 can periodically scan your disk looking for trouble spots.

The highlights of this hour include

- Why ScanDisk can salvage your disk files before you even know they have problems
- How the Disk Defragmenter speeds your disk access
- How the System Monitor graphically displays several graphs that monitor the system usage statistics
- How the Resource Meter appears on the toolbar to display the three primary resource statistics inside Windows 95

Check the Disk

Windows 95 supplies a program named *ScanDisk* that checks your disk drive for problems and potential problems so that you might avoid future troubles. ScanDisk contains two levels of disk drive inspection: a *standard scan* and a *thorough scan*. The standard scan checks your disk files for errors. The thorough scan checks the files and performs a disk surface test to verify the integrity and safety of disk storage.

ScanDisk is just one of the applications inside the folder labeled System Tools that you can install when setting up Windows 95 or when adding programs to Windows 95. Depending on your Windows 95 installation, your System Tools menu might contain one or more of the icons shown in Figure 21.1.

FIGURE 21.1

The System Tools menu contains several helpful utility applications

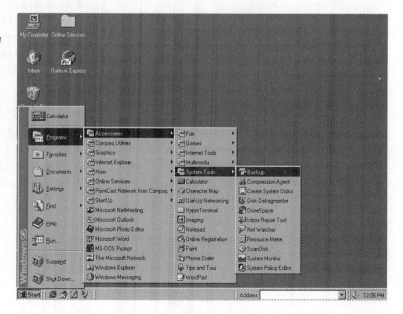

Run ScanDisk regularly (perhaps once or twice a week). As with all Windows 95 programs, you can multitask ScanDisk while running another program.

Task 21.1: Check a Disk with ScanDisk

Step 1: Description

This task explains how to use the ScanDisk application. ScanDisk is simple to use and often takes only a few seconds to load and run.

Step 2: Action

1. Display the Start menu.

2. Select the Programs command to display the next cascaded menu.

3. Display the Accessories menu.

4. Display the System Tools menu.

5. Click the ScanDisk menu item. Windows 95 displays the ScanDisk window shown in Figure 21.2.

FIGURE 21.2

The opening ScanDisk window for analyzing your disk drives

ScanDisk checks only hard disk or floppy drives, not CD-ROM drives.

6. The Standard option is initially checked by default. To perform a standard ScanDisk, press Enter to choose the Start command button. ScanDisk begins its chore of checking your files. The ScanDisk window displays a moving graphics bar to show how much time remains in each ScanDisk step, as well as a description of each step in the process.

21

> If ScanDisk finds a problem and you've checked the option labeled
> Automatically Fix Errors, ScanDisk attempts to fix any problems it finds
> using default repair tools. (You can change the way ScanDisk repairs the
> disk by pushing the Advanced command button described toward the end
> of this task.)

7. After ScanDisk finishes, you see a ScanDisk results window, such as the one
   shown in Figure 21.3.

FIGURE 21.3

*ScanDisk reports its
results to you upon
completion of the disk
scan*

The most important line in the results window is the number of bad sectors. Rarely
will the number be anything but zero. If bad sectors appear, ScanDisk attempts to
repair them and reports the results.

Press Enter to close the results window.

8. Click the Advanced command button. ScanDisk displays the ScanDisk Advanced
   Options dialog box shown in Figure 21.4. The default values are usually fine, but if
   you understand disk drive technology and file storage details, you might want to
   change an option. Click the OK command button to close the dialog box.

FIGURE 21.4

*The advanced
ScanDisk options that
you can control*

▼ 9. Click the Thorough option and click the Start command button to perform a thorough ScanDisk check. The thorough scan performs a more intense disk check than the standard scan. You see the results window when ScanDisk finishes.

Step 3: Review

The ScanDisk program is a dual-leveled disk checking program that searches for disk errors and, optionally, attempts to fix the errors. Run ScanDisk once or twice weekly to make sure your disk is as free from defects as possible.

If you want more control over the ScanDisk process, you can click the Options button to control these options:

- System and data areas: Scans your entire disk drive including the system areas.

- System area only: Scans your disk's system areas including the *FAT* (file allocation table, which controls how your files are placed on your disk) and directory.

▲ - Data area only: Scans only your programs and data and leaves the system areas unscanned.

Fill in the Holes

Over time, you create and delete many files. Although the deleted file space is released for other files, your computer's disk drive can become filled with many small holes so that subsequent files stored on the disk must fill, resulting in a slowdown (these holes create a *fragmented disk*). Windows 95 can close up these gaps and make larger and contiguous chunks of free disk space available so your files go to and from the disk quickly.

The *Disk Defragmenter* is a utility program, available on the System Tools menu. It fills in the gaps on your disks. As you add and delete files, the deleted space leaves free holes around the disk. Over time, your disk response time slows down as you add or delete document files to and from the disk drive.

> Disk defragmentation is *not* the same thing as Drive Space which is explained in Hour 12, "Back Up and Squeeze Disk Space."

Pick Up the Pieces

21

Windows 95 can store large files on a fragmented disk as long as there is enough free fragmented space to hold the file. Windows 95 stores the files in linked chunks across the disk drive, filling in fragments and linking them together.

The reason that disk access slows down on a fragmented disk drive is that Windows 95 must jump to each file fragment when retrieving a file. If you run the Disk Defragmenter program often enough (once or twice a month for the average user ought to be enough), Windows 95 keeps the fragments to a minimum and, thus, increases the disk access speed.

> Some people forget that the Disk Defragmenter helps speed diskette drives as well as hard disk drives. As a matter of fact, if you run Disk Defragmenter on diskettes that you use regularly, you can increase the speed of that diskette greatly.

> Although the Disk Fragmentation program works well and accurately in most cases, do yourself a favor and back up your system before starting the defragmenting process. Hour 12 explains how to use the Windows 95 Backup program to back up your files.

Task 21.2: Correcting Disk Fragmentation

Step 1: Description

This task explains how to defragment a disk drive. The task assumes that you'll begin by defragmenting a disk. If you defragment disk, you'll be able to run the Disk Defragmenter program several times (on different disks) if you want to.

Step 2: Action

1. Display the Start menu.

2. Select the Programs command to display the next cascaded menu.

3. Display the Accessories menu.

4. Display the System Tools menu.

5. Click the Disk Defragmenter menu item. Windows 95 displays the Select Drive window shown in Figure 21.5.

6. Insert a disk in your disk drive.

7. Open the drop-down list box and select the disk drive.

▼   8. Click the OK command button to start the defragmentation process. Windows 95 can multitask while defragmenting your disk space, so you can run other programs while Disk Defragmenter runs. At any point during the defragmentation, you can pause Disk Defragmenter or cancel the process. If the disk is not fragmented, Disk Defragmenter tells you so and asks if you want to run the Disk Defragmenter program on the disk anyway.

9. When it finishes, Disk Defragmenter lets you know that the defragmentation is complete. Click Yes to close the application.

FIGURE 21.5

The opening Disk Defragmenter window for analyzing your disk drives

Step 3: Review

Run Disk Defragmenter regularly to keep your disk running at its most optimum configuration. Disk Defragmenter rearranges information and blank spots on your disk drive and puts all the data in contiguous disk space and all the empty holes into one large con-
▲   tiguous block. After defragmented, your disk access will speed up.

Check Your System

Windows 95 contains two programs, System Monitor and the Resource Meter, that monitor your system resources. These applications are extremely advanced for most Windows 95 users because most users don't have to run them and analyze their results.

Windows 95 manages the system and memory *much* better than previous versions of Windows did, and you'll rarely run out of memory or resources when you work inside Windows 95. System Monitor tracks these three items:

* The *file system* comprised of disk access statistics
* The *kernel* comprised of the CPU's activity, as well as some multitasking activities
* The *memory manager* comprised of the various segments of memory that Windows 95 tracks

21

System Monitor graphically displays one or more of these items and continuously updates the graph to show how your system is being used. You can start the System Monitor and go about your regular Windows 95 work. If the system begins to slow and you want an idea as to which parts of the system are getting the most use, click on the System Monitor on the toolbar to have an idea of your machine's current workload.

When you run the Resource Meter, its program puts a Resource Meter icon next to the clock. You can click the icon to obtain statistics on these items:

- System resources, which describe the system's resource use percentage
- User resources, which describe your resource use percentage
- *GDI* (*Graphics Device Interface*), which describes your graphics resource use percentage

Task 21.3 demonstrates a simple use of the System Monitor and Resource Meter.

Task 21.3: Checking Resources

Step 1: Description

This task explains how to start System Monitor and Resource Meter. You can use output from these programs to check the efficiency of your computer system.

Step 2: Action

1. Display the Start menu.
2. Select the Programs command to display the next cascaded menu.
3. Display the Accessories menu.
4. Display the System Tools menu.
5. Click the System Monitor menu item. Windows 95 displays the System Monitor window. Start another program or two. Click the taskbar to return to the System Monitor graph every so often. As you will see, System Monitor updates its graph and eventually the graph fills the window, as shown in Figure 21.6.

To show the System Monitor running at extremes, the System Monitor in Figure 21.6 was produced on a fairly slow 486 33-megahertz computer, which had quite a drain on its resources. You can see the high and low extreme peaks in the graph as programs were used, paused, and closed.

FIGURE 21.6

The System Monitor screen updates regularly to show your resources

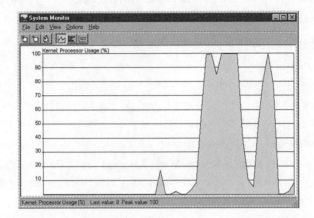

6. The default System Monitor displays only the kernel strain. Select Edit | Add Item or click the far left button on the toolbar. Click the File System in the left window and highlight every option inside the right window to request that System Monitor update all the file system statistics. Click OK.

7. Select Edit | Add Item again to add all the detail items for the Memory Manager. When you click OK, the System Monitor displays several small graphs. Watch the graphs update after they check the resources being analyzed. Your System Monitor window can get full as Figure 21.7 shows.

FIGURE 21.7

The System Monitor can display statistics for several items

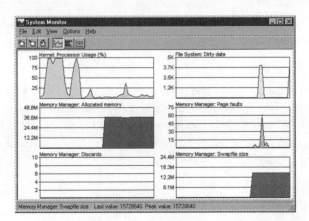

Click over any of the small graphs. System Monitor describes what the graph means in the status bar at the bottom of the System Monitor window.

21

▼   8. Select File | Exit to close the System Monitor so you can start the Resource Meter.

     9. Display the Start menu.

    10. Select the Programs command to display the next cascaded menu.

    11. Display the Accessories menu.

    12. Display the System Tools menu.

    13. Click the Resource Meter menu item. Windows 95 displays an opening description dialog box. Read the dialog box and press Enter to close the dialog box.

    14. Windows 95 displays the Resource Meter icon to the left of the taskbar clock.

    15. Right-click on the Resource Meter icon and select Details. Windows 95 displays a graph showing the current resource usage statistics for the three Resource Meter measurements as shown in Figure 21.8.

FIGURE 21.8

The Resource Meter window available from the taskbar

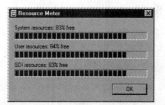

    16. As you work in Windows 95, you can check the Resource Meter graphs as often as you want to make sure you don't get close to running out of resources.

    17. Right-click the Resource Meter icon and select Exit to unload the Resource Meter program.

Step 3: Review

The System Monitor shows one or more graphs, depending on your options, that display usage patterns. The Resource Meter displays a graph of three resource utilizations as you work within Windows 95. If you run graphics- and processor-intensive programs, you can run System Monitor and Resource Meter to see how much of a load you are placing
▲   on Windows 95 and the hardware.

Summary

This hour described several system tools you can run to manage and monitor your disk, memory, and other system resources. The ScanDisk program detects errors on the disk drive and attempts to fix as many problems as it is capable of fixing.

The Disk Defragmenter program rearranges your disk files so that all the file space resides in one large block and all the free space is together. This speeds disk drive access and eliminates fragmentation. Run both ScanDisk and Disk Defragmenter every week or two to keep your disk drives as healthy as possible.

The System Monitor and Resource Meter programs work passively to display statistics about your memory, disk, and system usage. Windows 95 handles resources better than previous versions of Windows, but these tools give you two additional ways to monitor the usage.

Workshop

Term Review

Disk Defragmenter   A Windows 95 program that collects and removes blank disk space left from deleted files.

FAT   An abbreviation for file allocation table. Controls the placement of files on your disk.

file system   The collection of disk access routines and memory.

GDI   Stands for *Graphics Device Interface* and consists of your graphics resources.

kernel   The CPU's processor routines.

Memory Manager   Controls the various segments of memory that Windows 95 tracks.

standard scan   The quickest ScanDisk version that checks your disk files for errors.

System Monitor   A Windows 95 program that graphically illustrates your computer's resources as you use the computer.

system resources   The amount of CPU, memory, and disk space utilization consumed by Windows 95 and the applications you are running.

thorough scan   The slower, but more thorough scan that checks the files and performs a disk surface test to verify the integrity and safety of disk storage.

21

Q&A

Q **Should I worry about the advanced ScanDisk options that I don't under-stand?**

A Unfortunately, the advanced ScanDisk options are fairly advanced (that's why they're called *advanced* options!). The details of the options go beyond the scope of this book. Fortunately, you will rarely, if ever, need to modify any of the advanced options. Unless you learn a lot about the disk and the way that Windows 95 stores files on a disk, run ScanDisk using the default options; you'll virtually always run the proper ScanDisk.

Q **I don't know if my disk is fragmented, so do I still run Disk Defragmenter?**

A Run Disk Defragmenter whether or not your disk is fragmented. Disk Defragmenter will inform you whether you need to continue if the disk has few or no fragments to collect.

Q **How can I use the System Monitor and Resource Meter?**

A If you never run more than two or three programs at once, you may *never* need the System Monitor or Resource Meter. Both are necessary if your programs begin to put heavy strains on Windows 95 and the machine.

Multimedia-intensive programs often strain the system's resources. If you attempt to run a multimedia program, as well as one or more additional programs, you'll strain even the fastest of today's computers. The System Monitor and Resource Meter show you where that strain is coming from.

HOUR 22

Multimedia Is
Really Here

In the early 1990s, several companies, including Microsoft, got together to design a new multimedia standard. There are many ways to implement graphics, motion video, and sound. In fact, there are so many ways, virtually every company that was designing multimedia software implemented its multimedia differently from the others. The result was a confused marketplace where many companies' software would not work with very much hardware.

This hour describes the standard that resulted from an industry consortium of software and hardware developers led by Microsoft. As long as you have a computer with the standard hardware, you are certain to be able to run all software that conforms to the multimedia standard.

The availability and compatibility of multimedia hardware and software, combined with the increased power of today's computers and the decreased price associated with that power, make multimedia a reality. Windows 95 continues the tradition that earlier Windows versions began by adding multimedia capabilities never before available. This hour introduces you to Windows 95's multimedia capabilities.

The highlights of this hour include:

- What the MPC standard means
- How AutoPlay eliminates your usual CD-ROM startup keystrokes
- Where to enter the artist, title, and songs for your collection of CDs
- Why Windows 95 supports multimedia better than previous versions of Windows
- How to control the sound and display of full-motion video
- How to turn off AutoPlay temporarily and permanently

The MPC Standard

When Microsoft programmers developed Windows 3.1, they saw the need for an industry-wide multimedia standard. If that standard included Windows 3.1-compatibility, Microsoft would benefit nicely. The good news for the rest of us is that *we* would also benefit nicely if there were standards in place. We would then know that if we bought a hardware device or software that followed the standard, our investment would be safe because our software would work as expected and fewer conflicts would result.

As computers get faster, multimedia becomes even more important. Thankfully, the industry settled on the *MPC* standard. MPC stands for *Multimedia Personal Computer*. Every software product that is MPC-compatible is known to work, as long as you have MPC-compatible hardware.

 The multimedia consortium has now adopted a more advanced MPC standard called *MPC-3*.

To be MPC-compatible, your computer must be capable of running Windows 95 (it must be already if you've gotten this far) and contain a sound card (SoundBlaster-compatibility is always safe and almost all sound cards adhere to the SoundBlaster standard at a minimum), speakers, a CD-ROM drive, and a microphone. The technical requirements of MPC compatibility used to be more important than they are today because almost every computer sold since 1994 is compatible to the MPC standard.

Windows 95 goes beyond all other operating environments in its support of multimedia services to you as a user. Whether you play games, use motion graphics, or create online presentations, Windows 95 supports your needs and makes your Windows 95–compatible

22

hardware work better with multimedia products than previous versions of Windows did. Consider that data does not have to be text. Data can be video, sound, text, numeric, still graphics, or a combination thereof. Windows 95 blurs the distinction between data types and supports all of them.

Playing with AutoPlay

AutoPlay is a new feature of Windows 95 multimedia capabilities. If you've ever played a game or played an audio CD in your computer's CD-ROM drive, you'll appreciate AutoPlay very much indeed. AutoPlay automatically inspects your audio CD or CD-ROM as soon as you place it in the computer's CD-ROM drive. AutoPlay then does one of three things:

- Starts the installation on your CD-ROM if the program has yet to be installed
- Begins the CD-ROM's program if the program already is installed
- Starts the audio CD player if it is an audio CD

> Sometimes, a program's installation routine begins as soon as you insert your CD-ROM, even though you previously installed the program. If this happens, you have to cancel the installation routine. If you find this happening too often, hold your Shift key when you insert the CD-ROM and keep holding Shift until the CD-ROM drive light quits blinking. The AutoRun does not begin.

During the development of Windows 95, Microsoft decided that putting a CD-ROM (or audio CD) into the CD-ROM drive almost always meant that you were ready to do something with that CD-ROM. Of course, you could be inserting the CD-ROM in the drive for later use, but that's rare; most of the time when you insert a CD-ROM, you're ready to do something with it right away.

> Task 22.1 requires a CD-ROM drive. You must have a CD-ROM drive to be MPC-compatible and, in today's world, you can take advantage of very few multimedia services without a CD-ROM. If you have a CD-R device that both reads and writes CDs, or a DVD drive that supports large-capacity digital video disks, you can use that same drive for CD-ROMs as described in this lesson.

If you want to insert a CD-ROM but want to bypass the AutoPlay feature (perhaps you plan to access the CD-ROM later but prefer to insert the disc now), press Shift as you insert the CD-ROM. Keep holding Shift until the CD-ROM light goes out. Windows 95 does not start AutoPlay.

Task 22.1: Using AutoPlay to Play Music from a CD

Step 1: Description

This task demonstrates the AutoPlay feature as it works on an audio CD. Not only does Windows 95 provide for AutoPlay, but it also supplies all kinds of support for audio CDs and CD-ROMs that may surprise you when you see them.

Step 2: Action

1. Find an audio CD that contains music you like to hear.

2. Place the CD in the CD-ROM drive and close the door or push the CD-ROM drive's insert button to close the CD-ROM drive.

3. Windows 95 immediately recognizes that you've inserted the CD into the CD-ROM *and* begins playing the music! Notice the new CD Player button on the taskbar.

Depending on the date of your CD's release, something even *more* may happen: You might see a picture of the CD's cover on your screen! If so, move your mouse over the picture and click various parts of the screen to see information about the artist, song lists, the lyrics, and other things.

The feature you are viewing is called *Enhanced CD*, and audio CD makers are going to be adding Enhanced CD support to their audio CDs over time so that you can begin to fully integrate your PC, audio, and video capabilities. If the CD you place in the drive does not yet contain the Enhanced CD format, you can still add a title and song list as explained in the rest of this task.

4. Click the CD Player button on the taskbar. Windows 95 displays the CD Player window shown in Figure 22.1.

FIGURE 22.1

The CD Player window controls the CD's play

The CD Player acts like a physical CD player that you can control by pushing the buttons. It displays a Play button (grayed out because your CD is already playing); Pause, Stop, Previous and Next track buttons; Previous and Forward time buttons; and an Eject button that you can click when you're done listening to the CD. (Move the cursor over the buttons on the CD Player's window to see a roving help box that describes each button.)

Click the Pause button. Click the Play button. Press Alt+K to move the cursor to the drop-down list box and click the down arrow button to play a different track on the CD.

You can adjust the volume control by opening the speaker icon on the taskbar. Task 22.2 describes how to adjust the volume.

5. If your CD is not an Enhanced CD, something is missing because CD Player cannot know who the artist is or what the name of the songs are. *You* must tell CD Player what the artist's name is and what songs are on the song list.

Select Disc | Edit Play List. CD Player displays the window shown in Figure 22.2.

FIGURE 22.2

Describe the CD to the CD Player application

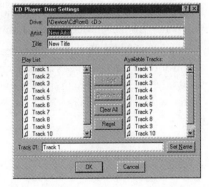

▼

> If you have more than one CD-ROM drive attached to your computer, you can select from among the various drives by clicking the list box labeled Drive.

6. Find the box your audio CD came in. Type the name of the artist in the text box labeled Artist. Type the artist's last name first, followed by a comma, and then the first name so that you can later compile an alphabetical list of artists.

7. Press Alt+T to enter the title of the CD.

8. There is a track listed for each song on the CD. Instead of the default titles of *Track 1* and *Track 2*, and so on, you can enter the actual song titles. Here is the easiest way to do that: Press Alt+K and type the first song title. Press Alt+N to add that title to the track list and enter the second song title. Press Alt+N to add the second title to the track list and enter the third song title. Continue entering all the titles. When you run out of tracks, you have entered all the songs.

9. The Play List and Available Tracks list boxes now contain the song titles. Don't do so now, but later you can select certain songs from the Play List and click Remove to remove those selected songs from the Play List (the song titles will remain in the Available Tracks list box). CD Player only plays those songs listed in the Play List.

   The CD Player remembers the artist, title, play list, and track lists by storing the information on your hard disk. Click OK to close the window and return to the CD control window. The window now contains a drop-down list box from which you can select specific songs you want the CD Player to play.

10. Display the various menu commands to see what else the CD Player can do. Display the Options menu to select Random Order, Continuous Play, or Intro Play to play the CD randomly, play the CD over and over from the beginning to end, or to play only the first few seconds from each track, respectively.

11. Select Options | Preferences to display the Options Preferences dialog box shown in Figure 22.3. You can control what the CD Player does upon completion of playing a CD, as well as several other items, including the amount of time the Intro Play plays each track's introduction.

▼

FIGURE 22.3

You can set various playing options

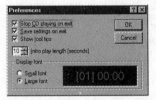

12. Click OK to close the window.

13. If you want to enter information about more of your favorite CDs, eject the CD and insert additional CDs to add their descriptions to CD Player's repertoire of CDs.

14. When you're done, eject the CD from the drive and select Disc | Exit to close the CD Player.

> CD Player recognizes each individual CD after you enter the CD's detailed information. In other words, you can insert a CD into the CD-ROM drive, and if you've entered that CD's information at any time in the past, CD Player remembers the CD and automatically displays that CD's descriptive title, artist, and song information.

Step 3: Review

The CD Player application not only plays as soon as you insert CDs, but CD Player also keeps track of artists, CD titles, and the CD song lists. After entering a CD's information, CD Player remembers that information. If you insert a CD that CD Player does not recognize, it still plays the CD, and you can subsequently enter the CD's information.

> The Internet contains all kinds of programs that extend the capabilities of Windows 95's Media Player.
> www.microsoft.com/windows/mediaplayer/default.asp is the Internet address where you can find a newer Media Player that supports more audio and video formats such as DVD-based discs. In addition, www.cddb.com contains audio CD song listings for virtually every CD published. You can download these song listings, and CD players that support these downloaded listings will automatically recognize a CD's song lists as soon as you insert the CD.

Full-Motion Video

Windows 95 supports full-motion video better than previous versions of Windows did. Windows 95 can display video in a full-screen resolution or smaller windows, if you prefer. The video is smoother than previous Windows versions because of the way Windows 95 handles the playback.

No matter how much Microsoft improves the Windows 95 video playback software, the ultimate quality of video playback depends on your computer's hardware speed. If you notice your video is sluggish, you might have to get a faster computer with a faster CD-ROM drive. Since its release, Windows 95 has included several forms of a video player. Video for Windows was the original video player that played sound and motion from a CD-ROM or a disk file. Newer Windows 95 versions include the Active Movie Control program that more smoothly plays video. You can access either program from the Multimedia menu on your Accessories menu.

Windows 95 uses the *Media Player* application to play video. Media Player is capable of playing all of the following kinds of items stored on the disk:

- Sound files
- Microsoft Multimedia Active Movie Player files
- Video for Windows files
- Movies in DVD format
- MIDI Sequencer files

Most full-motion video clips fall within one of these categories. Rarely do you have to know anything about the details of these files. Windows 95 recognizes the file formats and plays any of them.

Task 22.2 demonstrates an impressive full-motion video clip that you can play.

Task 22.2: Looking at a Full-Motion Multimedia Video

Step 1: Description

This task uses the Windows 95 installation CD-ROM that comes with your system. It demonstrates the full-motion video and sound that Windows 95 supports.

Step 2: Action

1. Locate your Windows 95 installation CD-ROM and insert it into your CD-ROM caddy.
2. After a brief pause, Windows 95 displays the Windows CD-ROM screen.

22

If you do not hear a musical sound when the CD-ROM's opening screen appears, you might not have turned on your speakers or the volume control on your sound card could be turned down too low.

3. Click the icon on the right, labeled Cool Video Clips. Depending on the release date of your Windows 95, you see a window that contains many, if not all, of the file folders in Figure 22.4.

FIGURE 22.4

Choose a video clip to play

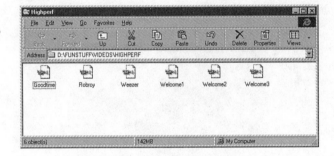

When you see document icons that contain a video camera, such as the ones shown in Figure 22.4, those documents are video clips. You can right-click on an icon and select Play or open the icon to play the video.

4. Open the icon labeled Weezer. You won't believe your eyes and ears! Figure 22.5 shows one shot of the video clip you see.

FIGURE 22.5

Have a happy day with this video clip

▼   5. Although the video clip window does not have a maximize button, you can resize the window to full-screen size by dragging the window's edges to the sides of the screen. You can also maximize the window to full-screen. Resize the window now to suit your viewing preference.

Depending on your video card and monitor's resolution, the video might look better in a smaller window size than a larger size. Use the play and pause buttons at the bottom of the video clip's window. You also can adjust the position of the play by dragging the play meter's indicator left and right.

6. If you want to adjust the volume, you can. Open the taskbar's speaker to see the series of volume controls and left and right balance controls shown in Figure 22.6. Depending on the type of multimedia sound you're listening to, you can adjust these volume and balance controls:

FIGURE 22.6

You can adjust volume levels for several controls

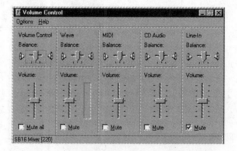

Volume	Controls the entire system's volume, no matter what is playing.
Wave	Controls wavetable sound volume. Wave sounds are realistic sounds unlike FM synthesis, which cheaper sound boards and older PCs use.
MIDI	Controls MIDI sound (stands for *Musical Instrument Digital Interface*) that reproduces musical instruments and other sounds.
CD	Controls the volume of your audio CDs when played with CD Player.
Line-In	Most sound cards contain a line-in port in which you can connect an outside sound source such as a stereo's output.

Adjust the volume to a comfortable level and then close the video window after you finish watching the video.

7. Close the Videos window, and then close the Windows 95 installation CD-ROM opening screen's window. You are now finished with the CD-ROM, so you can put
▼   the Windows 95 installation CD-ROM away for now.

▼ ## Step 3: Review

Full-motion video is a lot of fun to see on a computer. For too long, computer graphics have been low quality. Full-motion video requires ample storage space, so most video resides on CD-ROMs that can hold a lot of data. The Windows 95 Media Player applica-tion controls all full-motion video, and the volume control window lets you adjust the
▲ different kinds of volumes to the best levels.

Open the Multimedia icon inside the Control Panel to find a tabbed dialog box that lets you control audio, video, and CD-ROM settings. For example, you can select an option that displays all full-motion video clips full-screen by default.

Although the technology is still fairly advanced, you soon should begin see-ing powerful video-editing hardware and software interfaces for Windows 95. As disks get larger, the capacity to store video clips becomes more cost-effective. In addition, video hardware quality is getting better and less costly every day. The bottom line is that soon you'll be able to send your video camera's tape output to your computer; edit, rearrange, and add special effects to your home movies; and output a final produced and edited film. The new digital video cameras promise to help promote home video editing to a higher level.

Task 22.3: Unhooking Windows 95's AutoPlay feature

Step 1: Description

You learned earlier in this hour how to bypass the AutoPlay feature when you insert indi-vidual CD-ROMs. Windows 95 lets you turn off AutoPlay completely if you do not want to use AutoPlay.

Step 2: Action

1. Display the Start menu.

2. Select Settings | Control Panel.

3. Open the System icon.

4. Click the Device Manager tab.

5. Click the plus sign next to your CD-ROM drive; the CD-ROM drive's description
▼   appears.

▼   6. Click Properties.

7. Click the Settings tab. Windows 95 displays the Settings dialog box shown in Figure 22.7.

FIGURE 22.7

Turn off AutoPlay from the Settings dialog box

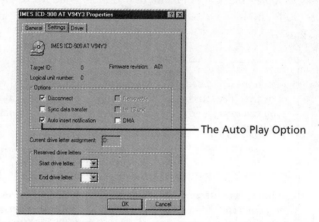

— The Auto Play Option

8. Uncheck the option labeled `Auto insert notification` to turn off AutoPlay. (If you subsequently check this option again, AutoPlay returns.)

9. Click OK to close the Settings dialog box.

10. Click OK to close the System dialog box. A dialog box prompts you to restart your system for the changes to take effect. If you select Yes, Windows 95 automatically restarts; if you select No, the change takes place the next time you start Windows 95.

11. Close the Control Panel window if you didn't restart your system in the previous step.

Step 3: Review

Although the AutoPlay feature is helpful, many Windows 95 users choose to turn off AutoPlay because they want to start the CD-ROM at a later time and are inserting the CD-ROM for subsequent use only. The Control Panel's System icon gives you access to

▲   the AutoPlay feature.

Summary

This hour described how Windows 95 finally integrated multimedia into the windowed multitasking environment. The multimedia capabilities of Windows 95 are advanced and provide for smooth video and sound. As computer hardware gets faster, Windows 95 will support better multimedia that uses the extra speed.

22

Windows 95's AutoPlay multimedia feature automatically installs CD-ROM software, loads and runs CD-ROM software, and plays audio CDs as soon as you insert the CD-ROM or CD into its drive. If you like, you can enter a description of the CD's artist, title, and tracks so that when you insert that same CD in the future, Windows 95 recognizes the CD and displays the lists from which you can select specific songs. The new audio CD format named *Enhanced CD* places text and graphics on the audio CDs you purchase at the music store.

Audio is only part of the multimedia glitz. Full-motion video capabilities allow for full-screen viewing of video clips using the Media Player. Windows 95 video is smoother than previous versions of Windows where video streams tended to be "chunky" and "stop and go."

Workshop

Term Review

Active Movie Control   The new Windows 95 video player. If you do not see the Active Movie Control on your Multimedia menu, you can contact Microsoft or check out their Web site for an update.

AutoPlay   The capability of Windows 95 to install or start a program from a CD-ROM as soon as you place the CD-ROM in the drive. AutoPlay plays audio CDs as well.

Enhanced CD   A new audio CD standard that puts graphics and text on the same CDs that your stereo plays.

FM synthesis   An older sound standard that produces non-realistic computer-generated sounds.

Media Player   The Windows 95 application that plays video clips.

MIDI   Stands for *Musical Instrument Digital Interface* and reproduces musical instruments and other sounds.

MPC   Stands for *Multimedia Personal Computer*. A computer hardware and software standard that has been in effect for several years. It determines the minimum hardware and software requirements for a product to be called a multimedia product that's endorsed by the MPC compliance committee.

MPC-3   A more modern version of the MPC standard that requires a double-speed CD-ROM drive.

Video for Windows   The internal player Windows 95 uses to produce full-motion video on your screen.

Wave   Also called *wavetable.* Sound stored in files with the .WAV extension that produces realistic sounds from your computer's speaker.

Q&A

Q How do I know if my computer is MPC-compatible?

A Most likely, you have an MPC-compatible computer if you've purchased your computer within the past few years and it has a sound card, speakers, a microphone, and a CD-ROM.

Perhaps the easiest way is to work through the two tasks in this hour. Your computer will probably have few or no MPC problems if the tasks work on your computer as described in the text.

Q Why do I not use the CD volume control to adjust a video playing from my CD-ROM drive?

A The volume control labeled CD is useful for controlling audio CDs that you play using the CD Player application. When playing videos, the computer uses one of the other volume controls such as the Wave or MIDI volume control.

Q Why are there so many kinds of sounds (CD, Wave, FM synthesis, and MIDI)?

A The different sounds produce different qualities of audio. Your hardware and software determine the kinds of sound that come out of your computer's speakers. Luckily, you probably won't have to worry about the different sounds because Windows 95 recognizes most sound sources and selects the proper playing software accordingly.

Hour 23

Hardware and Windows 95

This hour introduces you to the concept of *Plug and Play*. Plug and Play is the name Microsoft created to describe the steps you must go through when installing new hardware on your computer. Before Windows 95, you had to set jumper switches and make operating system settings. Often hardware and software conflicts occurred, creating many hours of debugging headaches. With Plug and Play, you simply plug new hardware components (memory, disk drives, CD-ROM drives, and expansion boards) into your computer, and Windows 95 immediately recognizes the change and sets everything up properly.

Plug and Play requires almost no thought when installing new hardware to your system. At least that's the theory. In reality, you might still encounter problems, as this hour explains. If Plug and Play does not perform as expected, Windows 95 provides a hardware setup wizard that you can use to walk you through the new hardware's proper installation.

Windows 95 has not only made it easier to change hardware on one system, but it has also added a program for aiding in the change of entire machines! Many people work on multiple PCs. Perhaps you have a laptop and also a desktop computer. Perhaps you work both at home and at the office. Whatever your situation, Windows 95 helps you transfer files between the two computers through a direct cable connection.

The highlights of this hour include:

- What Plug and Play is all about
- Which components must be in place for Plug and Play to work
- How Plug and Play benefits both you and hardware companies
- How to add new hardware to your PC
- How direct cable connection makes connecting together two computers virtually trouble-free

Plug and Play

Some computer users actually refer to Plug and Play as *Plug and Pray*; these users are actually making a good point. Despite the industry hype over Plug and Play, it simply does not always work. If you attempt to install an older board into your computer, Windows 95 might not recognize the board, and you could have all kinds of hardware problems that take time to correct.

Things do not always go right when installing non–Plug-and-Play hardware. You often have to set certain hardware switches correctly. And you might also have to move certain *jumpers* so that electrical lines on your new hardware flow properly to work with your specific computer. The new hardware can conflict with existing hardware in your machine. Most hardware devices, such as video and sound cards, often require new software support contained in small files called *drivers* that you must install and test.

Hardware designed before the invention of Plug-and-Play specifications is called *legacy hardware*.

Before Plug and Play can work in Windows 95, these two items must be in place:

- A Plug-and-Play-compatible Basic Input Output System (called the *BIOS*) in your computer's system unit. The computer manual's technical specifications or technical support should be able to tell you if the BIOS is Plug-and-Play–compatible.
- A Plug-and-Play-compatible device to install.

You are running Windows 95, which is Plug-and-Play–compatible. If you do not have the Plug-and-Play BIOS inside your computer (most computers made before 1995 have no form of Plug-and-Play compatibility), then you have to help Windows 95 with the installation process by answering some questions posed to you by a new hardware setup wizard. When you purchase new hardware in the future, try to purchase only hardware rated for Plug-and-Play compatibility.

> One key in knowing whether or not the hardware is designed for Plug and Play is to make sure the Windows logo appears on the new hardware's box or instructions. Before a hardware vendor can sell a product with the Windows logo, that product must support Plug-and-Play compatibility. Microsoft calls Windows 95-compatible hardware *PC 95 hardware*.

23

If you run Windows 95, own a computer with a Plug-and-Play BIOS, and purchase only Plug-and-Play hardware, the most you should ever have to do is turn off the computer, install the hardware, and turn the computer back on. Everything should work fine after that. (Perhaps to be on the safe side, you should also Plug and Pray.)

Plug and Play to Play and Play!

The Plug-and-Play standard should help both you and computer companies. Think of these benefits if Plug and Play delivers as designed:

- Installing new hardware will no longer be troublesome.
- You will have less computer downtime and will be able to get back to using your computer faster.
- Hardware companies will have to staff fewer technical support people.
- Hardware companies will not have to buy as many support phone lines.
- Hardware companies will be able to cut costs.
- Hardware products will come down in price due to the decrease in the support costs just mentioned.
- You will have more money in your pocket to vacation in Italy!

Plug and Play works both for newly installed hardware and for removed hardware. If you remove a sound card that you no longer want, or remove memory and replace that memory with a higher capacity memory, Plug and Play ought to recognize the removal and reconfigure the computer and operating system automatically. Again, Plug and Play is not always perfect and does not always operate as expected, but as long as you run a Plug-and-Play BIOS and install Plug-and-Play hardware, there should be little installation trouble ahead for you.

Plug and Play does *not* make legacy hardware obsolete. If you install Windows 95 in a computer that has older non–Plug-and-Play legacy hardware, Windows 95 and the hardware should work fine together.

Although most hardware sold today supports Plug and Play, some notable exceptions do not. For example, the Iomega Jaz and Zip high-capacity drives require several non–Plug-and-Play steps that you must go through to install these devices (the parallel port versions are simpler but are slower in their operation, so many users purchase the faster versions that require an expansion card).

Some Hardware Help

If you install hardware and find that Windows 95 does not properly recognize the change, open the Add New Hardware icon in the Control Panel window. Windows 95 starts the Add New Hardware Wizard, shown in Figure 23.1, which helps walk you through the installation process.

FIGURE 23.1

The Add New Hardware Wizard helps you install non–Plug-and-Play hardware

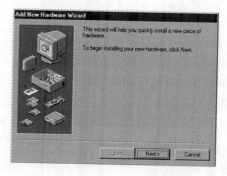

This hour is not as task-oriented as the rest because the hardware differences among all the readers would make following specific tasks virtually impossible.

Be sure to read your new hardware's installation documentation thoroughly before you begin the installation. Often, the new hardware comes with updated drivers that fix minor bugs and add features to drivers that Windows 95 already includes. Therefore, instead of letting the Wizard search for the new device, and instead of selecting from the list of supported devices (from the Wizard screen like the one shown in Figure 23.2), you might use a disk or CD-ROM that comes with the new hardware to add the latest hardware support for the device to Windows 95. Therefore, you have to click the dialog box's Have Disk button and select the hardware's disk or CD-ROM drive location to complete the installation.

23

FIGURE 23.2

Select from the list of known hardware or use your hardware's own installation files

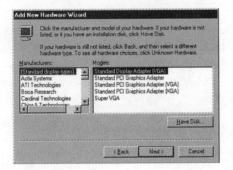

Most hardware and software vendors have Web sites where they put the latest bug fixes, patches, and updated drivers. The nature of the changing PC business is that change occurs frequently. Often, a hardware vendor must add driver changes so their hardware works with newer hardware and software that comes out after theirs. It's a game of continual catch-up. Therefore, as soon as you buy a new hardware device or software program, you should go to the vendor's Web site (usually listed in the manual or you can find it through a search engine) and look for newer versions of software or drivers that ease the installation and operation.

The wizard goes through a series of tests and attempts to detect the newly added hardware. Suppose you added an internal modem, but you cannot communicate with the modem. The Add New Hardware Wizard might realize that you have a new internal modem after running through its series of tests, but might not be able to determine exactly what kind of internal modem you have. You and the wizard together should be able to determine the proper configuration.

> If you add a new modem to a serial port or a printer to a parallel port, you should not run the Add New Hardware Wizard. The wizard works only for hardware you physically connect to the system unit. If you plug a modem into an existing serial port, that serial port is already installed, so you don't need to run Add New Hardware. You do, however, have to open the Control Panel's Modems icon and select your modem from the list of modems displayed. Windows 95 can usually recognize Plug-and-Play internal modems.

If you have a laptop or desktop with a PCMCIA card, you can plug PCMCIA cards directly into the laptop, changing a PCMCIA hard disk to a PCMCIA modem, and Windows 95 adjusts itself automatically. Hour 18, "Using Windows 95 on the Road," explains more about mobile computing and the hardware issues that you encounter when working with laptops.

Additional Hardware Support

Windows 95 uses a *Registry* and *hardware tree* to keep track of the current and changeable hardware configuration. The Registry is a central repository of all possible hardware information for your computer. The hardware tree is a collection of hardware configurations, taken from parts or all of the Registry, for your computer. (In addition, your Registry holds software settings as well.)

Luckily, you don't have to know anything about the Registry because Windows 95 keeps track of the details for you. If, however, you want to look at the hardware tree currently in place on your computer, you can display the Control Panel and open the System icon. Windows 95 displays the System Properties tabbed dialog box shown in Figure 23.3 when you click the Device Manager tab. The hardware tree shows the devices currently in use.

FIGURE 23.3

The Device Manager page under the Systems Properties dialog box shows a hardware tree

23

Working with a Second PC

When you purchase a second PC, such as a laptop or a second home PC, you might want to transfer files from your current PC to the new one. For example, you might have data files on the current PC that you want to place on the new one. Windows 95 supports a feature called *Direct Cable Connection* that lets you transfer files between computers without the need of a network and without moving data between the PCs with a disk.

If you attach a high-speed parallel or serial cable to two computers, those computers can share files and hardware resources with one another. This is a simple replacement for an expensive network if you only want two computers to share resources.

The Direct Cable Connection option should be available in the Accessories menu. (If the Direct Cable Connection option is not installed and you need it to be installed, run the Windows Setup option from the Control Panel's Add/Remove Programs icon.) After you select Direct Cable Connection, Windows 95 initiates the wizard shown in Figure 23.4. After answering the wizard's prompts, your two computers are linked together as Task 23.1 describes.

FIGURE 23.4

The Accessories menu contains the Direct Cable Connection wizard

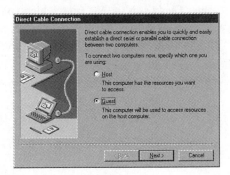

The two computers connected using a Direct Cable Connection must use the same type of port. Therefore, you must connect two parallel ports together or two serial ports together, but not a parallel port to a serial port.

Windows 95 supports a feature called *Dial-Up Networking* that lets you, when on the road, dial up your office or home computer and work just as if you were on the home or office computer network. The interface to you as a laptop user is no different than if you plugged the network cable into the back of your laptop. The only difference is that you might be 1,000 miles away, and things run as if you were attached to the office network. You can find a Dial-Up Networking Wizard in the Accessories menu.

Full dial-up networking is possible only if the computer that you call also is running Windows 95 or Windows 98.

Task 23.1: Making a Direct Cable Connection

Step 1: Description

The Direct Cable Connection lets you easily transfer files between two computers using both computers' parallel or serial ports. After you connect the two machines with the cable, you must start the Direct Cable Connection Wizard, select the sending and receiving computer, and select the files you want to send over the cable connection.

Step 2: Action

1. Connect your two computers with the cable.

2. Select the Start menu's Programs | Accessories | Direct Cable Connection option on both PCs to display the wizard's opening window, shown in Figure 23.4.

3. Select one PC as the host and one as the guest by clicking the appropriate options on the wizard's first page. The host is the PC from which you transfer the file (or files), and the guest receives those files. After you designate a host and guest, you cannot send information the other direction without restarting the wizard.

4. Click the Next button to select the port on which you've connected the computers from the dialog box that appears in Figure 23.5. You have to select the port on each PC.

FIGURE 23.5

Tell the wizard which port the cable connects to

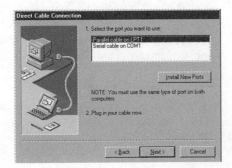

5. Click the Next button on both PCs so that the Finish button appears in the guest's window. The host dialog box displays a button labeled File and Print Sharing. Click this button to give access to both your files and printer from any guest PC that connects.

6. Click the host's File and Print Sharing button to specify whether you want to share files, your printer, or both. If you've never specified printer or file sharing, you might find that the host PC's wizard requires a system reboot to work after you've determined the file and printer sharing access. If so, you can restart the host PC's wizard and return to the final dialog box described in the next step without making a change on the waiting guest PC.

7. Click OK to return the host PC to the Direct Cable Connection Wizard.

8. If you want to require a password from the guest PC before allowing file or printer sharing (sometimes that is helpful when more than one person uses a computer connected to another person's computer), click the Use Password Protection option and click Set Password to enter a password that the guest PC user must type to gain access.

9. Click Finish to make the connection. If the two PCs recognize each other, you've made the connection properly. Otherwise, you might have to check cable connections and rerun the wizard to ensure that all the options are set. (For example, you want to make sure that both PCs are not set as host or both as guest.)

10. The guest's Windows Explorer or My Computer window now holds an icon for the host PC, and you can transfer files from the host as easily as you can transfer files from one of your disks to another. In addition, the guest's application programs can now print to the host printer because the host printer is available from all File | Print dialog boxes.

23

▼ Step 3: Review

The Direct Cable Connection provides a way for you to connect two computers to use the files and printer on one (the host) by the other (the guest). The Direct Cable Connection enables the guest computer to share the host's file and printer resources without requiring expensive and more elaborate networking hardware and software.

▲

> After you set up a host or guest PC, your subsequent use of Direct Cable Connection is easier. You then have to specify the dialog box settings only if you change computers or if you decide to change directions and switch between the host and guest when transferring files. Figure 23.6 shows the dialog box that appears when you start the host's Direct Cable Connection Wizard after you've initially set up the connection.

FIGURE 23.6

Subsequent Direct Cable Connections do not require that you specify the ports or cable type again

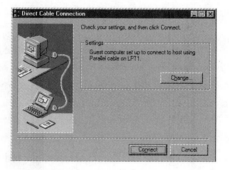

Summary

This hour got fairly technical during the discussion of hardware. An operating system must run through several operations before it can recognize and work with new hardware. Fortunately, the Plug-and-Play process makes such work slightly easier and sometimes trouble-free.

As long as you purchase Plug-and-Play hardware and have a Plug-and-Play–compatible computer, you can add all kinds of new hardware to your computer, and Windows 95 should be able to recognize the change and update itself accordingly.

If you do not use 100 percent Plug-and-Play hardware, the Add New Hardware Wizard will walk you through each installation and help make the hardware easier to install. If you are simply plugging devices into a serial or parallel port, you do not need to worry about installing new hardware, but you will have to set up a modem or printer driver using appropriate Control Panel windows.

The interconnection possible in Windows 95 offers you the convenience of networking two computers without the headaches! The Direct Cable Connection Wizard means that you'll be connecting computers more than ever before. You'll be able to transfer files and share printers easily from one to the other by attaching a cable between the parallel or serial ports of each machine.

Workshop

Term Review

BIOS   Stands for Basic Input Output System and refers to the system unit's ROM-based code that handles I/O devices.

Dial-Up Networking   The capability of a remote laptop computer to dial in to a network over the phone lines and work as if connected to the network by cable.

direct cable connection   The connection between two computers with a cable attached to both parallel or serial ports.

Drivers   Software files that often accompany hardware to tell the computer how to control the hardware when you install it.

hardware tree   A collection of hardware configurations, taken from parts or all of the Registry, that your computer may require.

I/O   Stands for *input and output*.

Jumpers   Special routing connections that a lot of older legacy hardware requires to change the electrical path flows so the hardware works properly on your specific machine.

Legacy   Older hardware that was designed before engineers invented the Plug-and-Play specification.

PC 95 hardware   Hardware that has been tested and approved by Microsoft to work with Windows 95 and support such features as Plug and Play.

Plug and Play   The name Microsoft gives to hardware that you can install without making any hardware or software changes. The Windows 95 Plug-and-Play feature will take care of setting up things correctly for you.

Registry   A central repository of all possible information for your hardware.

23

Q&A

Q How do I know if I have Plug and Play?

A You have Windows 95, which means that installing hardware ought to be easier than with previous operating systems and previous versions of Windows. Perhaps the best way to see if you have Plug and Play is to plug the next device you get for your computer into the computer, power on your machine, and see what happens. (Of course, you should read the new hardware's installation instructions to learn the correct way to install the device.)

If you turn on your computer and the computer responds to the new device properly, you have, for all intents and purposes, all the Plug-and-Play compatibility you need. You have Plug and Play, at least, for that one device. Just because Windows 95 and your BIOS are Plug-and-Play compatible, does not mean that the hardware you install will also be Plug-and-Play compatible. Some hardware might be Plug-and-Play compatible and some might not be.

Q I don't want to buy and install a network in my house, but how do I easily connect my laptop to my desktop to share files between them?

A Use the Windows 95 Direct Cable Connection. Connect a parallel or serial cable to both parallel or serial ports. Your laptop will be able to access the desktop's shared files.

HOUR 24

Windows 95 Tips and Traps

You've worked hard to master Windows 95! You've already mastered the basics of Windows 95 so now you're ready to move up to the level of *Windows 95 guru*. This hour teaches several practical tips that you are ready for now that you understand the ins and outs of Windows 95.

Due to the nature of tips, you won't find step-by-step tasks in this hour. Instead, this hour presents its Windows 95 tips in several categories. For example, if you are comfortable with Windows 95's interface, you can now turn to this hour's first section for some advanced tips that will help you manage the desktop.

The highlights of this hour include:

- How to use desktop tips to more quickly manage Windows 95
- When Internet Explorer tips save you online time
- Where Outlook Express's email shortcuts appear
- Which Windows 95 tips can help you when on the road with a laptop
- How to improve your Windows 95 Clipboard's effectiveness

Windows 95 Desktop Tips

When you master this section's desktop tips, you'll more quickly select programs and manage your desktop.

Rearrange Start Menu Items

If you don't like the location of a menu item on one of your Start menus, drag the item to another location. As long as you've activated the active desktop feature (see Hour 16, "Activating Your Desktop"), you can rearrange Start menu items with your mouse simply by clicking and dragging. After you've opened one of the Start menus, such as the Programs | Accessories menu, you can click and drag any menu item to any other menu.

Suppose you use Notepad a lot to edit text files and want to place the Notepad program at the top of your Start menu so you don't have to traverse all the way over to the Accessories menu. Open the Accessories menu and drag the Notepad option's icon to your Start menu. You might notice two things:

- The menu option's name does not drag but the mouse cursor displays a box showing the movement.

- You cannot drop the item onto the lower section of the Start menu (the section with the Settings and Programs options). The cursor turns into the international *Don't* symbol as you drag Notepad over the Start menu's lower portion. Only the top portion of the Start menu accepts new items.

When you release your mouse button, the menu option appears on the Start menu.

The menu item moves from its original location to the Start menu. If you want to copy a menu item to another location, leaving two of the same Start menu entries on your Start menu, hold Ctrl to make a copy of the menu item elsewhere.

To copy or move a menu item to a menu that is not open, drag the item to that menu and wait for a moment while that menu opens. You can then drop the item onto that open menu by releasing your mouse button where you want the item to appear.

Deleting Menu Items

To remove a menu item, drag the item to the Recycle Bin. When you release the mouse over the Recycle Bin, the item goes to the Recycle Bin and leaves the menu. If you change your mind about removing the item, you can restore it from the Recycle Bin up until the time that you empty the Recycle Bin. If too many desktop items cover up the Recycle Bin, you can first click the Show Desktop button to minimize all open windows and programs.

If you want to rearrange more than one or two items from your Start menu, consider selecting the Start menu's Settings | Taskbar & Start Menu option, clicking the Start Menu Programs tab, and clicking the Advanced button to display the Explorer menu shown in Figure 24.1. You can expand and collapse the Start menu structure by clicking the plus and minus signs just as you do in Windows Explorer to expand and collapse folders. The two panes let you move and rearrange entire menu groups. The click-and-drag approach to menu item management works well if you only need to move or remove a few menu items.

24

FIGURE 24.1

The Start Menu Explorer window lets you perform advanced menu editing

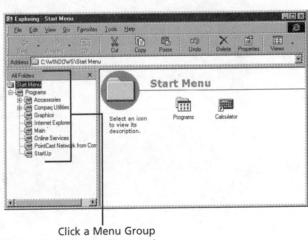

Click a Menu Group
to See its Contents in
the Right Pane

> The reason you can move menu options and send them to the Recycle Bin is because the Start menu contains *shortcuts* to programs. A shortcut is just a pointer to a program, not the program's filename. Therefore, when you drag a shortcut from one location to another, the pointer moves but not the file itself.
>
> You can even drag a menu item to your desktop. Subsequently, if you want to launch that program, you only need to open the desktop's icon. You don't have to traverse the Start menu every time to start the program.

Right-Click Menu Options

When you right-click on a Start menu option, Windows 95 displays a pop-up menu similar to the one in Figure 24.2.

FIGURE 24.2

The pop-up menus give you control over a menu option

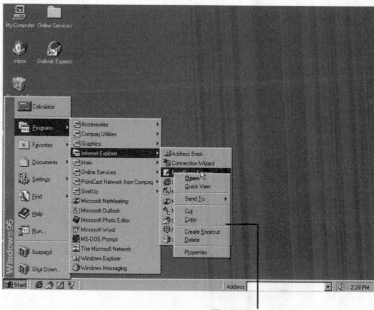

The Pop-Up Menu

You can delete or rename menu items with the pop-up menu as well as view the item's properties. The Properties option describes the menu option and its underlying file information.

Make a Startup Disk

During the course of using Windows 95, you will add hardware and software. Windows makes adding such components relatively easy, but in some cases, problems can occur. Perhaps you receive a bad installation disk or a hardware conflict arises that freezes up Windows 95.

By making a *startup disk*, you can safely get your computer started and access your hard disk when you otherwise cannot start your machine. The startup disk is little more than an MS-DOS boot disk, although the disk does contain several MS-DOS and Windows utility programs (such as the ScanDisk utility explained in Hour 21, "Fine-Tune with Advanced System Tools") that can help you locate disk and memory troubles that can cause boot problems.

Before making a startup disk, you must locate a high-density formatted disk. Make sure the disk contains no data that you need, because the startup process overwrites all data on your disk. Follow these steps to create the disk:

1. Click the Start button.

2. Select Settings | Control Panel to display the Control Panel window.

3. Double-click the Add/Remove Program icon.

4. Click the Startup Disk tab to display the Startup Disk page shown in Figure 24.3.

24

FIGURE **24.3**

*Create a startup disk
for emergencies*

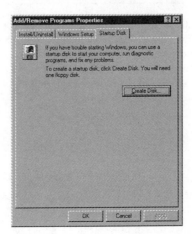

5. Click the Create Disk button. The dialog box lets you know when you need to insert the disk you'll use for the startup disk.

6. After the startup disk creation process ends, close the Control Panel and put the startup disk in a safe place.

When you create a startup disk, you have a disk in case of emergencies. If you find that you cannot access your hard disk or boot your computer because your system files are corrupt, you can regain hard disk access by inserting the startup disk and rebooting your computer. The startup disk cannot cure any problems, but you can get system access again so that you can begin tracking down the problems.

Don't Wait for a Disaster!

Most people back up regularly…after they've had a disaster! Don't wait. Master Hour 12, "Back Up and Squeeze Disk Space," and back up your system. The Windows 95 Backup program is adequate but includes few bells and whistles, such as full support for recordable CD drives. For a more complete backup program, consider going to your local software dealer and search through the many inexpensive programs on the shelves for one that looks as though it will suit your needs and hardware the best. Your disk drives are mechanical and will break down over time. Don't wait to make your first backup or you'll regret it the first time your disk has a problem.

Software is available that not only makes a backup of every file on your system but actually makes a disk drive image of your hard disk. From that saved image, you can restore your computer to its exact configuration if you ever have a disk breakdown. Look for products such as DriveImage (their Web site is www.powerquest.com for more information) if you want to make an image of your disk for backup storage.

Have the Latest?

To make the most of Windows 95, you should obtain a service release pack from Microsoft. A service release pack is a collection of patches, updates, and bug fixes that Microsoft wrote after the initial release of Windows 95. Many new hardware devices have been invented since Windows 95, and the service release packs attempt to support all the new devices.

If your Windows 95 came pre-installed on a PC when you purchased it, you might already have the fix. To see, select the Start menu's Settings | Control Panel option and open the System icon. On the page with the General tab, if you see the Windows 95 version number 4.00.950 A or 4.00.950 B, you do not need the service release pack. If you see any other number or letter, you can download the software and instructions by pointing your browser to this Web site:

```
http://www.microsoft.com/windows/software/servpak1/sphome.htm
```

You can also call Microsoft's phone support at (800) 360-7561, but you must pay $14.95 for the shipping of the CD-ROM that includes the service pack.

Make Yourself More Comfortable

What's the most important component in your PC system? It's not your system unit. It's not your CPU. It's not how fast Windows 95 performs. It's not your hard disk. It's not your printer. Your most important component is the very chair you sit in. The smarter PC users spend more on their chair than on their operating systems.

If you spend an hour or more a day at your PC, run, don't walk, to your local office furniture store and check out their desk chair selection. If you've never paid much attention, you'll be shocked at how many kinds of chairs that you find. Your back, arms, shoulders, and wrists (not to mention the body part on which you sit), deserve far better than the average chair most people place in front of their computer. You'll be more productive, work more accurately, and you'll take care of your body.

The better desk chairs provide separate controls for the arm rests, back and lumbar support, and height. Make sure that you can adjust these components easily *while sitting in the chair*. Look for a chair on wheels that roll easily so that you can move between your PC and writing area.

Internet Explorer Tips

With Internet Explorer 4, you have so many features that they are too numerous to learn all at once. As you use Internet Explorer 4 more and more, you'll pick up many new shortcuts along the way. To help you get started, the following sections explain how to make the most of Internet Explorer 4.

Start Internet Explorer from Any Window

Any time you open a Windows 95 window that displays a toolbar, such as the My Computer window, you have the immediate option to start Internet Explorer and log in to the Internet. Simply click the Internet Explorer icon in the window's upper-right corner (see Figure 24.4).

24

FIGURE 24.4

Click the Internet Explorer icon to surf the Internet from any open window

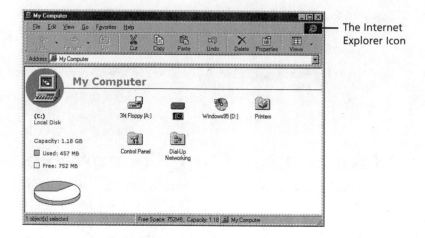

The Internet Explorer Icon

Learn the Web as You Use It

After you start Internet Explorer, select Help | Web Tutorial, and Internet Explorer starts an interactive Web tutorial that teaches you all about the Web.

Where Do You Want To Go?

Keep Internet Explorer's Go menu in mind as you traverse the Web and use Internet Explorer. The Go menu gives you quick access to these items:

- Email
- Newsgroups
- Your My Computer window
- Your Windows Address Book
- Internet phone calls with NetMeeting

Set Up Internet Explorer Security

When you select View | Internet Options, Internet Explorer displays a dialog box that lets you adjust Internet settings. Click the Security tab to display the dialog box shown in Figure 24.5. The four options in the center of the box determine how secure you want to be with your Web browsing.

FIGURE 24.5

Select the security you feel most comfortable with

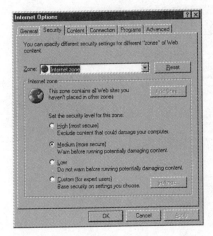

24

A high security protects your PC from incoming information that could possibly contain *virus*-laden files. A virus is a computer file that destroys other files. The problem with this high security level, however, is that you'll often access secure sites and want to purchase something or give other information and Internet Explorer will not let you send that information. You can always lower your security level when you know that a site is secure.

Keep More History for Faster Access

The General tab of the View | Internet Options dialog box lets you enter a value that determines the number of history days to keep track of. As you traverse the Web, Internet Explorer keeps track of where you've been in the history area. The more days of history that you keep, by adjusting the value in the option labeled Days to keep pages in history, you can make Internet Explorer keep more locations in case you return to recently visited pages.

Take a Look at Advanced Internet Explorer Options

Select Internet Explorer's View | Internet Options menu and click the Advanced tab to display the customization list shown in Figure 24.6. Each item in the list describes a different aspect of Internet Explorer that you can control, from browsing tasks to toolbar information.

FIGURE 24.6

*You can completely
customize Internet
Explorer*

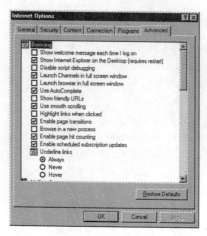

It pays to return to this dialog box every month or two. As you use the Internet in different ways, and as you develop procedures you routinely follow, you'll want to set options that help Internet Explorer work the way you do.

Type an Address

When you want to move to a Web site and have to enter that site's address because no hyperlinks to that site appear on the current page or in your Favorites list, press F6 to highlight the Address text box so that you can type an address into the box. By pressing F6, you don't have to point to the Address area with your mouse to place the text cursor in the box. After typing the address, press Enter to navigate to that site.

Disconnect Quickly

To disconnect your Internet dial-up connection, whether or not you are using Internet Explorer, double-click the taskbar's Web icon next to the clock (the Web icon shows two PCs connected together by a wire) to display a small connection dialog box window. Select Disconnect and Windows 95 immediately logs you off from your Internet provider.

Outlook Express Tips

You'll work in Outlook Express a lot due to the prevalence of email in today's online world. You can make Outlook Express more enjoyable by utilizing some of the following Outlook Express tips.

Compress Files

If you store a lot of sent and retrieved email messages or subscribe to a lot of news-groups, your disk space can fill up fast. To help, you can reduce the amount of space consumed by messages and newsgroup files by selecting Tools | Options | Advanced and click the Clean Up Now button. When you click the Compact button, Outlook Express compresses your message and file space.

If you click Remove Messages instead of Compact, Outlook Express removes the mes-sage bodies but retains all message headers (descriptions) so that you know which mes-sages you've already read. (Outlook Express places a read icon next to your read messages as long as you've saved the headers.)

If you click Delete, you save the most space because Outlook Express removes all news-group messages and files from your disk, but you have to download those newsgroup messages and files again if you ever need them again.

Create a Personal Signature

You cannot sign your email with your handwriting, but Outlook Express's *signature* fea-ture is the next best thing. An email signature is text that appears at the end of your email. Your signature might be just your name, or you might want to close all correspon-dence with your name, address, and phone number.

| You can choose not to enclose your signature with certain email messages. |

Outlook Express lets you add a signature to your email messages, your newsgroup post-ings, or both. To create the signature, select Tools | Stationery. Select the Mail or News page depending on which you want to add a signature for. You can select a default font to use for the message as well as a signature if you click the Signature button to display the dialog box shown in Figure 24.7.

Your signature can come from text you type at the Text option or from a text file on disk that you select at the File option.

24

FIGURE 24.7

Create a signature for the bottom of your messages and postings

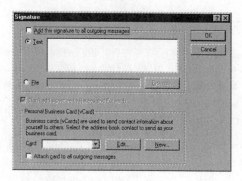

Outlook Express supports a special *vCard* (for *virtual card*) format for electronic business cards. Some Internet sites and applications support the new vCard standard from which you can send and receive business card information easily and in a standard format. You can create a vCard-based signature or edit one that's already on your system from the dialog box's Personal Business Card section.

Check Email Often

If you receive lots of email throughout the day, select Tools | Options and decrease the time that Outlook Express waits before checking for new email. If you only read your email once or twice a day, you might want to check for new email less often than the 30-minute default so that your system runs more efficiently when you don't want email. You must have Outlook Express running before Outlook Express can check for new email.

Outlook Express emits a sound if you get email. When you hear the sound, you know to check the Outlook Express Inbox for new messages. To request or cancel the new message sound, check or uncheck the second option on the Options General page, Play Sound When New Messages Arrive. (Open the Control Panel's Sounds icon to change the sound that plays when you get a new rmessage.)

Miscellaneous Tips

Although Windows 95 offers hundreds of shortcuts and tips that you'll run across as you use Windows 95, your 24 hours is about up and the day must end. The following tips round out the final Windows 95 tips offered here.

QBasic is Hidden but Still There!

Many programmers got their start writing simple *QBasic* programs. QBasic is a programming language designed for text environments. You cannot write Windows 95 programs with Qbasic, but you can run QBasic programs inside an MS-DOS window.

Learning programming takes some time and effort. If you begin with a simple programming language, such as QBasic, you don't have to wade through a complicated windowed environment, and you can concentrate just on the programming language. If you want to try QBasic, you need to insert your Windows 95 CD-ROM, start Explorer, and copy the two files that begin with QBasic from the CD-ROM's \Other\oldmsdos folder to your \Windows\Command folder.

To start QBasic, select the Start menu's Run menu, type **QBASIC**, and press Enter. QBasic begins with a Parameter dialog box that you can click OK to close; QBasic actually begins as shown in Figure 24.8.

24

FIGURE 24.8

QBasic appears on the Windows 95 CD-ROM

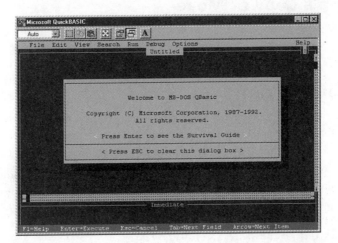

If you want to learn how to write programs in QBasic, check out *QBasic By Example, Special Edition* from Que Publishing.

Press Esc to remove the opening instruction screen and begin programming. When you finish, you can select File | Exit to return to Windows 95.

Save the Scraps

Suppose you work within a word processor and want to copy a paragraph or two from the word processor to several different programs over the next few days. The Windows 95 Clipboard holds data only as long you don't replace the Clipboard with additional contents or until you shut down Windows 95.

You can create a *scrap*, a portion of a data file, by dragging selected text and data from an application to your desktop. When you release the data, a scrap icon appears on the desktop. Keep in mind that a scrap is not a complete document but only text you've selected and copied to the desktop.

The scrap stays on your desktop until you delete the scrap. Therefore, as long as the scrap remains on your desktop, you can copy the scrap to any file.

Stop a Copy or Move

Sometimes, you begin a copy or move operation with your mouse by dragging something from one location to another and you realize that you want to cancel the copy or move. Press Esc to cancel the current copy or move in process.

Laptop Security

If you use a laptop, you can help get your laptop back if you lose it. Right now, before you forget, tape your business card to the bottom of your laptop. If you leave the laptop in an airport or hotel, the finder of your PC can contact you to return the laptop.

Sure, if a thief steals your laptop with a business card, she will know whom to thank! The thief won't return the laptop. It's the honest finder of your laptop who will act on the business card, as long as you've put one there.

Delay On-the-Road Printing

Without a laptop printer, you cannot get a *hardcopy* (a printout) of your data. You can, however, print all your data to an *offline printer*. When you print to an offline printer with your laptop, you appear to print but your laptop instead stores the printing for later.

To convert your laptop to offline printing, open your Control Panel's Printers folder and select File | Work Offline to check the offline printing option. All subsequent printing goes to the disk. You can print as much as you want, and Windows 95 stores up the output for when you eventually connect a printer to your laptop. When you get back to the office or home, plug a printer into your laptop, and then select the Printers File | Work Offline again, the laptop prints every file you sent to the printer while on the road.

Print to a Hotel Fax

When you create something with your laptop while you're on the road, you probably won't have your printer with you. Although you can back up your files to a disk, you might feel better if you print your data. You'll then have the printed *hardcopy* in case something happens to your disk. If you don't have a printer, fax your document to the hotel fax machine. You will, in a few seconds, have a printout of your document.

If you want to back up your files and you have a laptop modem, email your files to yourself! When you get home, you can download the mail or ignore it if your laptop files made it home safely.

24

Summary

This hour wrapped up your 24-hour tutorial with some tips that help you streamline your work. As you work more with Windows 95, you'll find many other tips that lighten your workload and some that can even make it more fun! Windows 95 itself is there to help you, not to hinder you. As you've learned throughout this 24-hour tutorial, Windows 95 often provides several ways to accomplish the same purpose. Although Windows 95 is powerful, it tries not to get in your way; instead, Windows 95 is there to help you get your work done faster.

Workshop

Term Review

hardcopy   Another name for printed output.

offline printing   The process of printing to a disk file when no printer is attached to your PC.

Qbasic   A simple programming language designed for newcomers to programming.

Scrap   A part of a data document you place on the Windows 95 desktop.

service release pack   A collection of patches, updates, and bug fixes Microsoft makes available to Windows 95 owners.

Signature   A text message that follows the email and newsgroup postings you send.

VCard   A standard format that represents common business card information.

Virus   A computer file that destroys other files.

Q&A

Due to the nature of this hour's material, questions and answers don't appear.

APPENDIX A

Understanding Your Computer

Perhaps you are brand new to computers. If so, you are in luck because Microsoft, the company that wrote Windows 95, wrote the operating system with you in mind. As a matter of fact, Microsoft used several new computer users to thoroughly test Windows 95 during the product's design.

This appendix will not make you an expert at computers. In fact, this appendix only briefly introduces computers. If, however, you have not used a computer much and have *no* idea what an operating system is, this appendix will certainly make you feel more comfortable in front of your computer. After you finish this appendix, you will have more insight into the world of computers, and you'll understand better how Windows 95 helps you work with your computer.

Often, desktop and laptop computers are called *PCs*, which stands for *Personal Computers*. Whether you have a full-sized desktop PC or a small laptop PC, the background in this appendix applies to both.

The Computer's Hardware

Your computer is made up of several *hardware* components. The hardware consists of the physical devices that you can touch and see. All of the following are hardware devices:

- The system unit
- The disk and CD-ROM drives
- The keyboard
- The screen
- The printer
- The mouse

Figure A.1 is a diagram that illustrates each of these hardware components. The disk and CD-ROM drives, keyboard, screen, printer, and mouse are often called *peripheral devices* because they plug into the system unit and support the computer's operation. Peripheral devices are either *input devices*, *output devices*, or *input/output devices* (sometimes called *I/O devices*) depending on the data flow direction between the device and the system unit. If data flows out from the system unit to a device such as the printer, that device is an output device. The keyboard is an input device because data goes from the keyboard into the system unit. Disk drives are I/O devices because data flows in both directions between the system unit and the disk drives.

FIGURE A.1

Your computer is made up of many hardware devices

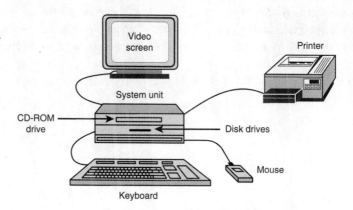

The System Unit

The system unit is the primary controlling unit of your computer. Often, the system unit is a large box that sits on the floor or on your desktop. Many people put their video screens on top of their system units. The system unit holds the following elements:

- The *CPU,* which stands for the *Central Processing Unit.* The CPU controls the rest of your computer and processes all the data that goes through the machine. The CPU resides on a wafer-like *integrated circuit chip* that is small enough to fit in the palm of your hand. The small size of the CPU makes laptop computers and pocket calculators possible.

- The *memory* that stores short-term data. There are two kinds of memory: *RAM* and *ROM.*

   The most important is RAM, which stands for *Random Access Memory.* Before your CPU can process data and run programs, that data and those programs must be in RAM. As an administrative assistant creates a document using a word processor, that document lives in RAM memory and is saved permanently, but only if the administrative assistant saves the document to a disk drive. When you purchase a computer, you should buy as much RAM as you can afford. The more RAM that your computer has, the faster the computer typically runs. Windows 95 requires 16 megabytes of memory to run well.

   ROM stands for *Read-Only Memory* and is a secondary memory that contains some system start-up instructions.

- The power supply that ensures your computer gets enough continuous power to perform its computing tasks.

The system unit is the actual computer. When you buy a computer, try to buy the latest system unit and as much memory as possible. Memory is inexpensive, and today's computers often come with 32 megabytes of memory.

Disk and CD-ROM Drives

Several kinds of disk drives exist. The two most common kinds are hard disk drives and floppy disk drives. *Hard disk drives* are non-removable, fast, and hold a considerable amount of information. *Floppy disk drives,* on the other hand, are slower than hard disks and do not hold as much information, but you can use removable *diskettes* in the floppy disk drives so that you can transfer and share data between two or more computers. Larger removable disks, such as those known as Jaz, Zip, and Syquest, are common and inexpensive today, and they offer up to 2 gigabytes of storage on removable disks not much larger in physical size than floppy disks

A

> The term *drive* refers to the box in which you insert disk and CD-ROMs.
> Hard disk drives contain non-removable disk platters that hold data and
> programs.

The disk drives provide for long-term memory. When you power off your computer, the
data on the disks remains on those disks. Like a cassette tape, the data leaves a disk drive
only when you issue commands to remove that data. Disk data is often called *non-
volatile memory*. In contrast, the contents of RAM disappear when you turn off your
computer.

The disks and RAM work in tandem with each other. When you need to run a program,
such as a word processor, you instruct the computer to load that program from a disk
drive into RAM memory. When it's loaded into RAM, your CPU can then execute the
instructions in that program.

> Programs are discussed more fully in a later section.

Today's marketplace offers many choices of data storage. CD-ROM drives hold compact
discs, not unlike your audio CDs. A CD-ROM drive typically contains over 600 million
characters of information. You can also purchase CD-R and CD-RW drives and record
your own CD-ROM discs, as well as get *DVD drives* (sometimes called *Digital Video
Disks)* that hold several billion characters of information—often more than the largest
hard disk or CD-ROM. All of today's CD-ROM, CD-R, and DVD-drives play music
from audio CDs as easily as they read data from CD-ROMs that contain computer data
and programs. In addition, movies are now available for DVD drives. Although CD-
ROM, CD-R, CD-RW, and DVD drives are slow compared to the speed of hard disks,
their capacity makes them almost a staple item for today's computers. *Multimedia* (the
audio and video capabilities of computers) often requires the huge storage capacities of
these media to hold motion video and sound.

Memory and disks are measured by their storage capacities. Generally, the more data they hold, the better and more the expensive disks and memory are. Today's disks and memory hold so much data that computerists have developed a shortcut that represents the amount of data a device can hold.

One character of storage is called a *byte*. One thousand bytes is often called a *kilobyte*. Actually, one kilobyte (or 1*KB* for short) is exactly 1,024 bytes because the internal nature of today's digital memory requires that memory amounts fall on a power of 2 boundary.

One million bytes is called a *megabyte* or *meg*, or *M,* for short. One billion bytes is called a *gigabyte*, or *gig* for short. Therefore, if a CD-ROM holds approximately 650 million characters of data, that CD-ROM is known as a *650-meg CD-ROM drive*.

New kinds of disk drives are appearing every day. Today, you can purchase a removable disk drive that falls somewhat between a hard disk and a floppy disk. The storage capacity comes close to that of many hard disks (you can get more than 2 gigabytes of removable disk storage), and these disk drives use removable disk cartridges that act and look a lot like floppy disks.

The Keyboard

New users rarely have a problem adapting to computer keyboards because the keyboard works almost exactly like a typewriter's keyboard. There are several *alphanumeric* keys that hold the numbers and letters laid out identically to a typewriter's alphanumeric keys. Figure A.2 shows a typical computer keyboard.

A

FIGURE A.2

Computer keyboards look like typewriter keyboards with some additional keys

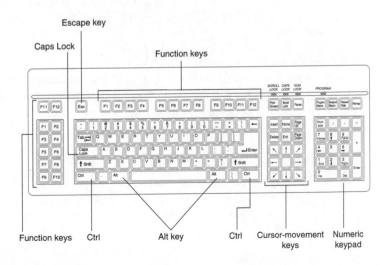

The Enter key often works like a carriage return key on a typewriter. You sometimes press Enter at the end of a line to signal that you're finished entering that line of text. In most word processors, you press Enter at the end of a paragraph of text, but not at the end of a line because the word processors usually offer a feature called *word wrap* that automatically brings the cursor to the start of the next line of text as you type.

Often, there is a *numeric keypad* to the right of the keyboard. The numeric keypad contains number keys as well as common operator keys that hold an equals sign, plus sign, minus sign, division sign (a slash), and multiplication sign (an asterisk). The keypad allows for quicker numeric data entry than is possible using the numbers across the top of the alphanumeric section of the keyboard.

There are usually two Shift keys for uppercase letters. To type an uppercase *A*, you hold Shift, then press A before releasing both keys. Often, such a combined keystroke is referred to as *Shift+A*. A Caps Lock key enables you to lock the keyboard into an uppercase state (all letters appear shifted) until you press Caps Lock again.

In addition to Shift, there are these additional *modifier keys*: Alt and Ctrl. The Alt key (meaning *alternative*) and Ctrl (meaning *control*) give two more levels of shift states. Therefore, you can press A, Shift+A, Alt+A, or Ctrl+A. Different programs use these modifier keys differently. For example, Alt+F might display a list of file options or select an item on the screen.

You'll find 10 or 12 keys labeled *F1* through *F10* (or *F12*). They are called *function keys*. A function key often performs several tasks depending on what you're doing at the time. Each program that you run responds differently to the function keys.

The Esc key (known as the *escape key*) often lets you back up one step when working on your PC. For example, if you start to print a document, you can often press Esc to cancel the printing. As with the function keys, each program that you run handles the Esc key differently.

There are always at least four keys with arrows on them. These are the *cursor-movement keys*. A cursor is a blinking underscore, straight vertical line, or box that indicates where the next typed character will appear on the screen. Often you can move the cursor around the screen using the Up, Down, Left, and Right arrow keys.

Actually, there are two cursors. The *text cursor* (more accurately known as a *caret*), normally a vertical bar, indicates where the next typed character will appear on the screen. The *mouse cursor* is usually a pointing white arrow (although Windows 95 lets you change the mouse cursor to a different shape) that indicates the current position of the mouse on the screen.

Four additional cursor-movement keys—the Home, End, PageUp, and PageDown keys—move the text cursor around on the screen. Each of these keys behaves differently depending on how the programs you run react to those keystrokes. During the movement of the text cursor, you can often press the Ins and Del keys to change text already on the screen by inserting and deleting text.

The NumLock key is used for converting the numeric keypad from numbers to cursor-movement keys and back again. Hour 11, "Aid Via the Accessibility Options," describes a second and more specialized use for NumLock. The ScrollLock key is not used much these days, but it sometimes controls the *scrolling* of the screen's display. If you are displaying a large document and only part of that document fits on the screen at one time, you can scroll the screen up and down the document to bring other parts of the document into view.

Windows 95 uses the PrtSc key (meaning *print screen*—it might be spelled out on your keyboard) to save a copy of the screen. You can later print or store that screen image to the disk drive. You also see special Windows keys on many keyboards that you can press to display the Windows 95 Start menu that you learn about in Hour 1, "What's Windows 95 All About?"

Keyboards sometimes come with built-in mice or trackballs that give you more room on your desk. In addition, companies are manufacturing more *ergonomically balanced* keyboards. Such keyboards are designed to ease strain on your hands and wrists, and they're a great help for people who use their computers a lot.

The Screen

The computer's video screen is sometimes called a *monitor*. These days, almost every screen is capable of displaying color graphics. Without color graphics, Windows 95 would be fairly useless. Windows 95 is known as a *GUI*, or *graphical user interface*, so graphics are an integral part of the nature of Windows 95.

The quality of graphics is measured by a screen's *resolution*. The resolution determines the number and density of dots that combine to create graphics and text. The lowest resolution sold today is called *SVGA* (which stands for *Super Video Graphics Array*), but most computers support higher resolutions as well as three-dimensional graphics. As long as your monitor is capable of displaying SVGA-resolution graphics, you can work with all Windows 95 features. In addition, at least a 17-inch monitor is needed to view many of today's applications easily.

A

Your computer's system unit usually contains a *video card* into which you plug your video screen. Both your video card and the monitor must be capable of displaying SVGA resolution before you will see SVGA on your screen.

The Printer

Many kinds of printers are available. Windows 95 supports over 1,600 printer makes and models. Although many printers exist, almost every printer connected to a PC today falls into one of these three categories:

- Dot-Matrix: A printer that produces graphics and text by printing dots on the page much like the way your screen displays output by combining small dots together. Dot-matrix printers are inexpensive and often support a *letter-quality* mode that helps smooth curved lines and make the printer's output look more like typeset letters. Although their popularity of the 1980s and early 1990s has now diminished, many people still use dot-matrix printers for multi-part forms due to the heavy impact these types of printers make on paper.

- Ink-Jet: This printer prints color text and graphics on the page by shooting ink onto the paper. Ink-jet printers are fairly inexpensive and produce high-quality output. The low cost and high quality of ink-jet printers has helped to lessen the demand for dot-matrix printers.

- Laser printer: This printer draws graphics and text on the print drum, or roller, and then heat burns the print into the page. The output quality of laser printers is extremely good, and laser printers are fast. Laser printers are often more expensive than dot-matrix and ink-jet printers, but their prices are coming closer to the lower-end printer prices every day.

You also can find color versions of laser printers. Color laser printers produce high-quality output, but are fairly expensive.

The Mouse

Although you can enter several kinds of information using the keyboard, the mouse is the fundamental controlling input device for Windows 95. Due to the graphical nature of Windows 95, you need the mouse for pointing and moving graphics around the screen.

Hour 1, "What's Windows 95 All About?" explains how to use the mouse.

If you have a desktop computer, be sure to clear plenty of room (about one square foot is good) for mouse movement. Some people use a *trackball,* which is a stationary mouse that takes up less desk space. Many of today's laptop computers contain mice or trackballs that are built into the keyboards or attached to the side of the computer.

The Computer's Software

The computer's software consists of programs and data. The term *program* has already been used often in this appendix during the discussion of hardware. Programs fall into the category of software and are sets of instructions that direct the computer. The CPU interprets those instructions and either activates one of the hardware devices (such as the printer) or processes data given to the program.

Programs and data reside both on disk drives and in memory. The software on disk drives is safe and remains stored on the disk until you erase the software and data. If you want to run a program (which causes the computer to execute the program's instructions), you have to instruct the computer to load the program from the disk into RAM. Only when the program is in RAM can the computer run it.

Windows 95 is an *operating system* that controls all the computer's input and output. An operating system is a base program that takes control of other programs and lets you control your computer. Windows 95 turns the computer into a *multitasking* computer, which means that you can run more than one program at a time. If you want to work on a word processor and print payroll checks, you can do both at the same time by starting the word processor program and the payroll program, without closing your word processor.

The checks produced by the payroll program, as well as the document that you create inside the word processor, makeup the data that resides inside the computer's memory at the time.

Figure A.3 shows what your memory looks like when using a computer and Windows 95. Notice that memory is consumed by Windows 95, by one or more programs, and by data sections that go with each program. The amount of memory not used is known as *free memory* and is available for other programs and data.

Figure A.3

The typical contents of RAM

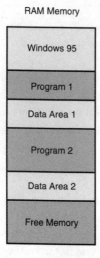

RAM Memory

Windows 95

Program 1

Data Area 1

Program 2

Data Area 2

Free Memory

If you do not have enough memory to run several programs at once, Windows 95 can often use disk storage to simulate memory. Windows 95 then swaps data and programs to and from the disk drive as you run the multiple programs. The more memory your computer has, the less swapping that Windows 95 has to perform, and the faster your programs will run.

All data and programs reside on your disk drive in *files*. A file is a program or a data document of related information. Files have unique names to distinguish them from one another.

Summary

Most of this appendix dealt with hardware because the rest of the book explains how to use your computer's software. Windows 95 is the controlling element, and Windows 95 must always be loaded and reside inside your computer before you can take advantage of its features, such as multitasking.

Now that you've been introduced to the computer's elementary hardware and software concepts, you're ready to begin using Windows 95. Turn now to the first hour and start Windows 95. You'll be a productive computer user (and computer lover) quickly!

INDEX